The Anti-Jewish Phenomenon

A Historical Torah Analysis

RABBI BENZION ALLSWANG, Ph.D.

FELDHEIM PUBLISHERS
JERUSALEM · NEW YORK

ISBN 978-1-59826-205-6

Page layout and design by E. Chachamtzedek

Published by:
FELDHEIM PUBLISHERS
POB 43163 / Jerusalem, Israel

208 Airport Executive Park
Nanuet, NY 10954

www.feldheim.com

Printed in Israel

This book is dedicated to
my grandmother

Anne E. Leibowitz ע״ה
חנה אסתר בת יצחק

who through her intellect, kindness and
compassion provided enduring spiritual and
moral support for generations

TOMORROW
by Anne E. Leibowitz

Eternal Jew, bowed down in sorrow
    Rise up and face a new tomorrow
    Discard they raiments, grief and fear
    Be brave of heart for hope is near.

Tortured Jew, though sad your plight
    Extinguish not brave hope's dim light
    The body's crushed, but not the soul
    This better day will be your goal.

Homeless Jew, no refuge yours
    Keep the courage that endures
    As far and near your footsteps wend
    Remember Jew, 'tis not the end.

For God works in mysterious ways
    His wonders to perform
    And out of darkened chaos
    A new day will be born.

Acknowledgments

I WOULD LIKE TO EXPRESS my heartfelt appreciation to Mr. Michael Wilens, Rabbi Yitzchak Sender, Rabbi Dr. Jerold Isenberg, Rabbi Gedalia Schwartz, Rabbi Yehoshua H. Eichenstein, Rabbi Boruch Hertz, Rabbi Dr. Chaim Erhman and Dr. Larry Hirsch for giving of their valuable time to read, comment and critique the manuscript. Their insightful comments added considerably to later drafts.

I am deeply indebted to the administration of Fasman Yeshiva (Hebrew Theological College). Without the intelligent and sensitive leadership of Rabbi Dr. Jerold Isenberg, Rabbi Moshe Wender and Mr. Sheldon Shaffel, this book would most probably never have resulted. In addition, I would like to thank my senior-class students over the past ten years. Their sincere questions, comments and urgings to produce another book, were the final catalyst for the book's eventual appearance.

I want to express my gratitude to Feldheim Publishers for their integrity and idealism in publishing my second book with them. In particular, I would like to mention my esteemed editor Eden Chachamtzedek for her honesty and professionalism in the production of the final draft. Her objective and intelligent critiquing throughout this long and arduous process has added greatly to the final product. Also, Harvey Klineman deserves much credit for his patience and expertise in developing a book cover which appears to catch the book's essence.

Many thanks to my professors at Loyola University at

Chicago (of twenty years past) for their contributions to the studies discussed in the book. Through the academic discipline imposed by their department, the studies attained a recognized level of methodological rigor and integrity.

In addition, I want to express my thanks to the many men and women who collected data during the months of interviewing, and to the Jewish Federation of Chicago for donating the telephones, the telephone lines and the space for conducting the interviews.

To a certain extent, this work was a family effort. My dear parents, Harry and Betty Allswang have been my greatest fans and sometimes strong critics. I could always count on my mother for a truly objective analysis, which only enhanced the book's readability and content. May God give them many more fruitful years of good health and happiness. My wife Rachel was, as always, a wonderful source of support and inspiration. Without her warm and understanding disposition this work could not have become a reality. Special thanks to my daughter Divora who was instrumental in her many typing services and my daughter Mielcah and daughters' in-law Tzivia, Rena and Menuchi for their assistance in the final stages of the book. And to all my beloved immediate and extended family, their care and good common sense enabled me to produce a book that, with the help of God, will help influence many lives for the better.

However, most importantly, is my gratitude, thanks and praise to the Almighty, Who has given me the strength, understanding and opportunity to produce a book of this nature.

Contents

Introduction

IN INTRODUCING A WORK OF this sort, it is difficult to know when the project actually began, for its true origins, analytically at least, can always go further and further back in time. Hence, without full rhyme or reason we'll begin in 1979 through 1982 when I was employed in Israel (Jerusalem and Beit Shemesh) as a school psychologist. My time was spent primarily in developing educational and behavioral programs and procedures. These programs were successful, and a desire to develop further expertise in the areas of statistics, methodology and social-science experimentation was the result.

Therefore, in 1982, I began a doctoral program in Applied Social Psychology at Loyola University at Chicago. Originally, my goal was to develop a branch of psychology based on traditional Torah literature which would result in my final dissertation. However, "many are the thoughts of man, but God's will prevails," and it was not meant to be (at least not then). For in 1982, Israel invaded Lebanon in order to root out Palestinian terrorists who were attacking its northern border. From any objective perspective, it was clearly a case of self-defense. Yet, during this period of time the American mass-media (television, radio, print) all seemed to wage an unholy propaganda campaign against the Jewish State of Israel. Having lived in Israel for many years prior, and having volunteered to fight in the 1973 Yom Kippur War, I found the situation very frustrating and disconcerting. Moreover, I had many Israeli relatives and

xi

friends who were forced to bear the consequences of international anti-Israel bias.

My academic direction was therefore reassessed and abruptly changed from the discipline of Torah psychology to the field of anti-Semitism. This metamorphosis of sorts culminated in my 1985 doctoral dissertation entitled "Anti-Judaism, Anti-Semitism, Anti-Zionism: A Theoretical and Empirical Analysis of the Anti-Jewish Phenomenon throughout Its History to the Present."

A few years later, the dissertation, with significant changes, resulted in the work *The Final Resolution — Combating Anti-Jewish Hostility* (Feldheim Publishers, 1989). My fling with the world of literature appeared completed, and for the next ten years I focused on making a living for a growing family. However, it was again not meant to be, for in 1998, after years employed exclusively as a clinical psychologist, I began teaching Jewish History at Fasman Yeshiva (Hebrew Theological College) and one of our textbooks just happened to be *The Final Resolution*. It soon became apparent, though, that my students found the book too difficult, too academic and branching off into too many diverse directions. Their constructive criticism, intellectually honest comments and sincere urgings for revision succeeded in convincing this author to revise the book, making it more palatable for the lay-person and, more specifically, for our Jewish history class.

I then began revising the book based on years of additions and deletions. As time progressed whole chapters were deleted and new ones appended. The remaining chapters underwent an overhaul in language, content, perspective and order. Hence, it was no longer a revised edition, but rather a separate book best described by its title *The Anti-Jewish Phenomenon — A Historical/Torah Analysis*.

*   *   *

In this work the term "anti-Jewish hostility" is used in lieu of the more commonly applied "anti-Semitism" to denote antipathy towards Jews. This is because the latter is a misnomer. The word "Semitism" comes from the name Shem, who was one of Noah's three sons. Therefore, according to the Bible (and assuming all sons were equally prolific), approximately one-third of the world's population today should be inhabited by Shemites (or Semites). In practice, anti-Semitism has been used exclusively to denote anti-Jewish prejudice and hostility, and directed against a people who account for considerably less than one percent of the world's population. In truth, the term anti-Semitism was coined in Germany in the 1870s to denote a "racial" enmity towards Jews, in place of the dated religious prejudice engendered in the past.

A further qualification: The book was compiled to flow as a complete unit from beginning to end, and any skipping or jumping around may arouse premature skepticism, without the required prerequisite understanding. Having said all that, I wish the reader an interesting and worthwhile experience and hope to receive stimulating feedback with its completion.

Benzion Allswang
Chicago, 5768/2008

1 | The Quest for Truth

Buy truth and don't sell.
(Proverbs 23:23)

FROM A JEWISH PERSPECTIVE, THE QUEST FOR TRUTH IS PARA-mount. Throughout the Bible, the virtue of truth is em-phasized. For example, we find in the book of Psalms: "All the ways of God are mercy and truth"[1]; the book of Exo-dus tells us, "Keep far away from anything false"[2]; likewise, in Zachariah it says: "Love truth and peace."[3]

The Oral Law—which, in traditional Judaism, is com-plementary to and no less important than the Bible—also emphasizes the importance of truth. It asserts that the world is established on three concepts: "on Judgment, *on Truth*, and on Peace."[4] Moreover, in several Talmudic tractates, God's seal itself is said to be Truth.[5]

Correspondingly, the ancient historian Josephus relates the following story of the Jewish leader Zerubabel who, in his youth, was a guard for the Babylonian-Median King Darius (circa 400 B.C.E.):[6]

1

> Once, when the king (Darius) lay wrapped in deep slumber, his guards wrote down what each of them considered the mightiest thing in the world, and he who wrote the wisest saying would be given a reward by the king. When each finished writing, he placed his answer under the pillow of the king, so that he would immediately be able to make his decision after he awoke.
>
> The first guard wrote: "Wine is the mightiest thing there is"; the second wrote: "The king is the mightiest on earth"; and the third, Zerubabel, wrote: "Women are the mightiest in the world, but *truth* prevails over all."
>
> When the king awoke, and perused the documents, he summoned the nobility of his realm, and the three guards as well. Each of the three was called upon to justify his saying. In eloquent terms the first described the potency of wine—when it takes possession of man's senses, he forgets grief and sorrow. Still more beautiful and convincing were the words of the second speaker...
>
> Finally Zerubabel depicted the power of women, who rule even over kings. "But," he continued, "truth is supreme over all; the whole earth asks for truth, the heavens sing the praise of truth, all creation quakes and trembles before truth. Unto truth is the might, power and glory of all times." When Zerubabel concluded his speech, the assembly broke out and exclaimed: "Great is truth; it is mightier than all else!"

Nevertheless, how practical is this quest for truth? Should we not involve ourselves with more pragmatic societal issues—such as feeding the hungry, clothing the naked, and, above all, spreading peace and fellowship among mankind?

In response, if truth was an abstract philosophical concept, removed from the daily activities of individuals and society, the answer might be yes. However, if feeding and clothing mankind are dependent upon truth — with its corollary in justice — and if genuine peace is likewise dependent on truth, then it is necessary to persevere and remain steadfast in this quest.

Rabbi Samson Raphael Hirsch, a profound Jewish thinker of the nineteenth century, discusses the correlation between truth and the Jewish exile, and explains that without a commitment to truth, real and enduring peace is unlikely to be achieved. He writes:[7]

> Has the exile ended? Has salvation arrived? Is there to be no more Exile? Will the gentiles' goodwill last? ...Is there reason to believe that such a time has come, or that it is even near? You can determine this by assessing whether and in what manner you love truth and peace! Truth and peace—first truth, and then peace; but if truth, then peace as well....
>
> Once the commitment to truth has been made, the attainment of peace follows. ... No strife or struggle is unwarranted in defense of truth, even if an entire world were the opponent....
>
> How does our time relate to truth? Is truth most precious to you? ... Or do you desire only that truth which is compatible with everything else in your life? *Would you bow only before that truth which has first bowed before you?*

According to Rabbi Hirsch, an everlasting peace can only result when based on truth. Conversely, a lack of truth may lead to extremely dire consequences. Historically, the Jewish People have suffered intensely from the dissemination of falsehood in both the political and religious spheres. In short, there has been a decided surplus of dishonesty in regards to both Jews and Judaism.

This issue was touched upon by the distinguished social philosopher Eric Hoffer, who was awarded the Presidential Medal of Freedom in 1983. In an article entitled "Israel's Peculiar Position," published in the LA Times (May 26, 1968), he speaks of the dishonest double-standard applied to both Jews and the State of Israel. He writes:

> The Jews are a peculiar people: things permitted to other nations are forbidden to the Jews. Other nations drive out thousands, even millions, of people and there is no refugee problem. Russia did it, Poland and Czechoslovakia did it, Turkey threw out a million Greeks, and Algeria a million Frenchman. Indonesia threw out Heaven knows how many Chinese—and no one says a word about refugees. But in the case of Israel, the displaced Arabs have become eternal refugees. Everyone insists that Israel must take back every single Arab. Arnold Toynbee calls the displacement of the Arabs an atrocity greater than any committed by the Nazis. Other nations when victorious on the battlefield dictate peace terms. But when Israel is victorious it must sue for peace.
>
> Everyone expects the Jews to be the only real Christians in this world. Other nations when they are defeated survive and recover, but should Israel be defeated it would be destroyed. Had Nasser triumphed last June (1967) he would have wiped Israel off the map, and no one would have lifted a finger to save the Jews. No commitment to the Jews by any government, including our own, is worth the paper it is written on.
>
> There is a cry of outrage all over the world when people die in Vietnam or when two Blacks are executed in Rhodesia. But when Hitler slaughtered Jews no one remonstrated with him. The Swedes, who are ready to break off diplomatic

relations with America because of what we do in Vietnam, did not let out a peep when Hitler was slaughtering Jews. They sent Hitler choice iron ore, and ball bearings, and serviced his troop trains to Norway.

The Jews are alone in the world. If Israel survives, it will be solely because of Jewish efforts and Jewish resources. Yet at this moment Israel is our only reliable and unconditional ally. We can rely more on Israel than Israel can rely on us. And one has only to imagine what would have happened last summer (1967) had the Arabs and their Russian backers won the war, to realize how vital the survival of Israel is to America and the West in general. I have a premonition that will not leave me: As it goes with Israel, so will it go with all of us; should Israel perish, the holocaust will be upon us.

Is hostility towards Jews a fact throughout history? Can anti-Jewish hostility be explained via logic and reason? Why have Jews been the target of such great dislike? What is the historical significance of hatred towards the Jewish nation, and is there a relationship between this social malady and peace on earth? Let us now pursue an understanding of truth stranger than fiction—let us pursue an understanding of the Anti-Jewish Phenomenon.

NOTES TO CHAPTER 1

1. Psalms 25:10.
2. Exodus 23:7.
3. Zachariah 8:19.
4. Mishnah *Avos* 1:18 (Jerusalem: Ortsel, 1960).
5. Talmud *Shabbos* 55a, *Yoma* 69b and *Sanhedrin* 64a.

6. Josephus, Antiquities XI, 3:3–9, in L. Ginzberg (ed.), *The Legends of the Jews* (Philadelphia: Jewish Publication Society of America, 1968).

7. Hirsch, S.R., "How Does Our Time Relate to Truth and Peace?" *Collected Writings of Rabbi Samson Raphael Hirsch* (New York: Feldheim Publishers, 1984), pp. 321–325.

2 | Ancient and Classical Anti-Jewish Hostility

They said, "Come let us build ourselves a city,
a tower whose top shall reach the heavens,
and let us make ourselves a name."
(Genesis 11:4)

THE ADVENT OF THE JEWISH NATION BEGAN WITH ONE MAN, Abraham the Ivri ("the Hebrew") in the seventeenth century B.C.E.[1] The Midrash explains that the word Ivri means "on the other side," for the idol-worshiping population at that time was figuratively on one side, and Abraham, through his monotheistic belief and ethical behavior, stood on the other.[2] Abraham suffered both persecution[3] and exile[4] because of his spiritual convictions and lifestyle.

Abraham was the first recorded iconoclast (literally, "idol breaker"). His intrepid ridicule of the government and idol worship of ancient Mesopotamia also endangered his material security and physical existence. The Midrash relates that when Abraham attained the age of twenty, his father

7

spoke to him and to his brother Haran:[5]

> "I ask you, my sons, to sell these idols for me."
>
> Haran executed his father's wish.
>
> However, when a man came in to buy an idol from Abraham, he asked him, "How old are you?"
>
> "Thirty," the man replied.
>
> "You are thirty years of age, and yet you would worship an idol that I made only today?" Abraham retorted.
>
> After the man departed Abraham took two idols, put a rope around their necks, and with their faces turned downward, dragged them on the ground, crying aloud: "Who will buy an idol wherein there is no profit? It has a mouth but it cannot speak; eyes, but it cannot see; feet, but it cannot walk; ears, but it cannot hear." ...
>
> As [Abraham] was walking through the streets, he met an old woman who approached him with the purpose of buying a large idol to be worshiped and loved.
>
> "Old woman, old woman," said Abraham, "I know no profit in [idols], either in the big ones or in the little ones, either for themselves or for others. And what has become of the large one that you bought from my brother Haran?"
>
> "Thieves came in the night," she replied, "and stole it while I was in the bath."
>
> "If that is so," said Abraham, "how can you pay homage to an idol that cannot save itself from thieves, let alone save others like yourself?"

Another Midrash relates how Abraham took a hatchet and broke all his father's gods, and when finished, placed the hatchet in the hand of the largest one.

Having heard the commotion, Terah, Abraham's father, ran into the room and arrived just as Abraham was about to leave:[6]

He asked, "What is this mischief you have done to my gods?"

"I set savory meat before them..." answered Abraham, "and they reached out their hands [to take from it] before the largest one had a chance.... Enraged, the largest one took the hatchet and broke them all! You see, the hatchet is still in his hand...."

Terah turned to Abraham, and said, "You speak only lies! Is there spirit, soul or power in these gods to do all that you have told me? Are they not wood and stone, and have I not myself made them? It is you who placed the hatchet in the hand of the large one."

Abraham then replied, "How, then, can you serve these idols, in whom there is no power? Can these idols, in which you trust, save you? Can they hear your prayers when you call to them?"

After speaking, he jumped up, took the hatchet from the big idol and smashed it as well.

The king, at the time, was the powerful Nimrod. Nimrod proclaimed himself a deity and was considered as such by his followers. Because of Abraham's heretical ideas and behavior, he was brought before Nimrod. He challenged Nimrod, requesting that the king change the course of the sun as proof of the latter's divinity. When Abraham's request was refused, he declared the king an imposter.[7]

Initially, Nimrod attempted through peaceful methods to draw Abraham to the "true" faith, and went to great lengths to convince him of his misplaced beliefs. Nimrod tried to show him the benefits of adopting the Mesopotamian people's beliefs and general customs. He even arranged a seven-day festival for Abraham's benefit, at which the king's noblemen were told to appear in their robes of state, their gold and silver apparel. By such display of wealth and power, Nimrod expected to attract Abraham and bring him back to the religion of the masses. He desired Abraham to see his greatness and wealth, the glory of his dominion, and the multitude of his princes and attendants. However, Abraham refused to come.[8]

According to the Midrash, fear then gripped the king, for more and more of his people were attracted to Abraham's heretical teachings. The king's power and influence were threatened. Therefore, in order to estrange Abraham from his idiosyncratic philosophy and behavior, he was cast into prison; and in order to uproot any remaining rebelliousness, he was denied food and drink.[9] When these strategies failed, Abraham was condemned to death.[10]

Nimrod's plans proved unsuccessful, but the vicissitudes of Abraham's life would become the prototypic path on which his progeny, over the course of the next 3,700 years, would tread. Abraham eventually escaped the wrath of Nimrod. At God's command, as recorded in the book of Genesis, he made his way to the land of Canaan (ancient and present-day Israel).

Abraham bequeathed his belief, philosophy and lifestyle to his son Isaac, and sent Ishmael away at the urging of his wife Sarah, which was afterwards justified by God Himself.[11] Isaac passed the tradition on to the younger of his two sons, Jacob (whose name was later changed to Israel), who passed it down to his twelve sons, the Twelve Tribes of Israel.

The Egyptian Sojourn   BECAUSE OF SIBLING rivalry, Jacob's sons sold their brother Joseph into slavery, in which state he was transported to Egypt.[12] Joseph became great in Egypt and attained the status of second-in-command.[13] He single-handedly saved from starvation not only the Egyptian people, but also the inhabitants of neighboring countries, while simultaneously procuring enormous wealth for Pharaoh.[14]

Due to the great famine, which had also swept the land of Canaan, Jacob and his family journeyed to Egypt at the urgings of his son. Initially, Pharaoh quite graciously granted to Jacob and his sons the best of Egypt, the fertile land of Goshen, to dwell in as free men.[15] In Egypt, Jacob's family grew by leaps and bounds,[16] and within a short period of time developed into the Hebrew nation.

With the passing of Joseph and his brothers,[17] the Hebrews began to adopt Egyptian customs — that is, they began to assimilate.[18]

The Midrash relates that the Hebrews became ardent cosmopolitans, and that their presence was conspicuous at the great cultural events of the day.[19] According to the historian Josephus, the industrious and successful nature of the Hebrew people made them the envy of Egypt.[20] Likewise, according to the Midrash, their remarkable rate of increase, coupled with feats of heroism, placed them in a highly visible and prominent position.[21]

Although the Hebrews were rapidly assimilating and becoming highly integral features of Egyptian society (the most sophisticated society at the time), the Midrash tells of two distinctive Jewish behaviors which, perforce, prevented total assimilation: (1) they retained their Hebrew names, and (2) they retained their Hebrew language.[22] Moreover, their belief system — originating from the Patriarch Abraham — clashed with the prevailing Egyptian religions.[23]

This clash of religious cultures is seen in the following narrative (some two hundred years later) from the Midrash:[24]

Now the two representatives of the Children of Israel stepped before Pharaoh, and said, "The God of the Hebrews has met with us; let us go...three days' journey into the wilderness!"

But Pharaoh answered, stating: "What is the name of your God? Of what does His strength consist, and His power? How many countries, how many provinces, and how many cities has He under His dominion? In how many military campaigns was He victorious? How many lands has He made subject to Himself? How many cities has He captured?"

Whereto Moses and Aaron replied: "His strength and His power fill the whole world... The heaven is His throne, and the earth His footstool. He nourishes and sustains the whole world, from the horns of the ram to the eggs of the vermin. Daily He causes men to die, and daily He calls men into life!"

Pharaoh answered: "I have created myself, and if you say that He causes dew and rain to descend, I have created the Nile, the river that has its source under the tree of life, and the ground impregnated by its waters bears fruit so huge that it takes two donkeys to carry it, and is palatable beyond description, for it has three hundred different tastes!"

Pharaoh felt threatened. The Hebrew populace was growing in size, success and prestige, while proudly and stubbornly remaining to some extent distinctively non-Egyptian. Pharaoh and his Egyptian nobility would not tolerate a distinct and competing Hebrew population in their midst. They determined that the Hebrew phenomenon had to be curtailed, and if the Hebrews would not relinquish their less progressive and obsolete cultural traditions, then other, more potent, methods would be implemented.

Pharaoh was struck by a seeming paranoia (a common theme throughout Jewish history), "Lest they multiply and endanger the land."[25] He said: "Let us deal wisely with them."[26] The Talmud explains that Pharaoh requested their help in building his storehouse cities.[27] The Children of Israel fell into the trap and worked diligently.[28] Gradually, the Hebrew people were pressed into involuntary servitude.[29]

To the dismay of Egypt, the Jewish People began to increase in proportion to the oppression.[30] The Egyptian plan to uproot the Hebrews' stubborn national identity via slavery proved unsuccessful. The Hebrew tradition — initiated by Abraham and predicated on ethical monotheism, with its ultimate fulfillment realized in the Land of Israel (as promised to Abraham[31]) — was too strong a bond for even Egyptian servitude to sever.

Egypt then implemented its second stage of attack, physical backbreaking labor.[32] If national identity could not be eradicated via forced labor, then bone-crushing measures were to be implemented in order to subdue the Hebrews' spirit — creating, in effect, national misfits. This second stage of attack was also unsuccessful, and consequently Pharaoh decreed the murder of all male infants at birth.[33] When the Hebrew midwives refused to carry out Pharaoh's command, he decreed that every newborn male be cast into the river.[34] Pharaoh's three-level strategy of oppression — (1) discrimination and subjugation, (2) spirit-crushing physical persecution, and (3) extermination — was to be the prototype for all subsequent anti-Jewish activity throughout history.

There were other similarities between Egyptian anti-Jewish hostility and those that followed. For example, Jews in Egypt were highly successful before their oppression. One of their founding fathers (Joseph) was second only to Pharaoh and revered by the Egyptian populace.[35] Similarly, when Joseph's father (Jacob) died, all of Egypt mourned for seventy days.[36] Pharaoh himself gave the Hebrews the finest land in Egypt, and offered them positions of prestige and power.[37] During the first eighty years of their sojourn, the Hebrews were highly successful; only afterwards were they bitterly oppressed. In other lands as well, Jews would, at first, succeed (when given the slightest opportunity) only to be eventually persecuted.

It bears mention, at this point, the difference between Jewish oppression and the oppression of other groups. Throughout history, other targeted minorities were often looked upon as being inferior, and thus their oppressors were not interested in having them integrate into the society at large. In contrast, Jews were always prime targets of assimilation, and only after they remained "stiff-necked" and refused to totally comply did discrimination and persecution ensue. What began as a self-imposed desire to be separate resulted in a universally accepted antipathy towards Jews.

Therefore, it is not difficult to understand why the persecution of Jews throughout history has transcended, in scope and intensity, the persecution of other minority groups. Discrimination and persecution of other groups was most often based on the majority population's superiority complex vis-à-vis the subjugants. Genuine hate and animosity was unusual while the subjugants knew their place and did not overstep their liberties. In such a state, these groups were tolerated.

Conversely, in ancient Egypt, only after it became clear that the Hebrews were not interested in becoming totally Egyptian — just as, in future times, the Jews would similarly resist Persian, Grecian and Roman efforts to assimilate them — did curtailment of freedom ensue. By refusing to assimilate, they seem to have inadvertently intimidated the ruling power. In effect, the threat of a successful and dynamic non-Egyptian population burgeoning in the midst of Egypt appears to have been the cause of Pharaoh's paranoia. Thus, he became hostile towards the Hebrews, which subsequently led to their subjugation.

Persian Anti-Jewish Hostility THE JEWISH HOMELAND was eventually conquered by the great Babylonian empire, and with the destruction of the First Temple in Jerusalem in 423 B.C.E. (This date is derived from *Seder Olam* which is considered an authoritative source of Jewish chronology.), the Jews were deported en masse to Babylonia.[38] Even after Babylonia fell to the mighty Media-Persian empire, the conquered Jews, living in the now conquered land, continued to remain voluntarily Jewish.

This distinctiveness was used against them by the infamous Persian prime minister Haman. In short, Haman claimed that by refusing to adopt the ways of the empire, the Jews were undermining the king's authority, and were therefore to be annihilated.[39] The Talmud relates the king's predisposition to Haman's plan,[40] and an edict was promulgated.[41]

From what we know of the period, it appears that the Jews were conspicuously successful in ancient Persia as they were, initially, in Egypt. For example, the leader of the Jews (Mordecai) was an official in the king's court[42] who had patriotically saved the king from assassination.[43] In addition, a Jewess (Esther) was the queen.[44] Furthermore, according to the Talmud[45] and Midrash,[46] the Jewish Elders were oftentimes consulted on issues of prime importance.

Assimilation, as a historical rule, follows societal success.

The Jews, as well, began adopting non-Jewish customs. For example, the Midrash relates that at the king's banquet tens of thousands of Jews became intoxicated and committed immoralities not unlike their indigenous Persian counterparts.[47] In addition, the traditional Jewish belief system — as originated by Abraham more than one thousand years prior — was gradually deteriorating.[48]

Notwithstanding the above, the Jews still maintained a distinctive Jewish character and national identity. This separatism is seen by Haman's denunciation of the Jews, which he presented before the king:[49]

> Haman appeared before King Achashverosh (Xerxes) claiming: There is a certain people, the Jews, scattered abroad and dispersed among the peoples in all the provinces of the kingdom. They are proud and presumptuous.... Their religion is diverse from the religion of every other people, and their laws from the laws of every other land.... Our religion finds no favor with them.... They do not give us their daughters as wives, nor do they take our daughters for wives. ... The seventh day they celebrate as their Sabbath... and their women pollute the waters with ritual baths. On the eighth day after the birth of their sons, they circumcise them mercilessly, saying, "This shall distinguish us from all the other nations." At the end of thirty days, and sometimes twenty-nine, they celebrate the beginning of the month. In the month of Nissan they observe the holiday of Passover. They put all the leaven in their homes out of sight saying, "This is the day when our fathers were redeemed from Egypt."
>
> In Sivan, they celebrate the holiday of Shavuos. They ascend to the roofs of their meeting places and throw down apples, which are picked up by those below, with the words, "As these apples are gathered up, so may we be gathered

together from our dispersion." They say they observe this festival, because on these days the Torah was revealed to their ancestors on Mount Sinai.

On the ninth day of the month of Tishrei they slaughter cattle, geese and poultry, they eat and drink and indulge in dainties — they, their wives, their sons and daughters. But the tenth day of the same month they call the Great Fast and all of them refrain from food and drink.

On the fifteenth of the same month they celebrate the Feast of Tabernacles. They cover the roofs of their houses with foliage, they resort to our parks, where they cut down palm branches for their festal wreaths, pluck the fruit of the Esrog, and cause havoc among the willows of the brook by breaking down the hedges in their quest after Hoshanos, saying, "As does the king in the triumphal procession, so do we." This is Sukkos, as they call it, and while it lasts they do none of the king's service — for, they maintain, all work is forbidden them on these days. In this way they waste the king's year with indolence and foolishness, only in order to avoid doing the king's service....

As in Egypt, Jewish success coupled with Jewish distinctiveness posed a grave psychological threat. In other lands as well, leaders and governments would be unable to tolerate a successful, yet distinct, Jewish minority — more specifically, a people who refuse to serve other gods.

After the king promoted Haman to second-in-command, an order was issued that all who saw him were to prostrate themselves. Of the king's court only Mordecai, the leader of the Jews, refused to obey.[50] And, as recorded in the Biblical Book of Esther, this seemingly presumptuous act was overly traumatic for the newly appointed prime minister,[51] and attempted genocide was the not too illogical consequence.

However, prior to Haman's bitter clash with Mordecai, the king attempted to erase Jewish separatism via more peaceful methods. For example, when the king prepared a banquet for all his citizens, he urged the Jewish population to attend. And in order not to offend their religious sensitivities, he had their food and drink prepared in accordance with Jewish law.[52]

Moreover, during the festivities the king even instructed that the Jewish, rather than Persian, manner of drinking be followed. In Persia, the custom prevailed that the participant would finish a large beaker of wine, exceeding his or her drinking capacity. Yet, at this banquet the Jewish custom prevailed.[53]

The Midrash states that the king was so sure that his overtures would be accepted that he said to his Jewish guests, "Will your God be able to match this banquet in the future world?" Whereupon the Jews replied: "Regarding the banquet that God will prepare for the righteous in the World to Come, it is written, 'No eye has seen it but God's; He will accomplish it for those who wait upon Him.' If God were then to offer us a banquet like yours, O King, we would then be able to say, 'Such as this we [already] ate at the table of King Achashverosh!'"[54]

However, peaceful methods were not the only methods used in endeavoring to erase Jewish separatism. For example, the Persian Queen Vashti, who reigned before Esther, had her own methods of uprooting Jewish distinctiveness. She would force Jewish maidens to spin and weave on the Sabbath day (something prohibited by Jewish law).[55]

After these various strategies failed to break the Jewish national and religious character, the following decree of genocide was issued:[56]

This herein is written by me, the great officer of the king, his second in rank, the first among the grandees, and one of the seven princes, and the most distinguished among the nobles of the realm. I, in agreement with the rulers of the provinces, the princes of the king, the chiefs and the lords, the Eastern kings and the satraps, all being of the same counsel and opinion, using the same expressions and the same language, write you at the order of King Achashverosh — this writing sealed with his signet, so that it may not be sent back — concerning the great eagle Israel. The great eagle had stretched out his wings over the whole world; neither bird not beast could withstand him. But there came the great lion Nebuchadnezzar, and dealt the great eagle a stinging blow. His wings snapped, his feathers were plucked out, and his feet were hacked off. The whole world has enjoyed rest, cheer and tranquility since the moment the eagle was chased from his nest until this day. Now we notice that he is using all efforts to secure wings. He is permitting his feathers to grow, with the intention of covering us and the whole world, as he did to our forefathers. At the insistence of King Achashverosh, where all magnates of the king are assembled, we are writing you our joint advice, as follows: Set snares for the eagle, and capture him before he renews his strength and soars back to his nest. We advise you to tear out his plumage, break his wings, give his flesh to the fowl of heaven...and crush his young, so that his memorial may vanish from the world. Our counsel is not like Pharaoh's; he sought to destroy only the men of Israel; the women he did no harm. It is not like the plan of Esau, who wanted to slay his brother Jacob and keep his children as slaves. It is not like the tactics of Amalek, who pursued Israel and smote the hindmost and feeble, but left the strong unscathed. It is not like the policy of Nebuchadnezzar, who

carried them away into exile and settled them near his own
throne. And it is not like the way of Sennacherib, who assigned a land for the Jews as fair as their own had been.
We, recognizing clearly what the situation is, have resolved
to slay the Jews, annihilate them, young and old, that their
name and memorial be no more, and their posterity be cut
off forever.

In the end, Haman's plan backfired, and Mordecai, following Haman's demise, succeeded him as prime minister.[57]

As in Egypt, the Jews' seeming inability to totally assimilate infuriated the ruling power. When attempts to break
the Jewish spirit by estranging them from their traditions
proved unsuccessful, the only recourse for these despots was
to annihilate the Jews. However, the Jewish People continued
to persevere in their already ancient traditions, and in their
relationship to the land promised them forever by God.[58]
In contrast, the Persian empire was eventually dissolved along
with its indigenous type of religion, form of government, and
societal mores.

Greek Anti-Jewish Hostility AFTER THE BABYLONIAN-PERSIAN exile, the Jews
were granted permission to return to their
land and rebuild their Temple. However, in
332 B.C.E. Alexander the Great of Macedo-
nia with his 40,000 soldiers attacked and defeated the larger
Persian army and conquered the land previously governed
by Persia, including the Land of Israel with its indigenous
Jewish population.[59] Alexander showed favor to the Jews,
allowing them to continue their autonomous rule, and even
extended their borders.[60]

Alexander's ambitions were cultural as well as military. He
expected the segments of his newly found empire to mingle

and evolve into a common civilization modeled after Hellenistic culture. The dissemination and influence of the Hellenistic spirit brought in its wake libraries, scientific research and technological advancement.[61] However, as time elapsed, this progressive spirit degenerated into an intensification of idol worship, with its concomitant corruption of morals.[62]

For 150 years Greek civilization and Jewish culture were able to coexist, but with the advent of Antiochus Epiphanes (175 B.C.E.) the relationship became badly strained. Antiochus believed himself Divine, and ordered all peoples under his rule to erect statues of him in their temples and prostrate themselves before his image. He imposed Grecian culture, and would not tolerate Jewish distinctiveness. He eventually decreed that Judaism be completely abolished.[63] He called for cessation of the service in the Temple, and in its place set up pagan temples throughout the country. He commanded that the Temple be converted into a pagan house of worship.[64] The observance of the Sabbath and Festivals, Jewish dietary laws, circumcision and the laws of family purity were all forcefully prohibited. All copies of the Bible were to be burned, and anyone found possessing them would be executed. Even to profess one's Jewishness was punishable by death.[65]

This form of oppression was different from the attempted Persian genocide. In Persia, the Jewish body was targeted, while under Greek rule the Jewish spirit was to be dismembered. Nevertheless, according to the Egyptian paradigm, both Persian and Greek forms of anti-Jewish hostility follow a common pattern. It began with an attempt to foster total assimilation. Then, Jewish law and lifestyle were attacked. Both the Persian and Greek empires — like their predecessor in Egypt — enacted oppressive legislation in their attempt to deal with the Jewish phenomenon. And both forms of oppression (i.e., of body and of spirit) were used one thousand years prior in ancient Egypt.

Yet Antiochus, like his predecessors, was unsuccessful in uprooting the Jewish spirit. Mattityahu the Hasmonean, with his five sons, led a group of militarily undisciplined zealots against the vastly superior Greek-Syrian army and miraculously prevailed.

Roman Anti-Jewish Hostility DURING THE NEXT hundred years, the Land of Israel (Judea) was ruled by a sovereign Jewish government,[66] but concurrently the Roman Eagle was conquering the already divided Grecian empire. In 63 B.C.E. the Roman general Pompey was invited, by the Jews themselves, to intervene in a battle for the kingship between two Jewish brothers (Hyrkanos and Aristobulus). Unfortunately for the Jewish People, Pompey did not leave, but subjugated the land in a battle which exacted tens of thousands of Jewish lives.[67] Once again the sovereign state of Judea was reduced to an autonomous vassal state, but this time under the auspices of mighty Rome.

Theoretically, the Jewish People should have been able to live peaceably under Roman rule despite economic hardships and loss of national sovereignty — as they did, for a time, under both Persian and Grecian rule.[68] Rome made several attempts to integrate Judea into its vast empire, but each attempt to erase Jewish national identity was countered by an equally strong Jewish resistance.

When Rome realized that Jewish separatism was not to be uprooted via peaceful methods, more forceful tactics were implemented. Accordingly, the Roman proconsul Gabinus abolished the spiritual core of the land which was the Sanhedrin (the Jewish Supreme Court). He reasoned that by stripping the court of its powers, the people would be lost, and hence become as docile as other conquered nations.[69] However his strategy was unsuccessful.

The years between 60 B.C.E and 70 C.E. proved a perilous period in Jewish history. The Romans were unrelenting in their efforts to subjugate the minds and bodies of the conquered. This set the stage for fierce battles between the two nations in which literally hundreds of thousands of Jews were slaughtered,[70] and reached its climax in the destruction of the Second Temple (70 C.E.).

In addition to the multitudes slain, many others were taken captive. Tens of thousands were sold into slavery, sent to toil in ships and mines, or presented as gifts to non-Jewish cities adjacent to Judea to fight against wild animals in their amphitheaters. Cities and villages were burnt and destroyed, either in the course of the war or afterwards, as acts of Roman revenge and intimidation.[71]

The tortures inflicted upon the Jews to compel them to transgress their tradition reached an apex of barbarity.[72] Not contented with these brutalities, the Romans sought out families said to be descended from the House of David, in order to eradicate any hope for the restoration of the Davidic Kingdom.[73]

The Jews' refusal to succumb and assimilate was poignantly depicted by the historian Josephus some 1,900 years ago. He wrote:[74]

> They have a passion for liberty that is almost unconquerable, since they are convinced that God alone is their leader and master. They think little of submitting to death in unusual forms...if only they may avoid calling any man master.

Similarly in another place he writes: [75]

> For it is no new thing for our captives...to be seen to endure
> racks and death of all kinds upon the theaters, that they
> may not be obliged to say one word against our laws and
> the records that contain them; whereas there are none at all
> among the Greeks who would undergo the least harm on
> that account.

The ancient historian Hecateus described the phenomenon in a similar manner:[76]

> When they [the Jews] are stripped...and have torments in-
> flicted upon them, and they are brought to the most terrible
> kinds of death, they meet them in an extraordinary manner,
> beyond all other people, and will not renounce the religion
> of their forefathers.

As unusual as it may seem, the Jews' already protracted
appearance in the annals of history was far from over. Although various Jewish sects (e.g., Sadducees) that had broken
from traditional Judaism were now abandoned, Jewish scholars were diligently reestablishing Jewish communal life in the
Land of Israel — but this time outside of Jerusalem, in the city
of Yavneh. During the ensuing sixty years (70 C.E. to 130 C.E.)
the Jews, once again, began buying up and cultivating the land
of Judea. They began flocking back to Jerusalem in the hope
of rebuilding the Holy Temple, though its construction would
be under the jurisdiction of the Roman emperor Hadrian.
Hadrian, however, abandoned his original plan of rebuilding
Jerusalem as a Jewish city, and continued its construction as
a pagan, Roman city.[77]

Within this sixty year interval, the Jewish People consoli-
dated their resources, and under Simeon bar Kosiba (Bar

Kochba) succeeded in liberating the whole of Judea, which for a short three-year period once again came under independent Jewish rule.[78] But, as before, the Roman empire prevailed, destroying hundreds of Judean settlements. Hundreds of thousands of Jews were again slaughtered and, according to the Talmud, on the ninth of Av (the summer of 135 C.E.), the anniversary of the destruction of both the First and Second Temples in Jerusalem, the remaining great Jewish city of Betar was captured.[79] The Romans laid the land waste, sent multitudes of Jews off to slave markets and, under Hadrian, launched an all-out war forbidding the study and observance of Jewish law. Jews were forbidden to live in Jerusalem, and in order to blot out all reference to the Land of Israel, Hadrian changed its name to *Syria Palaestina* (thereafter known as Palestine).

The great Roman empire eventually faded from history, and its indigenous and conquered populations adopted — or were forced to adopt — new political leadership, foreign ideologies, novel individual and group mores, and new religions. Ironically, however, its defeated opponent, the Jewish People, continued as a distinct civilization. Another remarkable phenomenon was that the Land of Israel, after being devastated by Rome, was to remain a wasteland for the next eighteen hundred years, and was never to become a sovereign or even autonomous political entity until the creation of the modern Jewish State of Israel in 1948.

Though Jewish suffering at the hands of Rome was more intense than that experienced before, Roman persecution did not deviate in kind from the Egyptian anti-Jewish paradigm. Again, the desire to uproot Jewish distinctiveness became the catalyst for destroying national identity and the Jewish religious spirit.

NOTES TO CHAPTER 2

1. *Encyclopaedia Judaica* (Jerusalem: Keter, 1973).

2. *Midrash Bereshit Rabbah* (Jerusalem: Vaharmon, 1965).

3. Ibid.

4. Genesis 12:1.

5. *Midrash Seder Eliyahu Rabbah* 5:27.

6. *Yashar Noah* 236–66.

7. *Midrash Bereshit Rabbah.*

8. *Midrash Beit HaMidrash* (Jerusalem: Wahrman-Books, 1967).

9. *Pirkei d'Rabbi Eliezer* (Jerusalem: M. Liman, 1969).

10. *Midrash Beit HaMidrash.*

11. Genesis 21:12.

12. Ibid. 37:28.

13. Ibid. 41:43–44.

14. Ibid. 47:14–26.

15. Ibid., ch. 47.

16. Exodus 1:7.

17. Miller, A., *Behold a People* (New York: Balshon, 1968).

18. See Ezekiel 20:5–7.

19. *Midrash Tanchuma* (Warsaw: Y.G. Monk, 1879).

20. Josephus, Antiquities.

21. *Midrash HaGadol* (Jerusalem: Mossad HaRav Kook, 1956).

22. *Midrash Mechilta*, in *Mechilta d'Rabbi Yishmael* (Philadelphia: Jewish Publication Society of America, 1976). *Midrash Yalkut Shimoni* (1:773) enumerates a third behavior: that they retained their distinctive Hebrew manner of dress.

23. *Midrash Shemot Rabbah*, in *Midrash Rabbah* (Jerusalem: Levin Epstein, 1965).

24. *Midrash HaGadol* 11:43.

25. Exodus 1:10.

26. Ibid.

27. Talmud *Sotah* 11a (Jerusalem: Ortsel, 1960).

28. *Midrash Shemot Rabbah.*

29. Genesis 41:35.
30. Exodus 1:12.
31. Genesis 17:8.
32. Exodus 1:13.
33. Ibid. 1:16.
34. Ibid. 1:22.
35. Genesis 41:43–44, 47:25.
36. Ibid. 50:3.
37. Ibid. 47:6.
38. Scherman, N. and Zlotowitz, M., *History of the Jewish People: The Second Temple Era* (New York: Mesorah Publications, 1982).
39. Esther 3:8–9.
40. Talmud *Megillah* 11a (Jerusalem: Ortsel, 1960).
41. Esther 3:12–13.
42. *Midrash Abba Gurion*, in A. Jellinek (ed.), *Beit HaMidrash* (Jerusalem: Wahrman-Books, 1967).
43. Esther 2:22.
44. Ibid. 2:17.
45. Talmud *Megillah* 12b.
46. *Midrash Esther Rabbah*, in *Midrash Rabbah* (Bnei Brak: Tiferet Zion, 1963).
47. *Midrash Abba Gurion*.
48. *Midrash Pesikta Rabati* (Vilna, 1880).
49. *Targum Yerushalmi*.
50. *Midrash Panim Acherim*.
51. Esther 3:5, 5:13.
52. *Pirkei d'Rabbi Eliezer*.
53. *Midrash Abba Gurion*.
54. Ibid.
55. Talmud *Megillah* 12b.
56. *Midrash Panim Acherim*.
57. Esther 10:3.
58. E.g., Genesis 17:8, Exodus 6:8, Jeremiah 7:7 and Ezekiel 28:25.
59. *Encyclopaedia Judaica*.

60. Scherman & Zlotowitz.
61. Mason, S.F., *A History of the Sciences* (New York: Collier Books, 1968).
62. Scherman & Zlotowitz.
63. Grayzel, S., *A History of the Jews* (New York: Mentor, 1968).
64. Miller, A., *Torah Nation* (New York: Balshon, 1971).
65. Scherman & Zlotowitz.
66. *Encyclopaedia Judaica.*
67. Scherman & Zlotowitz.
68. Ibid.
69. Ibid.
70. *Encyclopaedia Judaica.*
71. Ibid.
72. Josephus, *The Jewish Wars.*
73. Scherman & Zlotowitz.
74. Ibid.
75. Josephus, Contra Apion 1:8.
76. Hecateus, cited in A. Miller, *Rejoice O Youth*, pp. 128–129.
77. *Encyclopaedia Judaica.*
78. Ibid.
79. Talmud *Ta'anit* 26b (Jerusalem: Ortsel, 1960).

3 | Religious and More-Contemporary Anti-Jewish Hostility

Christian Anti-Jewish Hostility   THE NEXT EPOCH of overt anti-Jewish hostility, which lasted for at least 1,500 years, is probably the most unfortunate and paradoxical—unfortunate, because the non-Jewish world never had a chance to objectively observe and understand Jewish tradition; paradoxical, because the group carrying out this oppression was an offspring of Judaism itself, and when all auxiliary manifestations (which came about only afterwards) are removed, is not too distinct from other Jewish sects throughout history. However, whereas other Jewish sects disappeared, Christianity became a non-Jewish religion.

This new religion centered on the person of Jesus. Jesus, however, was not a Christian but a Jew. It appears, historically, that Jesus had no intention of ever breaking with Judaism, and that he would have been profoundly shocked to know that his teachings would be used to justify the rejection of Judaism and the persecution of its people.[1] For instance, in the book of Matthew the following passage is attributed to Jesus:[2]

> Think not that I have come to destroy the Law or the proph-
> ets; I have not come to destroy, but to fulfill. For verily I say
> to you, until heaven and earth pass, one jot or one title shall
> in no wise pass from the Law, till all be fulfilled. Whosoever,
> therefore, shall break one of these least commandments, and
> shall teach men so, he shall be called the least in the king-
> dom of Heaven; but whosoever shall do and teach [them],
> the same shall be called great in the kingdom of Heaven.

Jesus, it appears, was a force *within* Jewish society, and
was never against the Jewish People. This is further seen in
Matthew: "I am not sent but unto the lost sheep of the house
of Israel."[3] Similarly, the Apostles, the group of disciples chosen by Jesus to preach his gospel, were almost all Jewish, and
their message — in the beginning at least — was specifically
to the Jews. Only after the Jewish People refused to accept
this brand of Judaism (that is, they did not consider Jesus the
Messiah) did the Apostles (particularly Paul) venture out to
preach among the non-Jews. Other movements in Judaism
had sprung up over the centuries — particularly during Greek
and Roman persecutions — but none succeeded in swaying
popular Jewish opinion from the scholarly (Orthodox) tradition.

However, when confronted with Jewish resistance, this
Judeo-Christian movement turned to the non-Jews, but
their relationship to Judaism was far from severed. Initially,
the founding fathers of Christianity (i.e., the Apostles) were
split on the desired relationship to mainstream Judaism,
and two schools of thought — the Petrine and the Pauline
doctrines — competed to become the official dogma of the
up-and-coming Catholic Church.[4] The accepted dispute is
that the Petrine (as advanced by Peter) school of thought advocated a Judaized Christianity where both Jew and gentile

would be obligated to observe Torah Law, whereas the Pauline doctrine, which eventually prevailed, called for a total disassociation from Torah Law.

Although this has been the accepted understanding of the Pauline doctrine for millennia, it has been called into question by John G. Gager, who, in his book, *The Origins of Anti-Semitism*, brings substantive support to justify the claim that the Pauline doctrine was significantly doctored by later Church Fathers. In essence, in order to wean the people from any Judaizing influence, the Church Fathers recreated a Paul totally antagonistic to Pharisaical (Orthodox) Judaism.[5] Gager concludes that Paul's intent was most probably to propagate the message of Torah (based on Talmudic Oral Law) for Jews and Christianity for gentiles, but that any positive Judaizing influence on the new religion was too threatening for the Church Fathers and demanded total eradication.

According to Gager, both Petrine and Pauline doctrines — which lay at the foundation of true Christianity, as propagated by Jesus and his Apostles — were not anti-Jewish. Peter believed that both Jew and non-Jew were required to follow all the precepts of the Torah, whereas Paul, in contrast to what is commonly believed, advocated traditional, Talmudic Oral-Law Judaism for the Jewish People and a new religion, Christianity — based on Jewish spirituality without the rigors of the commandments — for non-Jews.

Historically, only after the Apostles — in the second and third centuries, when Christianity began severing itself completely from Judaism — did harsh intolerance of Judaism and the Jewish People commence.[6] The early Church Fathers, while trying to consolidate Christianity and formulate an official dogma, viewed the Judaizing influence as too intimidating. This was especially true all the while a dynamic

Jewish People, following their own traditions, continued to exist.[7] To sever the Jewish tradition from Christianity meant to uproot Christianity, but to accord it legitimacy meant to shed doubt on the Church's role as the "new Israel." A logical alternative was to claim that the Church had replaced the old Israel, because of the latter's grievous sins, and particularly the abomination of deicide.[8] Accordingly, only through conversion could Jews redeem themselves in this world and the next. In effect, it was this disassociation from its mother religion, Judaism, that supplied the rationalization for the ensuing discrimination, persecution and massacre of Jews in the name of Christianity.

The pattern of Christian anti-Jewish hostility reflects the pattern of oppression mentioned above in relation to Egypt, Persia, Greece and Rome, and only by virtue of its intensity and extensiveness does it qualify as something historically distinct. The themes of anti-Jewish hostility discussed above are also present here:

The Jewish refusal to assimilate — in this case, convert — into the ever-growing Christian empire. The Church then feels psychologically threatened and reacts by attempting to uproot any positive national identity via ghettoization and expulsion. The Church also attempts to break the distinctive Jewish spirit via book-burning (specifically the Talmud), forced conversions and physical persecution.

Yet, Judaism continues to flourish.

During the early Christian period (325–500 C.E.), after it had become the predominant religion of Rome:[9]

- ◆ Christians were forbidden to interact with Jews.
- ◆ State policy restricted the political and civil rights of Jews.

❖ Jews were forbidden to live in Jerusalem.

❖ Marriage between a Jew and gentile was punishable by death.

❖ Forced conversions were carried out.

❖ Sporadic Christian mobs would attack Jewish quarters and synagogues.

The Dark Ages (500–1000 C.E.) ushered in a new era of anti-Jewish hostility. In light of political instability in Europe, the Church became the major unifying and stabilizing force. At the time, Jewish settlements existed throughout Christendom in virtually every province and city. Although Jews were declared enemies of the state for refusing to convert to Christianity, the hostility was more an elitist phenomenon with an absence of popular anti-Jewish sentiment. Support for this comes from the repetitive royal and Church decrees, commanding the faithful and lower clergy to refrain from interacting and maintaining friendly relations with Jews.[10]

It is interesting to note the gradual development of Christian anti-Jewish hostility at this point, for it mirrors the above Egyptian paradigm. During the early Christian period (325–500 C.E.) activity was limited to discrimination in which Jewish national identity was threatened. The Land of Israel and Jerusalem were off-limits to the Jewish masses, and while residing in foreign lands their civil, economic, political and even marital rights were restricted. Subsequently, however, the Jews' refusal to convert brought in its wake further oppression, where the goal was no longer to break the Jew's national pride, but rather to destroy his Talmudic spirit, rendering him susceptible to Christian influence. Forced conversions, book burnings, child abductions, and prohibitions against the observance of Torah Law were the more salient forms of persecution. Accordingly, when this failed, the body of the Jew became endangered.

Though there appears to be little in the way of direct decrees issuing from the Church to annihilate Jews, the random torture and slaughter of literally hundreds of thousands of Jews during the Crusades (1000–1348), the Black Death (the Bubonic Plague, 1348–1357), the Inquisition (1366–1500) and the Eastern European pogroms (during the seventeenth and eighteenth centuries) all in the name of Christianity, appear to belie the Church's declared goal of spreading Christianity throughout the Jewish world.[11]

Muslim Anti-Jewish Hostility

ISLAM WAS THE second major religion to spring forth from Judaism,[12] but unlike Christianity, its founder was not a Jew, and it was not originally a Jewish sect. Islam also had a universal mission to save the world but, in contrast to Christianity, it was armed with the sword of the state almost at its inception.[13]

With the advent of Islam in the seventh century C.E., there was a large Jewish population in Medina, where the first Muslim community was founded.[14] Muhammad, the founder of Islam, was greatly influenced by Jewish practices and ideas.[15] In fact, Moses is mentioned in the Koran (the sacred text of Islam) over one hundred times and may be considered one of its predominant figures.[16] Accordingly, Muhammad declared: "Yet before it was the Book of Moses for a model and a mercy; and this is a Book (i.e., the Koran) confirming."[17]

Muhammad adopted the Jews' founding father Abraham as his new faith's founding patriarch, but in disregard for the Hebrew Scriptures — from which he based much of his new religion — inserted Ishmael as one of the Hebrew patriarchs,[18] and traced his own genealogy through Ishmael to Abraham. Muhammad granted theological legitimacy to Judaism and Christianity and though he denied the divinity of Jesus, considered Jesus the last of the Hebrew prophets, while claiming himself the messenger of God and "the Seal of the Prophets." While accepting most narratives of the Hebrew Bible, Muhammad accused the Jews of deleting Biblical predictions of his eventful coming.[19]

According to the scholar Abraham Katsh:[20]

> Muhammad never intended to establish Islam as a new religion. He considered himself the rightful custodian of the Book sent by Allah (God) to confirm the Scriptures. It is for this reason that in the beginning he saw no difference between Judaism and Christianity and believed that both Jews and Christians would welcome him. It is only later, when he realized that he could never gain support from either of them, that he presented Islam as a new faith.

For example, in the early days of Islam, Muhammad's followers prayed in the direction of Jerusalem, and observed the most solemn Jewish holiday, Yom Kippur. Only when Muhammad concluded that the Jews were unwilling to accept him as their prophet did he substitute Mecca for Jerusalem, and the Fast of Ramadan for Yom Kippur.[21]

No group could have validated Muhammad's claims as could the Jews, and no group could have so seriously undermined the new creed as could the Jewish nation. The consequences of rejecting Islam were inevitable: Muhammad turned against them. His hostile reactions were then recorded in the Koran, granting Muslims, throughout history, Divinely based antipathy towards Jews.[22] In response to the Jews' refusal to convert, Jewish communities in the area

of Medina were attacked and either slaughtered or forced
to leave. The Jews living further north were besieged by the
Army of Islam, and after Muhammad's death were expelled,
purging northern Arabia of all infidels.[23]

Although there were periodic physical persecutions, mass
expulsions and massacres of Jews in the name of Islam,[24]
the focus of Muslim anti-Jewish hostility was more of political subjugation, social humiliation and religious inferiority.[25]
Jews were allowed to reside in "Muslim lands" as "People of
the Book," as opposed to pagans who would have to choose
Islam or the sword. Officially, though not always in practice,
Jews were granted religious freedom, thus allowing them to
continue their traditions. Islam was not pressured to attack
the Jewish spirit via religious persecution, nor to annihilate
the Jewish collective body. Islam only required that Jews be
relegated to positions of inferiority vis-à-vis Muslims.

Official Islamic legislation, which delineated the restriction
of liberties and conditions of life for Jews, was promulgated
in the seventh-century *Covenant of Omar* (named after
Muhammad's second successor), which if transgressed was
punishable by death.

According to the Covenant, Jews were compelled to wear
a distinctive costume with a ribbon and a yellow piece of
cloth as a badge; they were not permitted to perform their
religious practices in public or to own a horse; they were
forbidden to drink wine in public; and they were required
to bury their dead without allowing their grief to be heard
by Muslims. Islamic law decreed the lightest of penalties for
killing a non-Muslim, and the testimony of a non-Muslim
against a Muslim was considered invalid. As payment for being allowed to live, the non-Muslim paid a special head and
property tax. These and other restrictions of the Covenant

remained in force for centuries, and were implemented with varying degrees of cruelty depending upon the particular Muslim ruler.[26]

Islam's guiding principle concerning the treatment of Jews (and Christians) was that Islam dominates and is not to be dominated. Once non-Muslims forfeited their civil liberties, they were allowed some degree of freedom. However, when Jews would receive equal status in "Muslim territory" and, needless to say, when they would forge their own independent state, the Jewish presence would no longer be tolerated.

This, in fact, occurred in the twentieth century. The demeaned subjects had the impudence to claim independence over Muslim land. As Yehoshafat Harkabi, a leading expert on the contemporary Arab world, put it: "A Jewish state is incompatible with the view of Jews as humiliated or wretched."[27] As long as the Jews were subjugated in Muslim lands, Islam could claim superiority as the true faith which had displaced the older monotheistic creeds. However, with the advent of Israel as an independent Jewish state, the foundations of Islam were shaken. The inferior somehow prevailed, casting doubt on Islam's superiority, and with each successive victory the dissonance intensified.

Accordingly, Ayatollah Khomeini proclaimed:[28]

> O brothers! Let us not regard this holy and sacrificial war as a war between Arabs and Israel. Let us regard it as a war of all Muslims together against Jews and their leaders.

The similarities between Muslim anti-Jewish hostility and its predecessors are clear. Judaism and the Jewish People were a threat to Islam from its inception. From the beginning, Jews refused to accept the majority religion. In addition, the type of anti-Jewish hostility that emerged was one of the three forms delineated earlier, where strict limitations on civil liberties and negation of Jewish statehood were diligently enforced. Though physical attacks have been constant since the early part of the twentieth century, these attacks are seemingly not targeted at the Jewish collective body, but rather at Jewish statehood which is anathema to any pious Muslim.

Another common trend is Jewish tenacity. Though it appears almost anticlimactic when compared with Jewish tenacity prior to Islam, the remarkable perseverance of the Jews can, as well, be seen here. It is particularly noticeable when compared to Christian communities of the Middle East. As mentioned above, Muslim oppression vis-à-vis non-Muslims applied also to Christians. However, although Jewish communities in Muslim lands often flourished (in spiritual terms), most Christian communities never even survived. This is often lost sight of when favorably comparing Muslim anti-Jewish activity with hostile Christian activity. However, the conversion to Islam of nearly every pre-Islamic Christian community in the Muslim world, bears testimony to what the Jews actually endured.[29]

Russian and Communist Anti-Jewish Hostility

PERVADED BY A spirit of enlightened liberalism, the nineteenth and twentieth centuries were to be a positive turning point for mankind in both Europe and America. With the advent of the industrial revolution, a promising economic order was created via capitalism and socialism. Unfortunately for the Jewish People, it turned in the wrong direction. For the Jew, the nineteenth, and particularly the twentieth century would bring with it

discrimination, persecution and massacre on a scale hereto-
fore never experienced.

Almost from the beginning of Russia's history, a tradition
of autocracy and devotion to Eastern Orthodox Christianity
shaped a policy of suspicion towards European influence,
and specifically towards Judaism.[30] This distrust was heightened to the point of paranoia when Poland was partitioned in
the late eighteenth century. Russia then became governor
of the largest body of Jews in the world. Simultaneous with
their admission into the Russian empire, Jews were restricted
to live in the "Pale of Settlement."[31] Even within the Pale, Jews
suffered economic restrictions, extra taxes and other hardships. For example, in 1808 Czar Alexander I issued an edict
calling for the expulsion of Jews from all villages; consequently half a million Jews were driven like cattle into the
cities, and left in the open squares to starve and freeze.[32]

Alexander's successor, Nicholas I, introduced hundreds of
disabling laws curbing Jewish activities and went further than
his predecessors who, for the most part, only stripped the
Jews of their civil liberties to live, own land and work where
and as they pleased. Nicholas I, determined to complete
the Russification of the Jews, attacked the Jewish spirit by
conscripting Jewish youths of twelve to an extended military
service of twenty-five years (the twenty-five year stint commenced once the boy turned eighteen). Jewish youth were
brought to the farthest outposts of the empire, to be beaten
and tortured in an effort to "persuade" them to convert to
Russian (Christian) Orthodoxy.[33]

When Nicholas failed to break the Jewish spirit (i.e.,
Jews were not converting) he turned his attention to Jew-
ish education. He decreed that Jewish children go to special
Jewish schools where Talmud was not to be taught, and

where Judaism, in general, was taught according to Russian Orthodoxy.[34] Nicholas eventually abolished these schools, for conversion was not being achieved.

In 1881, Czar Alexander II, under the influence of his chief advisor Pobedonstsev, formulated his "anti-revolutionary program," with Russian Jewry as its target. The Jewish problem was to be solved simply; one-third was to emigrate, one-third was to die, and one-third was to convert.[35] On Easter of 1881 the massacres commenced, and over a twenty-five-year period (1881–1906) thousands of Jews were murdered while tens of thousands were left maimed and destitute.[36]

In 1915 Grand Duke Sergei, the commander-in-chief of Russia's military, ordered the relocation of 600,000 Jews to interior Russia. Approximately 100,000 died from exposure or starvation during its implementation.[37] In 1917, during the Russian Revolution, massacres of Jews were organized and carried out by the Ukrainians and the Russian Whites. In the Ukraine 200,000 Jews were slaughtered, and 300,000 children were left homeless and orphaned. During the revolution and ensuing civil war Jewish populations were accused by both sides of being members of the opposing force, and were accordingly tortured. During this period it was considered a mercy to be killed outright, rather than to be tortured to death. Parents were forced to watch the torture of their children, and children of their parents. Jewish women were subjected to obscene acts and mutilation before being granted the privilege to die.[38]

It was within this historical context that the Russian people collectively "converted" to Marxism and set out, like their predecessors, to force their ideology on others in order to "save" the world. The "pious" Russian populace metamorphosed from devout religionists to progressive communists over a relatively short period of time. One major adjustment, however, was that pre-revolutionary Russia would only attack Jews residing within its borders, while communist Russia would strike at Jews and Judaism everywhere. With the adoption of Marxism, the Russian government no longer feared the indignation and repulsion of the Western world. They were now universalists, furthering the ideals of one of the century's leading thinkers, and this ideology just happened to be anti-Jewish.

Karl Marx, whose father had him baptized at the age of six in order that he not have to suffer anti-Jewish oppression,[39] became the new legitimizing force, aimed at uprooting and destroying the Jewish presence. Karl Marx, who himself descended from a long line of distinguished rabbis, argued that the Jew not be emancipated until he abandon his "exclusive religion, morality and customs."[40]

Marx theorized that the role of economics was the key determinant in the development of mankind. He argued that world peace and happiness would be achieved once man restructured the economic order. In composing passages like the following, he bequeathed legitimacy in the suppression and oppression of Jews and Judaism everywhere. He wrote:[41]

> It is from its own entrails that civil society ceaselessly engenders the Jew....
>
> Money is the jealous god of Israel, beside which no other god may exist.... The chimerical nationality of the Jew is the nationality of the trader, and above all of the financier.... As soon as society succeeds in abolishing the empirical essence of Judaism — huckstering and its conditions — the Jew becomes impossible, because his consciousness no longer has an object.

In the post-World War II era, the former Soviet Union attacked the Jewish People via various strategies. They attempted to break Jewish nationalism by defining Zionism as "a reactionary movement...which denies the class struggle and strives to isolate the Jewish working masses from the general struggle of the proletariat."[42] Their sophisticated propaganda apparatus consistently associated Zionism with Nazism, and often referred to the Jewish State as Hitlerian.[43] In addition, requests by Soviet Jews to immigrate to Israel were fraught with hardships ranging from losing one's job, to an extended prison term, to exile in Siberia.

The Soviets also attempted to destroy the Jewish spirit. Synagogues were seized and converted into Communist Youth Clubs. Rabbis and religious teachers were imprisoned. All forms of Jewish education were barred, and the teaching of Hebrew was outlawed.[44] Their attempt to annihilate the Jewish collective body, however, was more subtle. They did so by providing organizational and military training together with highly sophisticated military hardware to Israel's most hostile adversaries, while these adversaries called for the total destruction of the Jewish State.

German Nazi Anti-Jewish Hostility

THEORETICALLY, THE JUXTAPOSITION of Soviet communist leftist ideology with Nazi right-wing fanaticism appears absurd. Is it logical (save wartime alliances) for two radical movements which are ideologically at opposite ends of the spectrum and anathema to one another, to claim as their most natural enemy the same Jewish People? More ridiculous, it seems, is that each movement projects on the Jews the guise of the other. Soviet leftists would often refer to Jews as Nazi collaborators and to the State of Israel as a

Hitlerian state,[45] while Nazis did, and still do, refer to Jews everywhere as communists.[46]

However, this contradiction in doctrine is, at best, superficial. Just as the Russian incapacity to tolerate Judaism predated Communism, so too, did Hitler's pathological hostility towards Jews predate Nazi right-wing ideology. Both movements merely bequeathed to their adherents an ideological base from which to legitimize the discrimination and persecution of Jews.

Hitler's paranoia towards Jews was blatant from the start. Hitler's Nazism was not an independent movement which gradually incorporated anti-Jewish dogma. Rather, the foundation of Hitler's Nazism was specifically Aryan superiority over the Jew and the threat of the "Jewish peril." For example, as early as the 1920s, Hitler called for the total elimination of the Jews, who, in his words, were "contaminating the Aryan race."[47]

In *Mein Kampf*, which Hitler wrote while in prison in 1923–1924, he blamed the defeat of Germany in World War I on those "Marxist leaders" (the Jews) and stated that had "twelve or fifteen thousand of these Jews, who were corrupting the nation, been forced to submit to poison gas," the millions of deaths at the front "would not have been in vain."[48]

In Hitler's twisted mind, Jew-hatred came first and only afterwards, Nazi racial ideology. For example, neither the Japanese nor the Arabs were denigrated by the so-called racist Nazis (indeed, both were Nazi allies). According to Hitler, the racial impurities disseminated by Jews were their subversive value system and alien ideas. As he put it, "the Jews speak German, but they think Jewish."[49]

The racial war of Hitler was focused almost exclusively

on the Jew. Most everything Hitler did in the political arena
centered around the Jews. Hitler's first political speech as
well as his last will and testament contained explicit charges
against the Jewish People. Even the swastika represented for
Hitler the battle between the "pure" Germanic race and the
"inferior" Jew. In writing about the Nazi flag, he explained
that the swastika symbolized "the mission to struggle for the
victory of the Aryan man...which is eternally anti-Semitic
and always will be anti-Semitic."[50]

Albert Speer, one of Hitler's ministers, wrote in *Spandau:
The Secret Diaries*, that between the soup and the vegetable
course, Hitler was capable of tossing off quite calmly, "I want
to annihilate the Jews!"[51] Strange as it may seem, Hitler did
not attack Jews to achieve power, but was driven to power in
order to annihilate Jews.[52] For example, late in the war when
the Nazis were being defeated, German troops were taken
from Allied fronts in order to continue the mass murder
of Jews. In 1944, when the Germans required every train
to evacuate Greece, not one train was diverted from those
transporting Jews to death camps. And, while addressing
the German people for the last time in 1945, Hitler proclaimed:[53]

> Above all I charge the leaders of the nation and those un-
> der them to scrupulous observance of the laws of race and
> to the merciless opposition of the universal poisoner of all
> peoples — international Jewry.

The insanity of Hitler, abetted by a pervasive anti-Jewish
world,[54] set the stage for the unprecedented massacre of six
million civilian Jews in a war which consumed over fifty million people. In conclusion, Hitler himself best enunciated his
ultimate purpose:[55]

It is true we are barbarians; that is an honored title to us. I free humanity from the shackles of the soul, from the degrading suffering caused by the false vision called conscience and ethics. The Jews have inflicted two wounds on mankind: circumcision on its body and conscience on its soul. They are Jewish inventions. The war for domination of the world is waged only between the two of us, between these two camps alone; the Germans and the Jews. Everything else is but deception.

Hitler's paranoia would find no reprieve until all Jews were destroyed. In the end, however, the Hitlerian monster was exterminated, while his crippled and maimed arch-adversary lived on to create an independent Jewish state, after eighteen hundred years of wandering.

NOTES TO CHAPTER 3

1. Lamprecht, S.P., *Our Philosophical Traditions* (New York: Appleton Century-Crofts, 1955).
2. Matthew 5:17–19, *Self-Pronouncing* edition (Cleveland: World Publishing Co., 1941).
3. Ibid. 15:24.
4. See Ruether, R.R., *Faith and Fratricide: The Theological Roots of Anti-Semitism* (New York: Seabury Press, 1979); see also Gager, J.G., *The Origins of Anti-Semitism: Attitudes towards Judaism in Pagan and Christian Antiquity* (New York: Oxford University Press, 1983).
5. Gager.
6. Flannery, E.H., *The Anguish of the Jews.* (New York: Macmillan Co., 1965).
7. Ibid.
8. Ibid.
9. Grosser, P.E., and Halperin, E.G., *The Causes and Effects of Anti-Semitism* (New York: Philosophical Library, 1978).

10. Ibid.

11. Ibid.

12. Prager, D., and Telushkin, J., *Why the Jew? The Reason for Anti-Semitism* (New York: Simon & Schuster, 1983).

13. Grosser et al.

14. Prager et al.

15. Flannery.

16. Prager et al.

17. Koran, Sura 46:1, in *The Koran Interpreted* (New York: Macmillan Co., 1970).

18. Baidawi, cited in *Judaism and the Koran* (New York: A S. Barnes & Co., 1962), by A.I. Katch.

19. Katch, A.I., *Judaism and the Koran* (New York: A.S. Barnes & Co., 1962).

20. Ibid., p. 10.

21. Prager et al.

22. Ibid.

23. Grosser et al.

24. Ibid.

25. Peters, J., *From Time Immemorial: The Origins of the Arab-Jewish Conflict over Palestine* (New York: Harper & Row, 1984).

26. Ibid.

27. Prager et al.

28. In his book, *Confronting Israel*, quoted in *Myths and Facts 1985: A Concise Record of the Arab-Israeli Conflict* (Washington, D.C.: Near East Report, 1984), by L.J. Davis, p. 133.

29. Prager et al.

30. Flannery.

31. Ibid.

32. Grosser et al.

33. Ibid.

34. Ibid.

35. Flannery.

36. Grosser et al.

37. Ibid.

38. Ibid.

39. Prager et al.

40. Ibid.

41. Bottomore, T.D., *Karl Marx: Early Writings* (New York: McGraw-Hill, 1964).

42. Great Soviet Encyclopaedia (1952), cited in Prager et al.

43. Prager et al.

44. Fisch, D.A., *Jews for Nothing: On Cults, Intermarriage and Assimilation* (New York: Feldheim, 1984).

45. Grayzel, S., *A History of the Jews* (New York: Mentor, 1968).

46. Anti-Defamation League of B'nai B'rith, *Hate Groups in America: A Record of Bigotry and Violence* (New York: Anti-Defamation League of B'nai B'rith, 1982).

47. Goldberg, M.H., *Just Because They're Jewish* (New York: Scarborough House, 1981).

48. Dawidowicz, L.S., *The War Against the Jews, 1933–1945* (New York: Bantam Books, 1975, p. 3).

49. Prager et al.

50. Goldberg, p. 207.

51. Ibid.

52. Dawidowicz.

53. Ibid., p. 28.

54. See Morse, A.D., *While Six Million Died: A Chronicle of American Apathy* (New York: Random House, 1961); see also Wyman, D.S., *The Abandonment of the Jews* (New York: Pantheon Books, 1984).

55. Scherman N., Foreword in M. Prager, *Sparks of Glory* (New York: Mesorah Publications, 1985).

4 | Ancient and Classical Anti-Jewish Slander

Lies are pervasive, truth is rare.
(Talmud, Tractate Shabbos 104a)

C HAPTERS 2 AND 3 DELINEATED THE RECURRING PROCESS OF anti-Jewish hostility. However, the pattern falls short, for it fails to explain why the common people, the masses, have turned so violently against the Jews.

In short, attacks against Jews have historically been provoked by misinformation and slander about Jews and Judaism alike. The dissemination of malicious and denigrating statements about Jews appears to be the catalyst inciting the masses into action. The propagation of misinformation, misconceptions and outright lies have precipitated anti-Jewish hostility throughout history.

Through the spreading of hate and slander, anti-Jewish leaders have succeeded in directing the anger and frustration of the masses against both Jews and Judaism. Consequently, the continuous barrage of anti-Jewish rhetoric, throughout

millennia, has set the stage for subsequent slander and its
believability.

Ancient Egyptian Anti-Jewish Teachings   CONSISTENT WITH THE analysis in Chapter 2, the propagation of misinformation can already be seen in ancient Egypt. Only eighty years before Pharaoh began offering his rationale for enslaving the Jews, did Joseph single-handedly save Egypt from ruination.[1] Furthermore, the Hebrew people formed an integral part of cosmopolitan Egypt,[2] and their patriotism on behalf of Egypt, the fatherland, is documented.[3]

However, despite this scenario, Pharaoh, emperor of the most powerful and cultured nation of the time, declared:[4]

> Behold, the people of the Children of Israel are too many and too mighty for us; come let us deal wisely with them, lest they multiply, and it will come to pass that, when there happens any war, they will join our enemies and fight against us.

Though little is known of ancient Egyptian anti-Jewish propaganda, the above passage implies that without Pharaoh's incitement, against what he perceived as a Jewish threat in the midst of Egypt, the masses would have been less prone to subsequent anti-Jewish activity. Pharaoh required the "Big-Lie Tactic," something which would successfully play on the emotions and fears of the general populace. He did so by fabricating the Hebrews' anti-Egyptian leanings, with its logical consequence in time of war.

In essence, the Hebrews were portrayed as a powerful and inimical force, undermining Egypt's collective well-being and sovereignty.

Ancient Persian Anti-Jewish Teachings

HAMAN (THE PRIME minister of ancient Persia), with the explicit intent to annihilate world Jewry, persuaded the Persian King (Achashverosh/Xerxes) with the following argument, as recorded in the Midrash:[5]

There is a certain people, the Jews, scattered abroad and dispersed among the peoples in all the provinces of the kingdom. They are proud and haughty.... When they see us, they spit out before us. ... When we levy them for the king's service, they jump over the wall and hide to escape. If we try to arrest them, they turn to us and glare with their eyes, grind their teeth, and so intimidate us that we become virtually helpless....

If one of them is obligated to work for the king, he wastes the entire day. If they want to buy or sell with us they say, "This is a day for doing business." But if we request the same from them they say, "We cannot do business today." ...

On the first day of their New Year they go to their meeting places, read out of their books, translate pieces from the writings of their Prophets while cursing our king and execrating our government.... On the tenth day of the same month...they torture their children without mercy, forcing them to abstain from food. They again go to their synagogues, read their books, translate from the writings of their prophets, and curse our king and government by saying, "May this empire be wiped off from the face of the earth." ... They pray that the king may die, and his rule be made to cease.... On the twenty-first day of the same month they again go to their meeting places to pray, read from their books, and make circles with their willow branches while jumping and skipping, so that there is no telling whether they are cursing or blessing us.

Haman's vilification of the Jews was accepted,[6] and King Achashverosh thereupon issued his edict which read:[7]

> To all the peoples, nations and races: Peace be with you. This is to tell you that the Persian prime minister, Haman the Amalekite, the son of great ancestors, made a small request of me, saying, "Among us dwells a people, the most despicable of all, who have been a stumbling block throughout history. They are exceedingly haughty, and they know our weaknesses and shortcomings." Therefore...we have taken counsel, and have decided upon an irrevocable resolution, according to the laws of the Medes and Persians, to eradicate the Jews from among the inhabitants of the earth. We have sent the edict to all provinces of my empire, to slaughter them, their wives and their children on the thirteenth day of the month of Adar, none is to escape.

Greek Anti-Jewish Teachings   IN EXPLAINING JEWISH origins, Hecateus of Abdera, a Greek historian of the early third century B.C.E., stated that Moses "in remembrance of the exile of his people, instituted for them a misanthropic and inhospitable way of life."[8] Manetho, a Hellenist-Egyptian priest and historian, embellished the story by describing how the Jews, who in "actuality" were Egyptian lepers and diseased, were expelled by the Egyptian king and led by Moses, who taught them impudently "not to adore the gods."[9] The themes of leprous origins and misanthropy were rarely absent from Greek and Roman anti-Jewish literature.[10]

Following his predecessors, Democritus, in his *On the Jews*, claimed that Jews adore the golden head of an ass, and according to the historian Suidas, charged that "every seven years they capture a stranger, lead him to their Holy

Temple, and immolate him by cutting his flesh into small pieces."[11] The infamous ritual murder libel was born, and would be used in various forms against the early Christians and again against the Jews from the twelfth century and onward.[12] Apion, who transposed the story, reduced the interval of human sacrifice to once a year, and proved himself a most effective propaganda agent for the self-proclaimed divinity Antiochus Epiphanes. By explaining to his people the "barbaric" Jewish ceremonies, Epiphanes would be blameless for profaning the Temple and for his unbridled slaughter of Jews.[13]

Seeking out strategies to vilify Jews and Judaism, the Greek-Syrian government concocted stories and motifs which "proved" the "animalistic" nature of the Jewish People and their rites. Apion, as spokesperson for Hellenistic anti-Jewish rhetoric, attempts to explain the nature of Jewish ceremony. He writes:[14]

> Antiochus [Epiphanes] found in the [Jerusalem] Temple a couch, upon which a man was reclining. Before him was a table, laden with a banquet of fish of the sea, beasts of the earth and birds of the air; the poor fellow was gazing at it all in stupefaction. The king's entry was instantly hailed by him with adoration as about to procure him profound relief; falling at the king's knees, he stretched out his right hand and implored him to set him free. The king reassured him and bade him tell who he was, why he was living there, and what was the meaning of his abundant fare. Thereupon, with sighs and tears, the man, in a pitiful tone, told the tale of his distress. He said he was a Greek and that, while traveling about the province for his livelihood, was suddenly kidnapped by men of a foreign race and conveyed to the Temple; there he was shut up and seen by no one, but was

fattened on feasts of the most lavish description. At first, these attentions deceived him and caused him pleasure; suspicion followed, and then consternation. Finally, on consulting the attendants who waited upon him, he heard of the unutterable law of the Jews, for the sake of which he was being fed. The practice was repeated annually at a fixed season. They would kidnap a Greek foreigner, fatten him up for a year, and then convey him to wood, where they slew him, sacrificed his body with their customary ritual, partook of his flesh, and while immolating the Greek, swore an oath of hostility to the Greeks. The remains of their victim were then thrown into a pit.

Since Hellenistic culture considered itself the true standard of enlightened behavior, the Jews' refusal to assimilate on the grounds that the Greek gods were false and their ceremonies hedonistic was a cultural affront of no small measure. The insult was not to be taken lightly, and elaborate propaganda used to deprecate both Jews and Judaism was rigorously employed. For example, in Alexandria, Egypt — a bastion of Greek culture during that period — a literary tradition of anti-Jewish polemics was established. It was claimed, for example, that Jews had been a base and disease-ridden people who had integrated with the Egyptian slave population. Their exodus from Egypt was explained as forced by the Egyptians themselves, who drove them out in order to rid themselves of a leprous element. The Sabbath was no longer an honorable commemoration, but rather part of the "dirt-ridden" Jewish condition. The Jews, in fleeing from Egypt, could travel only six days at a time because they were afflicted with syphilis, and the Sabbath allegedly reflected this.[15]

Roman Anti-Jewish Teachings   ACCORDING TO THE Catholic priest Edward Flannery, Roman fabrications can be traced back to Cicero in 59 B.C.E. Occasion to vent his hostility was presented in a trial for the defense of the Roman official Flaccus, who had despoiled the Jewish treasury.

"Their kind of religion and rites," Cicero claimed, "has nothing in common with the splendor of the empire, the gravity of our name, and the institutions of our ancestors... and, conquered and enslaved, how little the immortal gods care for them."[16]

Further slander was expressed by the Roman historian Tacitus. According to this noted historian, Jews descended from lepers expelled from Egypt who followed a band of wild asses out of the desert. From these repugnant origins Jewish rites were derived. According to Tacitus, Jews worship the ass, which is consecrated in Jewish temples. They abstain from pork in remembrance of their leprosy. Their use of unleavened bread on Passover symbolizes the food they stole in Egypt, their Sabbath represents the day on which they escaped, and to which, in their indolence, they became attached. Their other institutions are "sinister, shameful and have survived only because of their perversity."

Among the Jews themselves, said Tacitus, "nothing is illicit, the first instructions they (i.e., the Jewish children) are given is to disdain the gods, abjure the fatherland, forget their parents, brothers and children."[17] They "reveal a stubborn attachment to one another...which contrasts with their implacable hatred for the rest of mankind."[18]

It is interesting to note that as Christianity became more and more differentiated from Judaism in the second and third centuries, they, too, were accused by Roman writers of ritual murder, infanticide, sexual perversion, worshiping the ass and cannibalism.[19]

The Roman intelligentsia provided ample justification for attacking the "perfidious" Jew with their "loathsome" beliefs and lifestyle. For example, the Roman rhetorician Marcus Fabius Quintilianus called the Jews a "pernicious nation" and their faith a "superstition."[20] To the Roman poet Martial, circumcision and the Sabbath were tantamount to everything despicable.[21] And Jewish education, according to the Roman satirist Juvenal, was described thus:[22]

> The Jewish child has been taught to adore nothing but the clouds and the divinity of the sky, and to make no distinction between human and porcine flesh. Brought up in contempt of Roman laws, he learns, observes and reveres only the Judaic law and all that Moses taught in a mysterious book — not to show the way to a traveler who does not practice the same rites, nor point out a well to the uncircumcised. And all this came about because his father passed each seventh day in idleness, taking no part in the duties of life.

Rutilius Namatianus, a Roman poet, wrote similarly:[23]

> An unsociable animal this Jew, to whom all human nourishment is repugnant. We [the Roman nation] answered him with injuries deserving his ignoble race, his shameless nation that practices circumcision and is the root of every imbecility....

Namatianus attacked other Jewish institutions, and concludes his polemic by denouncing the "curse" Judaism "inflicted" on mankind — Christianity.[24]

NOTES TO CHAPTER 4

1. Miller, A., *Behold a People* (New York: Balshon, 1968).
2. *Midrash Tanchuma* (Warsaw: Y.G. Monk, 1879).
3. *Midrash Yashar Shemot*, in *Sefer HaYashar HaShalem* (Jerusalem: Etz Chaim, 1968).
4. Exodus 1:9–10.
5. *Targum Yerushalmi.*
6. *Midrash Abba Gurion*, in A. Jellinek (ed.), *Beit HaMidrash* (Jerusalem:Wahrman-Books, 1967).
7. *Midrash Esther.*
8. Reinach, T., cited in *The Anguish of the Jews* (New York: Macmillan Co., 1965), by E.H. Flannery, p. 8.
9. Ibid.
10. Flannery.
11. Reinach.
12. Flannery.
13. Trachtenberg, J., *The Devil and the Jew: The Medieval Conception of the Jew and Its Relation to Modern Anti-Semitism* (Philadelphia: Jewish Publication Society of America, 1983).
14. Josephus, Against Apion.
15. Ruether, R.R., *Faith and Fratricide: The Theological Roots of Anti-Semitism* (New York: Seabury Press, 1979).
16. Flannery, p. 19.
17. Ibid., pp. 20–21.
18. Prager, D. & Teluskin, J., *Why the Jews? The Reason for Anti-Semitism* (New York: Simon & Schuster, 1983), p. 86.
19. Grosser, P.E. & Halperin, E.G., *The Causes and Effects of Anti-Semitism* (New York: Philosophical Library, 1978).
20. Flannery.
21. Ibid.
22. Ibid., p. 20.
23. Ibid., p. 21.
24. Ibid.

5 | Religious and More-Contemporary Anti-Jewish Slander

Christian Anti-Jewish Teachings

CONSISTENT WITH WHAT was stated in Chapter 3, Christian anti-Jewish slander does not appear to lay at the foundation of Christianity. Only after Christianity severed its close relationship with Judaism did Pontius Pilate, known throughout history for his ruthlessness, become vindicated in his execution of Jesus.[1]

Accordingly, early Gospels do not single out the Jews in general as at fault for the crucifixion, but the last in the series of Gospels to be written down does, and turns out to be the most anti-Jewish and pro-Roman of the Gospels.[2] Hence, Pontius Pilate is sympathetically portrayed as deferring to Jewish pressure, a deference he failed to exhibit in his other dealings with the Jews.[3] Thereafter, the Jew as "Christ-killer" (until he or she converts) became the progenitor for countless ritual murder, desecration of the Host, and Jew as devil charges.

In the fourth century, when the Church became dominant, attitudes towards Jews became increasingly deprecating. The most complete expression of Christian slander in its "century of victory" came from St. John Chrysostom. It was this type of mind-set which would dictate Christianity's relationship to Judaism throughout the following millennia. According to St. John, Jews are "inveterate murderers, destroyers, men possessed by the devil.... They have surpassed the ferocity of wild beasts, for they murder their offspring and immolate them to the devil." Their synagogue, said Chrysostom, is "the domicile of the devil," their rites "criminal," and their religion a "disease." Jews were depicted as degenerate because of their "odious assassination of Jesus..." and "vengeance is without end; Jews will always remain without Temple or nation."[4]

In 1965 the Catholic Church put to rest much of this slander with its statement on the Jews, issued by the Second Vatican Ecumenical council.[5] After eighteen hundred years, Vatican II broke the long-standing theme of Jewish collective and eternal complicity in the crucifixion of Jesus.

Lest one believe that Christian anti-Jewish rhetoric was exclusively a Catholic phenomenon, a summary of Protestant slander bears mention. Martin Luther, the founder of Protestantism, began his reformation with seeming pro-Jewish concern, but turned against them once he discerned their unwillingness to convert to his new brand of Christianity.

In the beginning, Luther was highly critical of the Church's historical anti-Jewish policies. He believed, like others, that if he courted the Jews, they would adopt his new reformed Christianity. In fact, in his essay entitled, "Jesus Christ Was Born a Jew" he wrote:[6]

> They (i.e., the papists) have dealt with the Jews as if they were dogs rather than human beings.... If the Apostles, who also were Jews, had dealt with us gentiles as we gentiles

> deal with the Jews there would never have been a Christian among the gentiles. In turn, we ought to treat the Jews in a brotherly manner in order that we might convert some of them...we are but gentiles, while the Jews are of the lineage of Christ. We are aliens and in-laws; they are blood relatives, cousins and brothers of our Lord.

However, when the Jews refused to convert and, worse, when some of Luther's disciples began displaying Judaizing tendencies, he turned against them. His later writings were so venomous that latter-day Nazis often cited them. In *Mein Kampf,* Hitler called Luther one of the three great German patriarchs together with Frederick the Great and Richard Wagner.

Luther renewed many of the old anti-Jewish libels. In his later writings, he labeled Jews "poisoners," "ritual murderers," and "parasites" preying on Christian society who were worse than the devil. They were, according to Luther, the embodiment of the anti-Christ himself, and were doomed to eternal hell.[7]

In his pamphlet entitled *Concerning the Jews and Their Lies,* he outlined the actions to be taken against them. They were:[8]

- ❖ Burn all synagogues
- ❖ Destroy Jewish dwellings
- ❖ Confiscate Jewish holy books
- ❖ Forbid rabbis to teach Torah
- ❖ Confiscate Jewish property
- ❖ Force Jews into physical labor
- ❖ Expel the Jews from all Christian-dominated provinces

Muslim UNLIKE CHRISTIANITY, THE negative stereo-
Anti-Jewish type of the Jew in Islamic literature is as
Teachings old as the religion itself. One need go no
further than the Koran (i.e., Islam's sacred
texts believed to contain Divine revelations to Muhammad)
to understand Islam's stereotype of the Jew. For example,
Muhammad charged the Jews with deliberately omitting the
prophecies of his coming:

❖ And when a Book came unto them from God, confirming
  the Scriptures that were with them, although they had
  prayed for assistance against those who believed not, yet
  when that came unto them which they knew to be from
  God, they would not believe therein: therefore the curse
  of God shall be on the infidels.[9]

❖ People of the Book! Why do you disbelieve in God's signs,
  which you yourselves witness? People of the Book! Why
  do you confound the truth with vanity, and conceal the
  truth and that wittingly?[10]

❖ People of the Book, now there has come to you a Messenger (i.e., Muhammad), making clear to you many
  things you have been concealing of the Book, and effac-
  ing many things.[11]

In other places Muhammad spoke unabashedly about the
"vile disbelieving" Jews:

❖ [They] brought upon themselves indignation on indignation; and the unbelievers shall suffer an ignominious
  punishment.[12]

❖ They are smitten with vileness wherever they are found;
  unless they obtain security by entering into a treaty

with God (i.e., converting to Islam)…and they draw on themselves indignation from God, and they are afflicted with poverty. This they suffer, because they disbelieved the signs of God, and slew the prophets unjustly; this because they are rebellious and transgressed.[13]

❖ You shall surely find the most violent of all men in enmity against the true believers (i.e., the Muslims) to be the Jews and the idolaters.[14]

Muhammad declared that Jews, like their Christian counterparts, were not true monotheists. He supported the charge by claiming that Jews believe the scribe Ezra to be the son of God. "The Jews say: 'Ezra is the son of God'…God assail them! How they are perverted!"[15]

Accordingly, all "God-fearing people" were exhorted to keep a distance from the "evil" Jews and Christians: "O believers, take not Jews and Christians as friends; they are friends of each other. Whosoever of you makes them his friend is one of them. God guides not the people of the evildoers."[16] The Jews' alleged hopes were also described by Muhammad: "Those unbelievers of the People of the Book and the idolaters wish not that any good should be sent down upon you from your Lord."[17]

For not believing in Muhammad, the Jewish People were depicted as diseased and corrupt:

❖ As for the unbelievers…they would trick God and the believers…. In their hearts is a sickness. and God has increased their sickness…for that they have cried lies. Truly, they are the workers of corruption.[18]

❖ Fettered are their hands, and they are cursed for what they have said. As often as they light a fire for war, God will extinguish it. They hasten about the earth to do corruption there.[19]

The Jews were portrayed as the enemy of God Himself:[20]

> Surely God is an enemy to the unbelievers. And we have sent down unto you signs, clear signs, and none disbelieve in them except the unGodly.... Those who were given the Book reject the Book of God behind their backs, as though they knew not, and they follow what the Satan recited over Solomon's kingdom.

According to the Koran, Jews were to suffer eternal damnation for refusing to relinquish their ancient beliefs:

- ◆ And the unbelievers, who cried lies to our signs — they shall be the inhabitants of Hell.[21]

- ◆ Those are they whose hearts God desired not to purify; for them is degradation in this world; and in the World to Come awaits them a mighty chastisement.[22]

- ◆ Abasement shall be pitched on them...they will be laden with the burden of God's anger, and poverty shall be pitched on them; that, because they disbelieved in God's signs.[23]

- ◆ Had God not prescribed dispersal for them, He would have chastised them in this world; and there awaits them in the World to Come the chastisement of the fire.[24]

- ◆ The unbelievers of the People of the Book and the idolaters shall be in the Fire of Gehenna (Hell), therein dwelling forever; those are the worst of creatures.[25]

Following therefrom, the relationship between the above religious declarations and more contemporary anti-Jewish, anti-Israel rhetoric by leading Arab-Muslim leaders, is clear.

For example:

◆ I declare a holy war, my Moslem brothers! Murder the Jews, murder them all!
  (*Haj Amim al Husseini, Mufti of Jerusalem, 1948*)[26]

◆ The Arab nation should sacrifice up to 10 million of their 50 million people, if necessary, to wipe out Israel.... Israel to the Arab world is like a cancer to the human body, and the only way to remedy it is to uproot it, just like a cancer.
  (*Saud ibn Abdul Aziz, King of Saudi Arabia, 1954*)[27]

◆ The existence of Israel is an error which must be rectified. This is our opportunity to wipe out the ignominy which has been with us since 1948. Our goal is clear — to wipe Israel off the map.
  (*President Abdel Rahman Aref of Iraq, 1967*)[28]

◆ All countries should wage war against the Zionists, who are there to destroy all human organizations and to destroy civilization and the work which good people are trying to do.
  (*King Faisal of Saudi Arabia, 1972*)[29]

◆ Perhaps the worst result of the shameful visit [to Jerusalem] is that the "faithful" president [Sadat] was mixed up in interpreting the word of God.... He praised the Jews in a manner that is contradictory to the Koran.... The late King Faisal [of Saudi Arabia] said he had reviewed the Koran from the beginning to the end and could not find one single sentence praising the Jews.... Does Sadat know more about the interpretation of the Koran than

King Faisal? Let us tell Sadat to go to hell in order to restore Arab solidarity, stronger than ever.

(*Syrian Minister of Defense, Mustafa Tlas, 1978*)[30]

❖ Jerusalem's occupation is a deep wound bleeding in our hearts and souls. We are determined to recover it and continue to pursue its recovery together with our beloved land Palestine. This, however, cannot be achieved by talking about it or by talking about peace, but through patience and sound planning and by efforts and jihad (holy war), and above all through unity of the word and the closing of ranks.

(*King Khalid of Saudi Arabia, 1980*)[31]

❖ The removal of the Israeli occupation from our occupied land Palestine is the first and basic condition for just peace.... The Islamic nation and just believers in any religion or creed will not accept the situation of the land of the Prophet's (i.e., Muhammad) flight to heaven and the cradle of prophets and Divine message being the captive of Zionist occupation.

(*King Hussein of Jordan*)[32]

In conclusion, the words of Dr. Maarouf al-Dawalibi, counselor to the Saudi royal court, and Saudi Arabia's delegate to the 1984 United Nation's Geneva conference on religious tolerance bear mention. At the conference Dr. Dawalibi explained: "The Talmud says that if a Jew does not drink the blood of a non-Jewish man every year, then he will be damned for eternity." The Talmud further states, he said, that "the whole world is the property of Israel, and the wealth, the blood and the souls of non-Israelis...are theirs."[33]

Russian and Communist Anti-Jewish Teachings

THE FATHER OF Marxist ideology and modern Communism was Karl Heinrich Marx (1818–1883). Marx's father converted to Christianity before Karl's birth in order to retain his law practice (forbidden to Jews under Prussian law) and baptized his children in order that they not have to suffer from anti-Jewish legislation.[34] The anti-Jewish rhetoric sowed by the "great emancipator" was to be used to justify the oppression and denunciation of Jews and Judaism everywhere. On the "Jewish Question" Marx wrote:[35]

> Let us consider the real Jew: not the Sabbath Jew...but the everyday Jew.
>
> Let us not seek the secret of the Jew in his religion, but let us seek the secret of the religion in the real Jew.
>
> What is the profane basis of Judaism: Practical need, self-interest. What is the worldly cult of the Jew? Huckstering. What is his worldly god? Money.
>
> Very well: then in emancipating itself from huckstering and money, and thus from real and practical Judaism, our age would emancipate itself....
>
> We discern in Judaism, therefore, a universal anti-social element of the present time, whose historical development, zealously aided in its harmful aspects by the Jews, has now attained its culminating point, a point at which it must necessarily begin to disintegrate. In the final analysis, the emancipation of the Jews is the emancipation of mankind from Judaism...

In fact, the former Soviet Union expended more energy in disseminating anti-Jewish/anti-Israel propaganda than it did in disseminating anti-American propaganda.[36] In his book, *The Creeping Counter-Revolution* (1974), the Soviet propagandist Vladimir Begun wrote:[37]

> If we view the Torah from the standpoint of modern civilization and progressive Communist morality, it proves to be an unsurpassed textbook of bloodthirstiness and hypocrisy, treachery, perfidy and licentiousness — of every vile human quality.

Similarly, the Soviet intellectual Yevegeny Yeuseev, in his book *Facism under the Blue Star* (1971), stated:[38]

> There really exists on earth a huge and powerful empire of Zionist financiers and industrialists. If we tried to depict it with the usual means of pictorial art, it would obviously look like a sticky spider's web enmeshing a good half of the globe; at its center swarm bloodsucking spiders, lying in wait for their prey.

Lev Korneev, a prolific Soviet propagandist, claimed that of the alleged 165 military-industrial monopolies that control Western Imperialism, 158 of them (no more, no less) were owned and controlled by Jews.[39] Paradoxically, during the Russian Communist Revolution of 1917 and subsequent civil war, over 250,000 Jewish civilians were massacred. They were slaughtered by the Ukrainians and Russian Whites, who were convinced of the Jews' Communist nature![40]

Lest the reader believe that Russian anti-Jewish slander began with the Russian Revolution, it is important to note other libels circulated by Russian governments of the past. For example, the infamous government-instigated anti-Jewish pogroms (1881–1906), which destroyed hundreds of Jewish communities, were legitimized in light of Jewish "exploitation" and for the killing of Jesus.[41]

In addition, *The Protocols of the Elders of Zion*, the forgery of the century, was the handiwork of Czarist Russia.[42] *The Protocols* first appeared in 1905, printed by the Russian government press, and was said to comprise extracts from the 1897 World Zionist Congress in Basel, which dealt with Jewish plans to conquer the world that dated back to King Solomon in 929 B.C.E. *The Protocols* were an alleged series of lectures on plans to subjugate the world and establish a Jewish world state. (This alleged conspiracy was similar to its medieval predecessor, where Jews were held responsible for the Black Death [Bubonic Plague] in their attempt to destroy all of Christendom.) Despite the fact that *The Protocols* was exposed as a crude forgery, it received excited attention throughout Europe and beyond, and reached its peak of influence in Nazi Germany.[43]

Nazi Anti-Jewish Teachings

THE FOUNDATION FOR most Nazi-German slander can be found in Hitler's *Mein Kampf,* which he wrote years earlier in prison. The book was an attempt to put forth his ideas in the form of an autobiography, ideological doctrine, and party manual in one. The following are selected excerpts:

◆ The effect of Jewry will be racial tuberculosis of nations.[44]

◆ If the Jews were alone in this world, they would stifle in filth and offal.[45]

Concerning democracy, Hitler maintained, "only the Jew can praise an institution which is as dirty and false as he himself."[46]

"The Jewish doctrine of Marxism," Hitler wrote, rejects

"the aristocratic principle of Nature." The goal of Marxism "is and remains the destruction of all non-Jewish national states." Marxism, Hitler believed, "systematically plans to hand the world over to the Jews."[47] Accordingly, he declared:

> It is the inexorable Jew who struggles for his domination over nations. No nation can remove his hand from its throat except by the sword. Only the assembled and concentrated might of a national passion rearing up in its strength can defy the international enslavement of peoples. Such a process is and remains a bloody one.... The Jew would really devour the people of the earth, would become their master.... The international world Jew slowly but surely strangles us.... The Jew destroys the racial foundations of our existence and thus destroys our people for all time.[48] ...
>
> Hence, today I believe that I am acting in accordance with the will of the Almighty Creator by defending myself against the Jew, I am fighting for the work of the Lord.[49]

On April 15, 1945, after six million Jews had been systematically annihilated, Hitler gave his final "military" assessment:[50]

> For the last time our mortal enemies the Jewish Bolsheviks (Communists) have launched their massive forces to the attack. Their aim is to reduce Germany to ruins and to exterminate our people.

Hitler's psychopathology filtered even into children's nursery rhymes. For example, a book of nursery rhymes, published during the Nazi regime, had on its first page in bold type:

THE FATHER OF THE JEWS IS THE DEVIL.[51]

Two years after Hitler took office, *The Protocols of the Elders of Zion* was required reading in all German schools. It was not surprising that in 1935 in Nuremberg, one million children swore eternal enmity towards the Jewish People.[52]

The efficacy of Nazi propaganda can be seen in the following school essay written in 1935, and reprinted in the German newspaper *Der Sturmer*. The student's class was assigned to write on the subject: "The Jews Are Our Misfortune." He wrote:[53]

Unfortunately many people today still say, "God created the Jews too. That is why you must respect them also." We say however, "Vermin are also animals, but we still destroy them." ... The Jews have a wicked book of laws. It is called the Talmud. The Jews look on us as animals as well and treat us accordingly. They use cunning tricks to take away our wealth.... In Gelsenkirchen, the Jew Gruenberg sold us rotten meat. His book of laws allows him to do that. The Jews have plotted revolts and incited war. They have led Russia into misery. In Germany they gave the Communist Party money and paid their thugs. We were at death's door. Then Adolf Hitler came. Now the Jews are abroad and stir up trouble against us. But we do not waver and we follow the Fuehrer. We do not buy anything from the Jew. Every penny we give them kills one of our own people. Heil Hitler.

NOTES TO CHAPTER 5

1. Goldberg, M.H., *Just Because They're Jewish* (New York: Scarborough House, 1981).

2. Ibid.

3. Ibid.

4. Flannery, E.H., *The Anguish of the Jews* (New York: Macmillan Co., 1965), p. 48.

5. Goldberg, p. 57.

6. Flannery, p. 152.

7. Ibid.

8. Prager, D. & Teluskin, J., *Why the Jews? The Reason for Anti-Semitism* (New York: Simon & Schuster, 1983), p. 107.

9. Grosser, P.E. & Halperin, E.G., *The Causes and Effects of Anti-Semitism* (New York: Philosophical Library, 1978), p. 376.

10. Koran 3:60, *The Koran Interpreted* (New York: Macmillan Co., 1970).

11. Ibid. 5:15.

12. Koran, in Grosser et al., p. 376.

13. Ibid.

14. Ibid.

15. Koran 9:30.

16. Ibid. 5:55.

17. Ibid. 2:95.

18. Ibid. 2:5–10.

19. Ibid. 5:65.

20. Ibid. 2:90–95.

21. Ibid. 5:10.

22. Ibid. 5:45.

23. Ibid. 3:105.

24. Ibid. 59:1.

25. Ibid. 98:5.

26. Cited in *Myths and Facts 1985; A Concise Record of the Arab-Israeli Conflict* (Washington, D.C.: Near East Research, Inc., 1984), by L.J. Davis, p. 198.

27. Ibid.

28. Ibid.

29. Ibid., p. 199.

30. Ibid., pp. 200–201.

31. Ibid., p. 202.

32. Ibid.

33. Kondracke, M., *Chicago Sun-Times*, January 25, 1985.

34. Prager et al.

35. Fisch, D. A., *Jews for Nothing: On Cults, Intermarriage and Assimilation* (New York: Feldheim, 1984), pp. 173–174.

36. The International Center for the Study of Anti-Semitism, *Anti-Semitism* (Jerusalem: Hebrew University).

37. Ibid.

38. Ibid.

39. Ibid.

40. Grosser et al.

41. Flannery.

42. Ibid.

43. Ibid.

44. Grosser et al.

45. Davidowicz, L.S., *The War against the Jews*, 1933–1945 (New York: Bantam Books, 1975), p. 21.

46. Ibid., p. 24.

47. Ibid., p. 26.

48. Ibid.

49. Ibid., p. 211.

50. Ibid., p. 220.

51. Ibid., p. 223.

52. Goldberg.

53. Ibid., pp. 205–206.

6 | Anti-Israel Hostility

*One of the lessons of the Holocaust is that
individuals and nations are often unwilling to
believe that people who threaten evil will some day
attempt to implement their hostile intentions.*
(Myth and Facts, 2001)

THE WESTERN WORLD TODAY MAY BELIEVE THAT PUBLIC
slander against Jews is no longer a serious threat.
Nevertheless, a preponderance of propaganda has, in
fact, been in vogue for at least the last forty years. However,
this time the allegations are not directed against a vulnerable
minority group, and this time the group is not portrayed
as attempting to undermine society. Today the allegations
are directed against the Jews of Israel, a group portrayed by
Arab-Muslim propagandists and their supporters as subdu-
ing and attempting to eradicate an entire nation.

A primary platform for disseminating this view is the
United Nations.[1] While addressing the United Nations
general assembly, Israel's former ambassador to the United
Nations, Yehuda Blum, declared:[2]

In this building (i.e., the U.N.), Southern Yemen, East Germany and Afghanistan are democracies. In this building, Libya, Vietnam and Iraq are peace-loving states. In this building, Cuba is a non-aligned country. In this building, the Soviet Union is the leader of an alleged peace camp, and any challenge in this regard is always refuted by the representatives of Budapest, Prague, Kabul and Warsaw, who can testify to the Soviet Union's peaceful intentions. In this building, the Arab aggressors — who are ganging up on my country since its establishment as an independent state, and who openly profess their desire to see it disappear from the face of the earth — are proclaimed as victims of aggression, and Israel, the target of their sinister design, is branded an aggressor.

Daniel Patrick Moynihan, former U.S. ambassador to the United Nations, wrote similarly:[3]

It would be tempting to see in this propaganda nothing more than bigotry of a quite traditional sort that can, sooner or later, be overcome. But the anti-Israel, anti-Zionist campaign is not uninformed bigotry, it is conscious politics. We are dealing here not with the primitive but with the sophisticated, with the world's most powerful propaganda apparatus — that of the Soviet Union and the dozens of governments which echo it.

Further, this fact of world politics creates altogether new problems for those interested in the fate of democracies in the world, and of Israel in the Middle East. It is not merely that our adversaries have commenced an effort to destroy the legitimacy of a kindred democracy through the incessant repetition of the Zionist racist lie. It is that others can come to believe it also. Americans among them.

Another former U.S. ambassador to the United Nations, Jeane J. Kirkpatrick, likewise declared:[4]

> The Holocaust did not begin with building gas chambers. It began with uttering evil words, with defamation. The United Nations, today, is following the same path by poisoning the atmosphere with hatred against Israel, Zionism and Judaism.

In brief, the anti-Israel theme disseminated in the West sounds something like the following:[5]

> At the onset of the British mandate of Palestine there were close to three-quarters of a million Arabs living in Palestine who had been on the land since time immemorial. The land of Palestine was a land flowing with milk and honey, adorned with beautiful mountains and luxurious valleys; the rocks producing excellent water; and no part empty of delight or profit. The Palestinian people were a socially, culturally, politically and economically identifiable people. A people with an indissoluble bond to the land.
>
> Zionism is not rooted in the history and culture of the Jews. It is a very recent movement. The advantage achieved by Zionism in Palestine resulted from the identification of the movement with Western imperialism, as it expanded and consolidated its dominance over the Afro-Asian world during the late nineteenth and early twentieth centuries.
>
> What the Jews failed to buy, they expropriated when they announced the establishment of the State of Israel. The Arabs fled their homes and possessions for fear of death. Jewish terrorism was the prime motivating force behind the Arab exodus.

This version of history has been taken up and embellished by Third World leaders of all kinds, by the Chinese, by the

Communist Bloc, by "progressive" Europeans and by United Nations officials. In the United States, elements of the left, liberal clergy and university students have been known to disseminate the above distortion of fact.

A problem in exposing current propaganda is that while it is popularly accepted, any effort to uproot it is itself depicted as a fabrication, politically serving the other side. For example, to have convinced the European populace of the Middle Ages that Jews were not responsible for the Black Death would have been near to impossible. In Nazi Germany, to have explained to the German masses that Hitler's accusations were based on little more than the man's diseased mind would have been futile. Likewise, to describe the "Palestinian problem" in contradiction to the Arab version may unfortunately appear to many as a second biased version of the same phenomena.

Historical accuracies seem to surface only after the issues lose political and social import, and only after the Jews have suffered the destructive consequences of the untruths. Nevertheless, according to this author, a more accurate version of the Palestinian refugee problem reads something like the following:[6]

> The land called Israel today was governed by the Jewish People from approximately 1250 B.C.E. to 70 C.E. — a period of roughly 1300 years. The Land of Israel was depopulated and laid waste by the Romans (second century C.E.), in which condition it remained, till mass Jewish immigration began in the latter part of the nineteenth century.
>
> Only after the Jews started cultivating and developing the land did Arabs immigrate, en masse, in order to find work. The Arab immigration process was fostered by the British

government, which stringently upheld the Jewish quota (despite the fact that masses of Jews were being slaughtered in German-dominated territories) but were flagrantly negligent with regards to Arabs.

Israel's independence was declared in 1948, and the infant state was immediately attacked by five Arab states in conjunction with the Arab population from within. Civilian Arabs were urged by their Muslim leaders (outside the land) to leave until victory was assured. After the predicted slaughter, they would return to gather the spoils.

The approximate 600,000 Arabs that left the land were then refused citizenship in all surrounding Arab lands except Jordan. They were placed in refugee camps by their own people. The 160,000 Arabs who remained are full Israeli citizens today. In contrast, over the following several years a corresponding minimum of at least 600,000 Jewish refugees fled their homes from Arab lands where they had lived for over a thousand years. The Jewish refugees, however, were granted immediate Israeli citizenship.

The result of growing up in Arab refugee camps — with their unique educational system, financed in great part by Arab countries, Western sympathizers and the United Nations — has been the establishment of various terrorist organizations and an educational process which glorifies the suicide bombing of civilians and whose primary goal is the total liquidation of Israel.

The consequence of adopting one of the above versions is profound. Acceptance of the pro-Arab version, which creates sympathy for the Palestinian national movement while condemning Israel's defensive activities, is the rhetorical rationale required to support (or ignore) another Jewish catastrophe. In short, the public's abandonment of Israel (via the pro-Arab version) would potentially lead to a world-supported Arab attack against an isolated (both economically and militarily) Israeli people. An Arab victory would not necessarily mean a viable state for the Palestinians, for both the late King Hussein of Jordan and Palestinian leaders have historically declared that "Jordan is Palestine and Palestine is Jordan"[7] — not to mention Syria's ambitions in the area — but it would mean the eradication of Israel as was officially canonized in the *Palestinian National Covenant.* Even a position of indifference, based on the middle-of-the-road belief that a symmetry of truth and non-truth exists in both versions, could produce dire consequences. This neutrality would pit an isolated Israel against Arab money and world-supported armaments. The situation becomes more dire when one realizes that the monetary and military resources the Arab states have at their disposal is virtually unlimited.

Consistent with the pro-Arab version is the view that the Palestinian refugee plight lies at the heart of the more general Arab-Israeli conflict. This theme is consistently and vociferously voiced by almost all Arab leaders and their sympathizers.[8] The implication is that the Arab states do not oppose the fact of Israel's existence, rather their hostility reflects the injustice done to their Arab brothers. The claim is that once the Palestinians have their own state, they will peacefully recognize Israel's right to exist.

However, historically the Palestinian refugee plight cannot be the source of the conflict, and the claim that the Arabs have initiated four wars with Israel on behalf of the refugees is historical nonsense.

For example, in 1937 the British government recommended a tripartite partition of western Palestine (eastern Palestine had already been severed by Britain in 1922, and today constitutes the Arab state of Jordan) which would have entailed the creation of a Jewish state, a larger Arab state, and a continued British Mandate over the Jerusalem-Bethlehem area, with a corridor to the sea. The Arabs, however, unanimously rejected this proposal, before any refugee problem ever existed.

In 1947 when the United Nations voted to partition western Palestine, giving both Jews and Arabs equal shares, the Arab world again rejected the opportunity. Moreover, in 1948 when the State of Israel was established, five Arab countries together with the Arab population from within, attempted to destroy the fledgling Jewish state — again, before there ever was a refugee problem. Furthermore, when the Arab state of Jordan had sovereignty over the West Bank from 1948 to 1967, no attempt was ever made to establish an independent Palestinian state. Jordan, in fact, annexed the West Bank, making it officially part of Jordan!

After the Six-Day War in 1967, the Arab leaders shifted from outraged proclamations calling for the total destruction of Israel to sympathetic rhetoric on behalf of their "Palestinian brethren." This new approach granted a legitimacy to those already opposed to the existence of a Jewish state and blurred understanding of the true conflict.

Yet from the inception of the problem in 1948 to the present, no Arab nation, except one, has been willing to grant the refugees citizenship — this, despite the Arab's vast oil resources, their limited populations, and their total area comprising 640 times more land than Israel. By refusing to absorb the Arab refugees they have, in effect, forced them to remain in their wretched camps. Jordan, the only country to actually grant the refugees citizenship, slaughtered thousands of the refugees in 1970–1971 and forced 20,000 others to flee.[9]

By way of contrast, the number of refugees throughout the world in 1982 totaled more than ten million, including over two million African refugees, one million Asians, and 2.6 million Afghans fleeing Pakistan. Yet the figure was significantly reduced from the number reported two years prior in 1980 where 12.6 million refugees, including six million Africans and two million Asians, were reported. As the United Nations High Commissioner for Refugees reported... "communities, institutions, cities and nations have generously opened their doors to refugees."[10]

Similarly, the United States Committee for Refugees noted that more than one million Indochinese refugees were resettled between 1975 and 1981. The report made mention that among the African refugees, "substantial numbers...are 'settled in place.'" To be "settled in place" or "resettled in a third country" was considered by the United Nations a durable solution for the Indochinese and the Africans.[11] Moreover, unlike the Afghans, the Ethiopians, the Vietnamese and the Cambodians, the Arab refugees, for the most part, went to places only a few miles from where they left, to be placed in camps by their own people. [12]

Arab anti-Israel rhetoric has led the world to believe that the Palestinian plight is the primary problem, and therefore Arab hostility towards Jews and Israel is granted legitimacy, while terrorism runs amok. At present, the United States is Israel's closest ally. Without American weaponry Israel would be at a serious disadvantage contending with its Arab neighbors and their allies. Though public and congressional support for Israel has been strong over the past twenty-five years,[13] Arab propaganda has made significant inroads via the mass media and among senior government officials. For example, the American news media's latent dislike of Israel surfaced during Israel's 1982 incursion into Lebanon. During the three- to six-month interval following the incursion, the news media appeared to unite in an unholy war aimed at condemning the State of Israel. Gross exaggerations of casualties, fatalities and displaced persons were a common phenomenon during this period.[14]

An example of this type of news coverage was reported by Ilya Gerol, a correspondent for *The Citizen* daily newspaper of Ottawa, Canada. Mr. Gerol visited Lebanon a few months after the invasion. He wrote:[15]

> With a group of other Western correspondents, I crossed the Israeli-Lebanese border expecting to see destroyed cities, burned villages and other signs of fierce battles. Like everybody in the Western world, we arrived there after watching daily reports from Lebanon via NBC, CBS, or ABC. Only a few days before my departure for the Middle East, NBC commentator John Chancellor was talking about the destroyed cities of Sidon and Tyre. The films of destroyed houses, falling bombs, the sounds of screams and fear were shocking indeed. Who would have doubted Chancellor's statements about tens of thousands of civilian victims and cities being in ruins during the first weeks of the Lebanon conflict?
>
> Those were my thoughts when I arrived in the city of Tyre. For the first few minutes after driving through the streets it looked as if we had missed our road and were maybe even in a different country.
>
> There was no destruction. The cafes were full of people, schools were operating, stores were open and Lebanese policemen regulated the traffic. We asked one policeman how to get to the mayor's office. "It's just around the corner," he said. "Not far from Television Alley."

> Later the mayor showed us "Television Alley" — the only
> street where several blocks had been destroyed by bombs.
> He said: "All eleven destroyed buildings were occupied by
> the PLO headquarters and officers."
>
> The mayor was very busy. After our conversation, he had
> to accompany a new group of television crews to the same
> famous alley to film the "total destruction" of Tyre. I asked
> an ABC man: "How did you manage to make a picture of
> apocalyptic destruction out of only eleven ruined houses?"
>
> "We just had to film them from different angles," was the
> answer.

A further example was seen in the media's coverage of the
Sabra and Shatilla refugee camp massacres. In early September 1982, approximately 500 people were killed by Lebanese
Christian units. Four of America's leading dailies (i.e., the *Los
Angeles Times*, the *New York Times*, the *Washington Post*, and
the *Christian Science Monitor*) devoted nearly eight thousand
column-inches of news copy to the massacres, focusing primarily on Israel (which was only indirectly involved). Yet, the
same four newspapers allocated only six thousand column
inches of news space to the combined coverage of the ten
bloodiest massacres of the past decade, in which a total of
over three million men, women and children were put to
death. In addition, the word "massacre" appeared at least
ninety-nine times in headlines related to Sabra and Shatilla,
while showing up in only twenty-four headlines pertaining
to the other ten massacres combined.[16]

The media also failed to report Israel's invasion in its
proper historical context. For instance, had Americans known
of the continuous bombings of civilian targets in northern
Israel,[17] Palestinian terrorist attacks against Jews and non-

Jews throughout the world,[18] massive stockpiling of arms in southern Lebanon,[19] the Palestinian's official platform to liquidate the State of Israel,[20] the terrorizing of Lebanon from 1975 to 1982,[21] and the use of large civilian populations as human barricades against advancing Israelis,[22] public support for Israel most probably would not have dropped to a ten-year low.[23]

Consequently, Jews are again victims of negative propaganda, in this case as a result of the media's distortion of Middle East events and history. And once again the majority of the world accepts the slander and misinformation as fact.

In light of this disturbing distortion of truth, studies were implemented (as part of the author's doctoral dissertation) to discern the level of misinformation prevalent among the general American public. The findings are discussed in the following chapter.

NOTES TO CHAPTER 6

1. See *The Anti-Zionist Complex* (Englewood Cliffs, N.J.: SBS Publishing, 1982), by J. Givet; see also *United Nations: Perfidy and Perversion* (New York: M.P. Press, 1982), by H. Seidman.
2. Seidman, p. 5.
3. Givet, pp. xii-xiii.
4. Seidman, p. vii.
5. See *The Transformation of Palestine* (Evanston, IL: Northwestern University Press, 1971), Abu-Lughod, L.A. (ed.); see also *The Question of Palestine* (New York: Times Books, 1979), by E.W. Said.
6. See *Myths and Facts, 1982: A Concise Record of the Arab-Israeli Conflict* (Washington, D.C.: Near East Research, Inc., 1982), by L.J. Davis & M. Decter; see also *From Time Immemorial: The Origins of the*

Arab-Jewish Conflict over Palestine (New York: Harper & Row, 1984), by J. Peters.

7. Davis et al.

8. E.g., Interview with King Hussein, *Time Magazine,* July 26, 1982, p. 23; Johnson, M., *Time Magazine,* August 9, 1982, p. 24; Muller, H., *Time Magazine,* October 18, 1982, p. 34.

9. Muller.

10. Peters.

11. Ibid.

12. Ibid.

13. Kessler, J.S. & Schwaber, J., *The AIPAC College Guide: Exposing the Anti-Israel Campaign on Campus* (Washington, D.C.: American Israel Public Affairs Committee, 1984).

14. Muravchik, J., *Misreporting Lebanon* (Washington, D.C.: Heritage Foundation, 1983).

15. Gerol, I., "TV Exaggerates Lebanese Damage," *The Citizen,* October 30, 1982, B2.

16. C.O.M.A., *Media Onslaught on Israel* (Santa Monica, CA: Committee on Media Accountability, 1983).

17. Davis et al.

18. Merari, A., *PLO: Core of World Terror* (Jerusalem: Carta, 1983).

19. Mandel R., "Israel in 1982: The War in Lebanon," in M. Himmelfarb & D. Singer (eds.), *American Jewish Yearbook,* 1984 (New York: American Jewish Committee, 1983).

20. Palestinian National Covenant (1968), in Davis.

21. "Britain Israel Public Affairs Committee," *The PLO Exposed* (London, Britain: Israel Public Affairs Committee, 1982).

22. Tal, E., *Now the Story Can Be Told* (Tel Aviv: Achduth Press, 1982).

23. Kessler et al.

7 | The Study: Anti-Israel Perceptions

MUCH MONEY IS ALLOCATED YEARLY TO ASCERTAIN THE public's perceptions and attitudes towards Israel (e.g., Gallup Polls) but little is known of the public's knowledge of the Arab-Israeli conflict. Therefore, the following study, as part of the author's 1985 doctoral dissertation from Loyola University at Chicago, measured the American public's knowledge of the conflict, and correlated it statistically with attitudes towards the State of Israel.

A second objective of the study concerned the news media itself. The contents of four magazines representing American, Arab, Jewish liberal, and Jewish religious orientations were analyzed with regard to their portrayal of the Arab-Israeli conflict during the 1982 Israeli invasion of Lebanon. (The media's coverage of the present-day Middle-East situation leads the author to believe that little has changed over the past twenty years.)

The Study THE STUDY WAS based on an American non-Jewish and non-Arab random sample of four hundred participants from Chicago proper. The participants, ages 25 and up, were interviewed by telephone.

The following demographics describe the study's sample.

Gender	**Race**
Female = 53%	White = 57%
Male = 47%	Black = 36%
	Other = 7%

Religion	**Age**
Catholic = 46%	25 to 40 = 49%
Protestant = 39%	41 to 54 = 32%
Other = 15%	55 and over = 19%

Country of Citizenship	**Born in U.S.**
U.S.A. = 98%	Yes = 92%
Other = 2%	No = 8%

Last Year of Formal Education

Grade 1 thru 11	= 13%
High School Degree	= 27%
Some College	= 26%
Bachelors Degree	= 16%
Some Graduate School	= 5%
Masters or Doctorate Degree	= 12%

The first analysis measured the public's awareness of the Arab-Israeli conflict. Eight questions were constructed. Response categories were "True" (T), "False" (F), or "Don't Know" (DK). The following represents the complete scale, with response breakdown for each item. (All percentages were rounded off.)

The correct answer to items 4, 7, and 8 is "True," and "False" is correct for the remaining five.

1. Palestine was an independent Palestinian state over the last three hundred years until the creation of the State of Israel. Is this true or false?

   Response breakdown: T = 37%   F = 28%   DK = 36%

2. From the time many Jews started arriving in Palestine in the late 1800s until the creation of the State of Israel in 1948, thousands of Arabs were kicked out of the land by the Jewish settlers. Is this true or false?

   Response breakdown: T = 35%   F = 32%   DK = 33%

3. Arab hostility towards Jews began with the start of Jewish nationalism in the late 1800s. Is this true or false?

   Response breakdown: T = 25%   F = 36%   DK = 40%

4. Middle-East Arab nations openly hostile to the State of Israel have spent over three times the amount of money in military equipment than has Israel. Is this true or false?

   Response breakdown: T = 41 %   F = 25%   DK = 34%

5. Over the last ten years, Saudi Arabia's voting record in the United Nations has shown a strong connection between itself and the United States. Is this true or false?

   Response breakdown: T = 40%   F = 25%   DK = 36%

6. Israel's past actions have expanded its borders so that it now almost equals in size the area of all its Middle-East enemies put together. Is this true or false?

   Response breakdown: T = 23%   F = 48%   DK = 29%

7. Over the last ten years, Saudi Arabia has been openly dedicated to the destruction of Israel. Is this true or false?

   Response breakdown: T = 40%   F = 37%   DK = 24%

8. In 1948, Israel took control of less than one-fifth of the land identified by the League of Nations as Palestine. Is this true or false?

   Response breakdown: T = 45%   F = 15%   DK = 41 %

The frequency breakdown for the complete scale was:

N (Number of Participants)	=	400
0 to 2 correct	=	41%
3 to 4 correct	=	38%
5 to 6 correct	=	18%
7 to 8 correct	=	3%

In brief, 79% of all participants scored 50% or lower. The results demonstrate that, despite much Middle East news coverage, little is actually known. Based on the theory that misinformation correlates with attitudes,[1] the participants' knowledge of the Middle East was predicted to correlate significantly with their attitudes towards Israel. During the survey each participant was questioned regarding his attitudes towards the modern-day State of Israel.

The results supported the above hypothesis: Those who had more knowledge of basic Middle-East historical facts (based on their responses in the above survey) had a more favorable attitude towards Israel, whereas the less informed had a more negative attitude.

These findings imply that attitudes towards the Jewish state would be significantly enhanced if more were known of principal Middle-East facts.

However, in only four of the eight questions (items 1, 2, 3 and 6) was there a significant correlation between the respondents' knowledge of the facts and their attitudes towards Israel. Attitudes and the other four items were not significantly correlated.

Hence, it was the basic knowledge of those issues that seemed to have significantly influenced respondents' attitudes towards the State of Israel. The four items are discussed in the following:

Seventy-three percent of respondents did not know the correct answer to the first significantly correlated item:

> #1 Palestine was an independent Palestinian state over the last three hundred years until the creation of Israel. Is this true or false?
>
> **False.** In fact, there never was a separate Palestinian Arab nation. Palestinian Arab nationalism is a post-World War I phenomenon. In actuality, only after 1948 — primarily in the refugee camps — did a distinct Arab-Palestinian national character take form. In other words, understanding that present-day Palestinian nationalism is in actuality only a hostile response to an independent Jewish state has far-reaching consequences in terms of influencing public opinion for or against the modern-day State of Israel.

Sixty-eight percent did not know the correct answer to the second significant item:

> #2 From the time many Jews started arriving in Palestine in the late 1800s until the creation of Israel in 1948, thousands of Arabs were kicked out of the land by the Jewish settlers. Is this true or false?
>
> **False.** Arabs were not kicked out of the land, but according to British census figures — which failed to take into account the myriad of Arabs who, with the help of the British, succeeded in entering the land illegally[2] — the Arab population in Palestine during the British mandate period rose by 75.2% as compared with a 25% increase in relatively fertile Egypt. More interesting was that the Arab increase was greatest in areas of

intensive Jewish development (where they could find employment). For example, the Arab population in Haifa increased by 216%, and in Jaffa and Jerusalem by 134% and 90% respectively. In contrast, where there was an absence of Jewish settlement, the Arab population increased substantially less. For example, in Nablus, Jenin and Bethlehem increases over the same period were 42%, 40% and 32% respectively.[3]

Sixty-four percent did not know the correct answer to the third significantly correlated item:

> #3 Arab hostility towards Jews began with the start of Jewish nationalism in the late 1800s. Is this true or false?
>
> **False.** This inaccuracy is profound in light of the oppressive and hostile relationship Arab Muslims have had historically towards Jews, as explained earlier in Chapters 3 and 5.

Fifty-two percent did not know the correct answer to the fourth significantly correlated item:

> #6 Israel's past actions have expanded its borders so that it now almost equals in size the area of all its Middle East enemies put together. Is this true or false?
>
> **False.** If we would take into consideration the total land of Israel's more active and verbal enemies in the Middle East, the land ratio would be more than 200 to 1 — to the disadvantage of Israel. The importance of this datum is that despite detailed American news coverage concerning Israel, the ignorance of fact is pervasive.

Effects of   DEMOCRACY IN THE United States is based on
the Media   the faith that an individual's best thinking
       will emerge if he is adequately informed of
the facts. "Informed people will be more likely to decide on
reasonably practical, just and humanitarian policies, because
in the long run it is in their interest and their country's to
do so."[4]

If the purpose of disseminating news information is, in
the words of the Federal Communications Commission, "the
right of the public to be informed, rather than any right
on the part of the government, any broadcasting license or
any individual members of the public to broadcast his own
particular views on the matter,"[5] then the transmission of
factual, unbiased and historically accurate news is para-
mount.

However, in regards to the media's coverage of Israel this
standard has rarely been met. For example, in the case of
Israel's incursion into Lebanon in 1982, non-factual news
reports and biased opinions were circulated by the most re-
spected and influential news media. The media's portrayal of
"friendly moderate" Arab states and a "belligerent" State of
Israel was a clear distortion of reality — a distortion which
continues to this day.

Therefore, because of the role slanderous material and
misinformation have played historically in the expression
of anti-Jewish hostility, the content of four news periodicals during a time of international crisis — the seven months
following the initial Israeli incursion into Lebanon in
1982 — was examined. The periodicals represented the following orientations: American (*Time Magazine*), Arab (*Arab
Perspectives*), Jewish-liberal (*The [Chicago] Sentinel*) and Jewish-religious (*The Jewish Press*).

The magazine representing America-at-large (based on national circulation) and the magazine representing Jewish liberal interests (the Jewish periodical most widely read by a random sample of over eight hundred Chicago Jews) were content analyzed for their portrayal of the Arab-Palestinian problem. Over 80% of their weekly issues, from June 1982 to January 1983, were reviewed. The other two periodicals were a pro-Arab monthly (recommended by the PLO office in Chicago) and a religious Jewish weekly (a widely circulated Jewish/English newspaper) were similarly analyzed.

The results showed that the Jewish-religious periodical presented the Arab-Palestinian problem in a significantly more pro-Israel light than did the other three.

Curiously, there were no statistically significant differences among the American, Arab and even Jewish-liberal magazines' portrayal of Israel during that time period. The results imply that during times of international crisis and general condemnation, both the American media and the American-Jewish secular media will tend to support anti-Israel positions.

Possible Reasons for the Media's Anti-Israel Bias

Arab Money: Based on the Arabs' pocketbook power and their special relationship with large American corporations, it is not unprecedented to suggest that the major American news media are cooperating. For example, according to a 1974 report of the Senate Foreign Relations Subcommittee on Multinational Corporations, the ARAMCO consortium (Exxon, Mobil, Texaco, and SOCAL) attempted to block America's emergency airlift to Israel in 1973 during exceedingly desperate times (i.e., the beginning of the Yom Kippur War). During the same war, these companies cooperated closely with Saudi Arabia to deny oil and fuel to the United States Navy.[6]

Physical Intimidation: The question of how media giants could distort reality is indeed interesting. An understanding of Middle-East news, which sheds light on the above question, is furnished by Zeev Chafetz, in his book *Double Vision*. He writes:[7]

> During the past decade no region in the world has been more important to the United States than the Middle East.... And yet, despite the torrent of media coverage and commentary, surprisingly little is actually known about the region.
>
> This has a great deal to do with the fact that American journalists in some parts of the Arab world have been the victims not only of exclusion but of physical intimidation. The Syrians, the Palestine Liberation Organization and, to a lesser extent, some other Arab regimes have practiced terror as a tool of news management. They have subjected unfriendly reporters to threats, harassment, assault and even murder.
>
> As John Kifner of the *New York Times* once wrote (in February, 1982): "To work here [in Beirut] as a journalist is to carry fear with you as faithfully as your notebook. It is the constant knowledge that there is nothing you can do to protect yourself, and nothing ever happened to any assassin. In this atmosphere a journalist must decide when, how and even whether to record a story."
>
> The decision to practice self-censorship is often humiliating and many reporters justify it to themselves by rationalization. "Faced with undefined threats," says Mort Rosenblum, "reporters may inadvertently withhold sensitive information by convincing themselves that their perfectly reliable sources are not good enough."

To work in Beirut one needed the help and sponsorship of the PLO. Bill Marmon put it this way: "The PLO was able to play on the willingness of journalists to meet it more than half way. Generally in the Arab world it is necessary, to an extent unknown in Israel or the West, to prove you are a friend, and you try to do this to the extent possible without totally sacrificing your integrity. I did it myself. Often you must have a patron. He's crucial, and sometimes that relationship comes at the expense of hard-hitting journalism."

After a while, though, the pretense of friendship and sympathy can ripen into the real thing! There is a sort of contract you make with organizations like the PLO — and they are skillful at extracting a good price from the press. One way it's done is through the "I'm a friend, you should talk to me" kind of arrangement. You know, you tell the guy, I'm pro-PLO and anti-Israel, that sort of thing. The problem is that once you start that, some people really begin to believe it. If the press in Beirut was not fully reporting out of fear of Arab reprisal, then Israel was being forced to fight the war for Western public opinion with one hand tied behind its back.

People who knew little of the PLO's operations in southern Lebanon or its connections with international terrorist groups or about the internal situation in Syria often found Israel's concern about these matters "paranoid" and its attempt to deal with them over-reactive. Moreover, when Israel tried to point out what was happening in Lebanon or Syria, its arguments had little credibility — after all, people reasoned, there were plenty of American and European reporters in Beirut who would surely be aware of a Palestinian "mini-state" in south Lebanon if one existed, or of large-scale massacres in Syria.

Identification with the Left: Jews are sufficiently aware that they are not the only group reviled, but few are aware that only against them has discrimination been officially sanctioned by both the reactionary right and radical left.[8] The following excerpt by Jack Newfield, in the leftist periodical *The Village Voice*, speaks of the leftist trend towards Jews and Israel. It is this left-wing perspective which the American and Jewish liberal news media, in general, identify with.

> The thing that troubles me about a part of the American left doesn't have an official sociological name. It's more than anti-Zionism and different from traditional anti-Semitism. Its impact is often in omissions — the injustice not mentioned, the article not written, the petition not signed. It is often communicated in code words. But it is essentially a series of dual standards. It is a dual standard for the human rights of Jews in certain countries. It is a dual standard that questions Israel's right to exist by denying to Zionism the same moral legitimacy that is granted to every other expression of nationalism in the world. And it is an amnesia of conscience about the creation of Israel, and about the Holocaust, symbolized by Noam Chomsky (a Jew himself) writing an introduction to an insane, anti-Semitic book that alleges the Holocaust is a Zionist hoax. And by Jesse Jackson saying he is sick and tired of hearing about the Holocaust.[9]

Jewish Self-Esteem: A disproportionate number of Jews hold important and influential positions in the American news media today.[10] Why then would Jews, in both the American and Jewish liberal media, misrepresent their own people? An answer to this question may be found in Jean-Paul Sartre's *Anti-Semite and Jew*, in which Sartre speaks of the assimilated, liberal Jew. He writes:[11]

He [the assimilated Jew] has allowed himself to be persuaded by the anti-Semites; he is the first victim of their
propaganda. He admits that if there is a Jew, he must have
the characteristics with which popular malevolence endows
him, and his effort is to constitute himself a martyr, in the
proper sense of the term — that is, to prove in his person
that there are no Jews.

They have allowed themselves to be poisoned by the stereotype that others have of them, and they live in fear that
their acts will correspond to this stereotype.... Thus many
inauthentic Jews play at not being Jews....

The Jew who encounters another Jew in the drawing
room of a Christian is a little like a Frenchman who meets
a compatriot abroad. Yet the Frenchman derives pleasure from asserting to the world that he is a Frenchman,
whereas the Jew, even if he were the only Israelite in a
non-Jewish company, would force himself not to feel that
he was a Jew. When there is another Jew with him, he feels
himself endangered before the others, and he who a moment before could not even see the ethnic characteristics
of his son or his nephew now looks at his co-religionist
with the eyes of an anti-Semite, spying out with a mixture
of fear and fatalism the objective signs of their common
origin....

He is so afraid of the discoveries the Christians are going
to make that he hastens to give them warning, he becomes
himself an anti-Semite by impatience and for the sake of
others. Each Jewish trait he detects is like a dagger thrust,
for it seems to him that he finds it in himself, but out of
reach, objective, incurable and published to the world...in
anti-Semitism he [the Jew] denies his race in order to be no
more than a pure individual, a man without blemish in the
midst of other men.

NOTES TO CHAPTER 7

1. Quinley, H.E. & Glock, C.Y., *Anti-Semitism in America* (New Brunswick, NJ: Transaction Inc., 1983).

2. Peters.

3. Palestine Royal Commission Report, in Davis.

4. Cirino, R., *Power to Persuade* (New York: Bantam Books, 1974), p. 30. Epstein, E.J., *News from Nowhere* (New York: Vintage Books, 1974).

5. Epstein, E.J., *News from Nowhere* (New York: Vintage Books, 1974).

6. Davis et al.

7. Chafetz, Z., *Double Vision: How the Press Distorts America's View of the Middle East* (New York: Wm. Morrow & Co., 1985), pp. 17,19,51,52,78,93.

8. Perlmutter, N. & Perlmutter, R.A., *The Real Anti-Semitism in America* (New York: Arbor House, 1982).

9. Newfield, J., *The Village Voice* (New York, 1981).

10. Chafetz.

11. Sartre, J.P., *Anti-Semite and Jew* (New York: Schocken Books, 1976), pp. 94–96,102,103,109.

8 | Prerequisites to Understanding Anti-Jewish Hostility

It is a nation who will dwell alone.
(Numbers 23:9)

MORE THAN FORTY YEARS AGO, THE CATHOLIC PRIEST Edward Flannery, in his introduction to *The Anguish of the Jews*, declared:[1]

> Christians, even highly educated ones, are all but totally ignorant of [anti-Semitism] — except for contemporary developments. They are ignorant of it for the simple reason that anti-Semitism does not appear in their history books. Histories of the Middle Ages — and even the Crusades — can be found in which the word "Jew" does not appear, and there are Catholic dictionaries and encyclopedias in which the term "anti-Semitism" is not listed.

Unfortunately, even in our day most Jews, as well, know little of the sorrow which befell their ancestors throughout recorded history. The vicissitudes of the Jewish Patriarchs and Matriarchs are little known, and the sojourn in Egypt is, in general, trivialized. Accordingly, the Assyrian expulsion, some twenty-seven hundred years ago, is not recognized by most Jews, and any reference to the great Babylonian and/or Persian exile conjures up only those images emphasized in general history textbooks (of the Birth of Civilization).

Ancient Greek and Roman savagery against our people remains a possession of the historian. Who is aware that nineteen hundred years ago the Romans were crucifying Jews daily? And who knows that for over fifteen hundred years, Jews, en masse, were pillaged, expelled and slaughtered in the name of Christianity? How many Westerners understand Islam's approach towards Jews and Judaism, an approach which views Jewish subjugation and degradation as sacred?

Who has heard of the Russian folk hero and "freedom fighter" Chmielnicki, who in the seventeenth century fought the Polish (non-Jewish) aristocracy and in the process wittingly massacred hundreds of thousands of Jewish civilians? And what of the Russian pogroms, the Russian revolution and its ensuing civil war which produced the wholesale slaughter and torture of over a half-million Jewish peasants?

Correspondingly, common among Jews today is to focus almost exclusively on the Nazi-German Holocaust, while bypassing three millennia of brutal anti-Jewish persecution. It has created a mind-set incapable of understanding the phenomenon in its proper perspective. This emphasis on the Holocaust has puzzled young Jew and gentile alike, whose perception of the contemporary Jew from an economic, academic and militaristic perspective is more to be envied than pitied. This constricted focus makes it difficult to understand the problem adequately, and any constructive plan of action following therefrom would be deficient. This does not imply that the bestiality of the German people during World War II deserves a respite from condemnation, but that the

attempted genocide, carried out by one of the most sophisticated nations of the twentieth century, was little more than
the culmination of a millennia-old, social cancer.

A further problem concerns the type of analyses that have
been presented. Since World War II, there have been many
English works delineating anti-Jewish occurrences, but these
works do little more than describe its many unfortunate details.[2] The factual descriptions presented in most works have
depicted mankind's depravity, but have failed in describing
the uniqueness of anti-Jewish hostility. The universal message
of group bigotry, via the Jewish experience, is deemed most
important. Accordingly, Jews are depicted as qualitatively
replaceable by other persecuted and discriminated against
groups such as Blacks, women, the American Indian, etc.
The focus on anti-Jewish hostility is due only to the intensity
and extensiveness of the persecution that Jews have endured,
which best seems to expose mankind's sadistic nature.

Thus, according to most authors, anti-Jewish hostility
appears no different, in kind, from other forms of group-
hostility, and lessons to be learned are not and never intended
to be specifically Jewish, but rather universal in scope and
application. It has been this intention of admonishing the
world (via the Jewish experience) which has precluded the
analysis of anything distinctively Jewish.

The present work is different. Rather than addressing the
reasons why minorities are persecuted, the question asked
here is: What is fundamentally different about anti-Jewish
hostility? While other writers present a sad commentary on
society, where Jews are little more than arbitrary stimuli
on whom frustration and contempt are heaped, the present analysis describes the anti-Jewish experience as an
exclusively Jewish phenomenon. Where other writers derive

universal lessons from Jewish history — which they hope will benefit other persecuted and discriminated against minority groups — the present work derives Jewish lessons which may serve universal ends (that is, for both the oppressed and the oppressors). Therefore, it is little wonder why most historians and social scientists fail to discern the following very distinctive Jewish anomalies.

Anomaly No. 1: The Longevity of the Jewish Nation   THE QUESTION SHOULD not be why Jews have been oppressed throughout millennia — for other groups and nations have suffered at the hands of the more powerful — but rather how they continued to remain a distinct people, under the most unbearable and ironic of circumstances and most of the time in a foreign land. For example, when Alexander the Great conquered much of the known world, multitudes of ancient cultures were supplanted by the victorious Hellenistic culture. However, this relatively easy process of transplanting Grecian culture throughout the world was ineffective with regard to the Jews and Judaism. The Jews, in general, were unwilling to exchange their modes of thinking and behavior for the seeming progressive and sophisticated Hellenistic culture.

When mighty Rome prevailed, all succumbed except for the stubborn Hebrews. (It should be noted that Christianity was originally a Jewish sect. After estranging itself from Judaism, it had no national character or lifestyle other than a system of beliefs not too disparate in kind — in the beginning at least — from its mother religion Judaism.) Over the three-hundred-year period of Roman rule the Jewish People would, once again, learn the cruel lesson of being different. In fact, the Jewish nation appears to have been the only nation exiled, en masse, from its homeland (by the Roman legions) with the intent of destroying, once and for all, Jewish nationalism.

During the Dark and Middle Ages, it was the Christian Church which united Europe. Remnants of the Roman Empire, together with groups of invading barbarians relinquished their age-old religions in order to embrace the new creed, as embodied in the Jew from the Land of Israel, Jesus. All, that is, except for the Jews, who again refused to bow to any bodily form. Over the course of the next fifteen hundred years, their refusal to accept Christianity would cost them dearly in wealth, security and blood.

Accordingly, from the eighth century onward, the conquering Islamic armies converted whole tribes and nations throughout North Africa, Asia Minor and the Middle East — all, that is, except the Jews (and to a much lesser extent the Christians) who persistently weathered second-class citizenship, with its cruel ramifications, for more than one thousand years thereafter.

Where are the great cultures of the ancient world with their indigenous language, religion and group mores? Where are ancient Sumeria, Mesopotamia, Amon, Moab, Aram, Egypt, Babylonia, Media, Nubia, Persia, Greece, Palmyra, Parthia, Lydia, Akkadia, and Rome? Where are the ancient nations of the Phoenecians, Amalekites, Hittites, Assyrians, Canaanites, Midianites, Aegeans, Minoans, Nabataeans, Mayas, Aztecs, Cassites, Cimmerians, Dorians, Etruscans, Incas, Hyksos, Jebusites, Zidorians, and Sycthians? And what about the not-so-ancient groups such as the Mongols, Huns, Avars, Bulgars, Carians, Franks, Vandals, Ostrogoths, Samanids, Goths, Visigoths, Lombards, Celts, Saxons, Berbers, Picts, Tartars, Gauls and Vikings — where are they today?

The answer to this question is clear: These nations and many others have been absorbed culturally, religiously and even ethnically within the flow of history.[3] All other ancient nations have relinquished their national and/or religious identity — when given the opportunity — to become one with the majority or conquering power. Only the Jewish People, amidst untold discrimination and persecution, retained their language, religion, national consciousness and civil laws for over three thousand years, while oftentimes becoming an integral part of the larger non-Jewish society.

The Jewish People had only to accept the majority culture and/or religion, and seemingly, would have been saved untold accounts of pillage, torture, exile and slaughter. Why were the Jews so different from other nations and cultures? Were the Jewish leaders throughout history so uncommonly ingenious and convincing that they succeeded, in highly disparate lands, in holding the Jewish nation together for over three thousand years while the disintegration of other nations was only a matter of military conquest, ideological infiltration, or exile? Were the Jewish People so different in kind that only they were able to persevere, whereas other nations — under significantly less severe conditions — were, in due time, fully integrated and absorbed within the prevailing society?

History pundits, however, are fast to downplay the Jewish longevity phenomenon in light of other ancient peoples currently extant, whose histories also predate three millennia, such as the Chinese or Kurds. Superficially, their arguments seem logical, and in order that one group not deviate from the norm, the issue is usually not scrutinized. However, before comparing the historical continuity of the Jewish nation with others like the Chinese and Kurds, the following questions need to be asked:

QUESTION: *Have those nations had the luxury of living continuously on their indigenous soil throughout millennia?*

ANSWER: *Yes.*

Both the Chinese and Kurds have always lived in one general geographical area. In contrast, since the destruction of the First Temple (some twenty-five hundred years ago) and all the more so after the destruction of the Second Temple (over nineteen hundred years ago), the Jewish People have been scattered literally throughout the world.

QUESTION: *Is the continuity of these nations due, for the most part, to their cultural and physical isolation?*

ANSWER: *Yes.*

For example, the Chinese had no substantive interaction with Western or Middle-Eastern culture up to the nineteenth century. The Kurds, too, had minimal interaction with the West. In comparison, the Jews have not only witnessed almost every Western and Middle-Eastern military and cultural revolution over the past three thousand years, but have, oftentimes, been an integral player in non-Jewish society.

QUESTION: *Have the belief systems (that is, the religions) of these ancient nations remained intact?*

ANSWER: *No.*

Currently, religion in China is communist controlled, and the ancient Kurds today are Muslim. The Jews, by comparison, follow the same basic Judaism with the same Written

Law (the Bible) and Oral Law (Talmud) that they have throughout millennia. (Historically, Jewish groups or sects which deviated from the Written and Oral Law have been short-lived.)

QUESTION: *Has this people constituted a majority throughout its history?*

ANSWER: *Yes.*

The Chinese in China have always been the majority. The Kurdish people as well (within their own national geographic boundaries) were the majority until Turkish occupation in the sixteenth century. In contrast, for over eighteen hundred years, until the creation of the modern Jewish State of Israel in 1948, Jews were always the minority.

QUESTION: *Have dissimilar physical characteristics created an assimilation barrier?*

ANSWER: *Yes.*

Regarding the Chinese this is clearly the case. The Kurds, too, are distinctively Middle Eastern in appearance. In contrast, European and American Jews are more physically similar to their gentile neighbors than they are to Middle-Eastern Sephardic Jews.

In short, once the above criteria are taken into consideration, the longevity phenomenon takes on an exclusively Jewish character.

The celebrated nineteenth-century American author, Mark Twain, in his essay "Concerning the Jews" marveled, as well, at this phenomenon; he wrote:[4]

If the statistics are right, the Jews constitute but one quarter of one percent of the human race. It suggests a nebulous dim puff of star-dust lost in the blaze of the Milky Way. Properly, the Jew ought hardly to be heard of, but he is heard of, has always been heard of. He is as prominent on the planet as any other people, and his importance is extravagantly out of proportion to the smallness of his bulk. His contributions to the world's list of great names in literature, science, art, music, finance, medicine and abstruse learning are also very out of proportion to the weakness of his numbers. He has made a marvelous fight in this world in all ages, and has done it with his hands tied behind him. He could be vain of himself and be excused for it. The Egyptians, the Babylonians and the Persians rose, filled the planet with sound and splendor; then faded to dream-stuff and passed away; the Greeks and the Romans followed and made a vast noise, and they are gone; other peoples have sprung up and held their torch high for a time but it burned out, and they sit in twilight now, or have vanished. The Jew saw them all, survived them all, and is now what he always was, exhibiting no decadence, no infirmities of age, no weakening of his parts, no slowing of his energies, no dulling of his alert and aggressive mind. All things are mortal but the Jew; all other forces pass, but he remains. What is the secret of his immortality?

In the time that has passed since Mr. Twain wrote his essay, in the 1800s, hundreds of thousands of Jews were massacred in Russia (in the early twentieth century) and the Nazis succeeded in annihilating a third of the Jewish People. The twentieth century brought with it, as well, the creation of the third Jewish commonwealth. At its inception the tiny Jewish state, composed primarily of refugees, succeeded in repelling the combined forces of five Arab nations, whose numbers and armaments vastly exceeded the fledgling Jewish force. The Jewish state would be required to fight several other battles and wars over the next sixty years, while its unrelenting but defeated adversaries — with their vast lands, riches, manpower and military equipment — continue to call for its total liquidation. What would Mr. Twain say today?

In addition, despite the fact that the vast majority of American Jews came to America no earlier than the turn of the twentieth century (and, at present, comprise less than 2% of the American population) in 1970, before the saturation of Jewish baby-boomers, they accounted for 9% of all American physicians and 20% of American lawyers. In universities their percentages were even more disproportionate. In 1971 they comprised 22.4% of all medical university faculty members, and 24.9% of all law faculties.[5] Moreover, from 1901 to 1981 (a period of Jewish carnage and crises in Russia, Germany, Eastern Europe and the Middle East) the number of Jews to become Nobel Prize recipients was twenty-five times greater than their world proportion.[6]

Today (2007) Jews constitute only about one-fifth of one percent of the world's population. However, in the first half of the twentieth century, despite pervasive social and legal discrimination, and despite the Holocaust, Jews won 14% of Nobel Prizes in literature, chemistry, physics and medicine/physiology. In the second half of the twentieth century, when Nobel Prizes were then awarded to people from all over the world, that figure rose to 29%. So far, in the twenty-first century, it has been 32%.[7]

The Jewish People also turned out a plethora of intellectual and humanitarian giants during this same time period, and all this only after Mr. Twain's essay on the inexplicable Jewish phenomenon!

Anomaly No. 2: The Gentiles' Desire for Jews to Assimilate

A SECOND ASPECT which distinguishes the oppression of Jews from that of other groups who have been discriminated against (e.g., Blacks, American Indians, etc.) and likewise is overlooked by historians and social scientists, concerns the origins of this discrimination. Historically, most other oppressed groups were initially not given the choice to assimilate as equals. For example, Blacks, when taken from Africa, were never given the option to be like their white Christian or Arab Muslim captors. For them slavery was the only offered alternative.

In contrast, the Jews have always had the opportunity to become one with the majority. In certain lands this opportunity was abrogated (e.g., Nazi Germany) but even there the possibility of total assimilation had, at one time, existed. Not only had Jews the chance to assimilate, but the assimilation of Jews was often a priority of the ruling power. It was only after the fact, when the Jews refused to totally relinquish their Jewish identity, that discrimination and persecution ensued.

Hence, by failing to distinguish between anti-Jewish hostility and other anti-minority group persecution we are, indeed, learning about the sorry state of mankind, but little concerning anti-Jewish activity. In fact, by lumping anti-Jewish oppression with others — as most scholars do — we are, in effect, leading the serious student astray.

Anomaly No. 3: The Continuity of Torah (Oral Law) Judaism

THE THIRD ANOMALY, which follows from the first, concerns the one particular form of Judaism that has maintained itself throughout the millennia. Though historically there have been different sects of Judaism (e.g., Sadducees, Nazarenes, Karaites, etc.), only one group — which has been called in different eras Pharisaical, Rabbinic and Orthodox Judaism — has consistently kept the spark of Judaism alive in divergent lands and cultures.

Although other Jewish groups throughout history, claimed to be a more progressive form of Judaism, whose destiny it was to replace the "antiquated" or "corrupt" Torah (Oral Law) tradition, their claim was never actualized. When a particular period in history ended, so did the various Jewish sects. The only group to survive, through every age and culture (for over 3,200 years) was the Judaism which claimed that its detailed interpretation of the Bible was, in addition to the Bible, handed down to Moses from God.

Other Jewish groups never claimed that their interpretation of Scripture was transmitted uninterruptedly from God to their respective era; rather they claimed that the Oral Law tradition was also man-made. The corollary of their assertion was evident: If the Jewish Sages could make up their own interpretations and details, why should others be prevented from doing the same?

Irrespective of their claims, the Oral Law tradition has been the only continuous form of Judaism in every era and culture, whereas the others have disappeared. This point becomes extremely important when Jewish longevity becomes a major factor in interpreting the anti-Jewish phenomenon. It demonstrates that Judaism's anomalous longevity is inextricably related to the Jews' adherence to the Oral Law.

Although most people are familiar with the Bible, its Oral Torah interpretation is little known among secular American Jewry, and even less so in the non-Jewish world. In light of the relationship between the Oral Law and Judaism's longevity, it is necessary to present a brief summary describing its origins and legislation.

According to the Talmud, which is the embodiment of the Oral Torah: "The Holy One, Blessed be He, did not establish His covenant with Israel except by virtue of the Oral Torah."[8] Support for the claim that there was a concomitant body of legislation inseparable from the Written Law (the Bible) comes from the fact that it is impossible to make tangible pragmatic sense of the Written Law without some accompanying interpretation. More specifically, there are terms in the Bible which are undefined. For example, the term "work"[9] in Sabbatical law or the term "slaughtering"[10] in the dietary laws are undefined, and only through a supplementary body of law can these concepts be practically applied. In addition, there are basic legal concepts and institutions, the existence of which is assumed by the Bible, but are not defined. For example, without previously specifying the formal institution of marriage and divorce, the Bible states that a husband cannot remarry the wife he has divorced if in the meantime she has been married to another man.[11] Only through the Oral Torah are these Biblically assumed concepts explained.

The Talmud relates the story of a non-Jew who approached the two leading sages of the time, Hillel and Shammai. When he asked Shammai how many Divine bodies of legislation there are, the latter replied, "Two — the Written Law and the Oral Law."

"The Written Law I believe in, but the Oral Law I don't believe in," retorted the non-Jew. "Convert me on the condition that I accept the Divinity of only the Written Law." The non-Jew was led out.

He then approached Hillel and made the same request;

Hillel began teaching him the Hebrew alphabet. The following day Hillel taught him the alphabet in reverse order. The man exclaimed, "But yesterday you taught me the opposite!"

"You now realize," replied Hillel, "that it is necessary to rely on authority even for this (that is, even for understanding the letters of the alphabet). Therefore, you must rely on me with respect to the Divinity of the Oral Law, as well." In other words, there must be a reliance upon authority before anything can be learned.[12]

According to the philosopher, physician and Talmudist Moses Maimonides (1135–1204) the Oral Torah, as its name indicates, was passed down orally from generation to generation by the leading scholars and their educational institutions for over 1,400 years (circa 1250 B.C.E.–200 C.E.). The public redaction of the Oral Law, which became known as the Talmud (and comprises both the Mishnah and Gemara) began in the days of Rabbi Yehudah haNasi (circa 200 C.E.) in the Land of Israel, and was eventually completed in Babylonia (circa 500 C.E.). The Jewish leaders, with their numerous student-scholars, collected, sorted, debated, edited and redacted the ocean of Oral Law legislation before the Talmud was finally redacted and completed.

In addition to Sinaitic legislation (i.e., laws given to Moses by God) the Talmud is replete with rabbinic legislation which, in most cases, are protective fences enacted to safeguard Sinaitic law. The Talmud is also a conglomerate of philosophy, history, science, anecdotes and even humor.

Emphasis placed on the ethical quality of Oral Torah teachers—and not on the quality of teaching alone—is a primary feature of Oral Law Judaism.[13] It is also a reason why it was originally prohibited to be publicly written down.[14]

Its redaction would enable any scholar, whatever his bias, to present himself as authoritative. Conversely, when the Law is handed down orally, it is unlikely that it would be accepted from an individual of dubious character.[15]

NOTES TO CHAPTER 8

1. Flannery, E.H., *The Anguish of the Jews* (New York: Macmillan Co., 1965), p. xi.

2. E.g., Flannery. Grosser, P.E. & Halperin, E.C., *The Causes and Effects of Anti-Semitism* (New York: Philosophical Library, 1978). Ruether, R.R., *Faith and Fratricide: The Theological Roots of Anti-Semitism* (New York: Seabury Press, 1979).

3. See Tapsell, R.F., *Monarchs, Rulers, Dynasties and Kingdoms of the World* (New York: Facts on File Inc., 1983).

4. Twain, M., "Concerning the Jews," *Harpers Magazine*, September, 1899.

5. Lipset, S.M. and Ladd, E.C., "Jewish Academics in the United States: Their Achievements, Culture, and Politics," in *American Jewish Yearbook*, 1971 (Philadelphia: Jewish Publication Society of America, 1971), M. Fine and M. Himmelfarb (eds.).

6. *Encyclopedia Judaica: 1973–1982 Decennial Book* (Jerusalem: Keter, 1982).

7. Murray, C., "Jewish Genius," *Commentary* (April 2007).

8. Talmud *Gittin* 60b (Jerusalem: Ortsel, 1960).

9. Exodus 31:14.

10. Deuteronomy 12:21.

11. Ibid., 24:1–4.

12. Talmud *Shabbos* 31a.

13. Talmud *Sukkah* 28a.

14. *Sefer HaIkkarim* (Jerusalem, 1960).

15. Schimmel, H.C., *The Oral Law: A Study of the Rabbinic Contribution of Torah SheBe'Al Peh* (Jerusalem: Feldheim, 1971).

9 | Insufficient Solutions

There is nothing new under the sun.
(Ecclesiastes 1:9)

I N CHAPTERS 2–7 WE ATTEMPTED TO DESCRIBE IN BRIEF THE extensiveness of the anti-Jewish phenomenon over a period of more than three thousand years. Chapter 8 explained major differences between hostility towards Jews versus other minority groups and emphasized key points in the anti-Jewish process which most historians and social scientists have ignored. Before describing a Torah (Oral Law) understanding of this most grave and serious issue, it is interesting to view other perspectives. These perspectives have developed their own theories concerning the causes and concomitant solutions to the anti-Jewish phenomenon. It bears emphasis that these perspectives or theories, despite their historical and logical inconsistencies, appear to represent the present-day status-quo thinking on the subject.

Christian and Muslim Solutions — CHRISTIANITY'S INTERPRETATION of Jewish suffering was enunciated by St. John Chrysostom and St. Augustine in the fourth century. Both envisaged that the Jew would suffer an endless state of misery for his purported role in the crucifixion of Jesus. This rejection and dispersion by God would only be terminated by the Jews acceptance of Jesus.

The Koran explains that because the Jews were unwilling to accept Allah's revelations, as communicated by his prophet Muhammad, they were cursed for all time to live an existence of humiliation and wretchedness. The curse is not binding, however — once the Jew converts to Islam.

Christian and Muslim explanations for Jewish suffering are problematic for at least two reasons: (1) The discrimination, persecution and expulsion of Jews predates both Christianity and Islam by several hundred years; and, (2) from the inception of Christianity and Islam up to the present twenty-first century, the majority of discrimination and persecution, throughout millennia, has been meted out in the name of these two religions themselves (i.e., self-fulfilling prophecies).

The Academic Approach   SOME SIXTY YEARS ago, social scientists, interpreters of the anti-Jewish phenomenon, described the primary cause in terms of psychological maladjustment and/or social discontent.[1] That is, individual and/or societal ills were depicted as precursors for the breeding of prejudice with all its tragic corollaries (e.g., oppression, segregation and the like). Anti-Jewish hostility was posited as dependent upon individual and social well-being. Theoretically, healthy individuals and societies would not commit anti-Jewish crimes. Their solutions, however, were based more on imagination than fact, for a modern world or nation free, for any extended period of time, from significant social and/or psychological malaise is historically unfounded. In fact, an argument may be made that despite the vast amounts of monetary and human resources devoted to societal ills over the past fifty years — particularly in America — collective and individual distress has, paradoxically, increased.

Alternatively, over the past forty years the cognitive (phenomenological) approach has superseded the above type theories in terms of professional credibility.[2] According to this approach, the solution is not some elusive strategy to prevent or alleviate universal distress (which would presumably curtail the anti-Jewish cancer in the process) but rather the concrete implementation of educational campaigns to directly combat misperceptions about Jews, Israel and Judaism. In other words, if the basis of hostility and prejudice towards Jews is cognitive in nature, then a re-education program is the logical solution.

Unfortunately, these latter theorists failed to see the inadequacy of their solution. If they would have researched the problem historically, they would have discovered that slander and misinformation about Jews, which has resulted in untold oppression, was almost always initiated and augmented by the totalitarian-type leaders then in power. Had these despots not been so preoccupied with condemning Jews, anti-Jewish hostility would have been, in fact, relatively innocuous (as in the United States today). In a society where the ruling power is not psychologically threatened by the Jewish presence and anti-Jewish hostility is of a relatively minor nature, a mass re-education program can indeed be implemented. However, in a government-backed anti-Jewish environment, where this educational process would indeed be of utmost necessity, any effort to educate the masses would immediately be blocked by the ruling power. In other words, the places these educational programs would be most needed, are the very places they could never be actualized in practice.

The Assimilationists' Proposition

ACCORDING TO ASSIMILATIONISTS, Jews should completely integrate within the larger general society. If only the Jew would relinquish his distinctive Jewish identity, he would free himself and posterity from further oppression. According to this view, in the enlightened twenty-first century, the Jew must make every effort to disband and become one with the majority, like all other culturally interactive groups. The Jewish culture could remain in the form of historical archives (as is the case with every great ancient culture) where all humanity could unabashedly learn, if desired, from traditional Jewish culture without the unpleasant consequences of being different. In this way, Jews would be able to live unmolested and without fear in the real world.

De facto, this is currently being implemented. For example, there are roughly fourteen million Jews worldwide. Approximately five to six million reside in the United States, where intermarriage is rampant; that is, well over fifty percent of American Jews today are marrying non-Jews.

According to this approach, Jews in Israel could assimilate with their Arab cousins. This type of tactic was considered a viable option by the founder of secular Zionism himself, Theodore Herzl. Initially, Herzl suggested that Jews, en masse, convert to Christianity. He envisaged "a voluntary and honorable [mass Jewish] conversion" to Christianity. He even depicted, in his notes, the ceremony thereof: "in the broad light of day, at noon on a Sunday, a solemn and festive occasion accompanied by the pealing of bells...proudly and with a gesture of dignity."[3] Only after realizing that the Jews at that time were unwilling to convert, did Herzl argue for a return to the Jewish homeland.

What if Herzl had known that a Jewish state would fail

to desegregate the Jewish nation, that it would continuously be surrounded by enemies attempting to destroy it and its inhabitants, and would be refused normal diplomacy with the majority of the world's nations? Moreover, what if he knew that the nations of the world would refuse to recognize the Jewish state's historical and present-day capital, that the assembly of nations (the present-day United Nations) would label the movement he himself founded as racism, that after sixty years the Jewish state would still be required to justify its existence, that Jews world-wide would be threatened by ever-increasing terrorism, and that despite constant efforts by Jewish and Israeli liberals, the Jewish state would be a pariah among nations? Would Theodore Herzl not have retracted his proposal for a Jewish state, and instead have opted for his original proposal (of total assimilation)?

The Historical Paradox HOWEVER, A PARADOXICAL phenomenon, mitigating against the above solution, relates to the inconsistent policy non-Jewish national or international powers have historically had towards Jews. This inconsistency is not mentioned in most, if any, analyses of anti-Jewish hostility. As previously discussed, anti-Jewish powers, throughout history, have fervently attempted to assimilate the Jews into their respective empires and have, most often, been met by intransigence. However, during the various periods of history when large Jewish populations were visibly in the process of relinquishing their Jewish identity (e.g., late medieval Spain, nineteenth- and twentieth-century Russia, and twentieth-century Germany), inexplicably, in those very lands where total assimilation seemed to be a foregone conclusion, they, the Jewish People, were met by extreme and unnatural hostility and persecution.

Moreover, the antipathy towards Jews during those times of mass assimilation was aimed primarily at the assimilated Jew (e.g., in late medieval Spain, those who chose to convert rather than be exiled; and in Germany, the Reform Jews). Albeit, all Jews suffered — that is, both the assimilated and non-assimilated — however the primary focus of rage and hostility appeared to be against the Jew who attempted to identify with his non-Jewish compatriots. The import of this historical phenomena rests in its ability to counter the claim that Jewish suffering is a direct consequence of Jews' historical stiff-necked separatism. Ironically, the very forces which so feverishly tried to assimilate Jews were now the chief antagonists obstructing the rapid assimilation process, and creating a division between Jew and non-Jew which even Jewish separatism, in its most extreme form, could not parallel.

NOTES TO CHAPTER 9

1. Fromm, E., *Escape from Freedom* (New York: 1941); Maslow, A.H., *The Journal of Social Psychology*, 1943; Adorno, T.W., *The Authoritarian Personality* (New York: 1950).
2. Quinley, H.E. & Glock, C.Y., *Anti-Semitism in America* (New Brunswick, NJ: Transaction Inc., 1983).
3. Sachar, H.M., *A History of Israel: From the Rise of Zionism to Our Time* (New York: Alfred A. Knopf, 1981), p. 38.

10 | Biblical Authenticity

The vast number of archeological discoveries in Israel have tended to vindicate the pictures that are presented in the Bible. If, therefore, the Bible has been proven true concerning the past, we cannot look lightly at any prognostication it makes about the future.
(Chaim Herzog, Past President of Israel)

A GREAT DEAL ABOUT ANTI-JEWISH HOSTILITY CAN BE UNDERstood from the Jewish Bible. The Bible sheds light on the issue of Jewish suffering and gives solutions for dealing with the problem. Because the Bible may play a major role in helping us understand and eradicate anti-Jewish hostility, it behooves us to have some fundamental intellectual acceptance of Biblical authenticity. Without an open-minded stance as to the veracity of Biblical narratives and exhortations, any knowledge gleaned therefrom may be immediately dismissed as mere superstition. Therefore, before proceeding to discuss a Torah perspective in dealing with the problem, it is important to first delineate Biblical authenticity.

Another point to bear in mind is that the Jewish Bible lies at the foundation of both Christianity and Islam, and that without the validation of the Jewish Bible there could be neither Christianity nor Islam. This means that the majority of the Western world believes, at least *de facto*, in the Jewish Bible.

Many scholars, in the physical and social sciences alike, tend to ignore religious sources, as if science and religion are mutually exclusive. The Jewish sojourn in Egypt, as Biblically recorded, is a case in point of how this perspective can create an impasse in understanding the anti-Jewish phenomenon. For example, according to the analysis in Chapters 2 and 4, to omit the episodes in Egypt and Mesopotamia only because they are based on Biblical and Oral Law sources, would be to omit the prototype for all subsequent anti-Jewish epochs.

This lack of perspective when dealing with anti-Jewish phenomena becomes all the more salient when one remembers that both traditional Christianity and Islam have never contested the events in Egypt and its subsequent culmination at Mount Sinai. On the contrary, both Christianity and Islam are dependent on the Egyptian phenomenon, and invoke it as one of the most convincing proofs of God's existence and His relationship to the social world of man.

When viewed objectively, the episode in Egypt satisfies most criteria needed to validate an authentic historical event. An event claimed to have been attested to by some six hundred thousand adult men[1] (in addition to women and children) that changed the way of life of a nation and, eventually, the world, could not logically have been smuggled into the annals of history for all time. Similarly, we accept as fact that there was a Roman emperor called Julius Caesar and a founder of Islam named Muhammad, because it is nearly impossible to introduce fictitious events, witnessed by the masses, into recorded history. This is further corroborated by the fact that those who witnessed the events in Egypt were not members of a primitive servile tribe, but rather a stiff-necked, independently-spirited people. In fact, the Bible itself describes the Hebrews' contentious and skeptical nature.[2]

Further support for the events in Egypt concerns the Bible's unflattering description of how the Jewish nation developed. A national history claiming to have evolved via slavery is not to be dismissed lightly. Based on the psychology of political entities — which tend to exaggerate their past in the positive direction — the Jewish People's publicizing of their uncomplimentary origins in their own national history book is not easily discredited.

Moreover, after the recorded Exodus from Egypt, historical Egyptian culture and society seems to come to an abrupt halt, and was not heard from again until hundreds of years later[3] — a further indication that an event of significant proportions occurred at that time.

Biblical Criticism   THE FACT THAT historians and social scientists are reluctant to deal with Biblical history in any depth appears to be a consequence of the pseudo-science known as Biblical Criticism, which was popularized in Germany in the nineteenth century. In brief, Biblical Criticism denied the historical accuracy of the Bible and claimed multiple authorship at various stages in history. Its critique, based on Hegelian philosophy, viewed civilization as advancing from the primitive stage and progressively moving westward, until it reached its apex in Hegel's Germanic culture. Accordingly, Israel's Bible and its history were reconstructed to fit this chauvinistic mold. Everything was neatly arranged in logical progression, and Israel's religion was depicted as having developed gradually from primitive idolatry to the advanced monotheism of the Prophets.[4] Theories of Biblical Criticism were expanded and refined by various scholars throughout the nineteenth century, and reached their classical formulation in the works of Julian Wellhausen (1844–1918).

What was believed then in the nineteenth century, when there were but few examples of ancient writings, was that phonetic script dated back only to the year 1000 B.C.E. Accordingly, Biblical narratives such as the Jewish Exodus from Egypt, the wars of Joshua, and various other Biblical happenings were considered mythologies, written at a later date than traditionally claimed. The common custom in other cultures of recording retroactively one's oral traditions provided the basis for this assumption. In the course of time, however, ancient manuscripts were discovered which set the inception of script back to at least 1500 B.C.E. In other words, Biblical Criticism today is unable to deny that during the period of the Exodus and of Joshua written records did, in fact, exist.[5]

Wellhausen tried to explain, in natural-rational terms, the formation of the Jewish Bible and the development of Judaism itself. His arguments created a base on which to erect his quasi-intellectual edifice. Yet over the last century, his foundations have been completely undermined, and have collapsed one after another. Proponents of Biblical Criticism today are forced to admit that their arguments are not valid.[6]

The elaborate edifice of Biblical Criticism was crumbling as quickly as it was being built. One of the first signs came in 1887 when the Tel el-Amarna letters were discovered. The letters revealed a well-developed culture in the ancient Middle East as early as the fourteenth century B.C.E. It portrayed a world advanced in intellect, commerce, trade and diplomacy, and demonstrated that Israel's history began long before the advent of Moses — as is corroborated in the Bible. Since then, the science of archaeology has made hundreds of discoveries that appear to support the times and happenings cited in the Bible.[7]

One of the foremost authorities on the archaeology of Israel and the Middle East, Professor W. F. Albright of John Hopkins University wrote in his book, *Archaeology and the Religion of Israel*:[8]

> The Mosaic tradition is so consistent, so well attested by different Pentateuchal documents, and so congruent with our independent knowledge of the religious development of the Near East in the late second millennium B.C., that only hypercritical pseudo-rationalism can reject its essential historicity.

Similarly, Professor Albright also relates:[9]

> According to our present knowledge of topography of the eastern delta, the account of the start of the Exodus, which is given in Exodus 12:37 and Exodus 13:20, is topographically absolutely correct. Further proofs of the essentially historical nature of the Exodus-story and the journey in the area of Sinai, Midian and Kadesh can be supplied without great difficulty, thanks to our growing knowledge of topography and archaeology.
>
> We must content ourselves here with the assurance that the hypercritical attitude, which previously obtained in respect to the historical traditions of Israel has no longer any justification. Even the lon7isputed date of the Exodus can now be fixed within reasonable limits. If we put it at about 1290 B.C. (the approximate time period posited by Judaism) we cannot go far wrong.

Concerning the various difficulties raised by many of the proponents of Biblical Criticism, Professor Albright explains:[10]

> Hebrew national tradition excels all others in its clear picture of tribal and family origins. In Egypt and Babylonia, in Assyria and Phoenicia, in Greece and Rome, we look in vain for anything comparable. There is nothing like it in the tradition of the Germanic peoples. Neither India nor China can produce anything similar.
>
> In contrast to other peoples, the Israelites preserved an unusually clear picture of simple beginnings, of complex migrations, and of extreme vicissitudes — which plunged them from their favored status under Joseph to bitter oppression after his death.
>
> Until recently it was the fashion among Biblical historians to treat the patriarchal sagas of Genesis as though they were artificial creations of Israelite scribes...or tales told by imaginative rhapsodists around Israelite campfires during the centuries following their occupation.
>
> Eminent names among scholars can be cited regarding every item of Genesis (Chapters 11–30) as reflecting a later invention, about which nothing was thought to have been known. Archaeological discoveries since 1925 have changed all this.
>
> Aside from a few die-hards among older scholars, there is scarcely a single Biblical historian who has not been impressed by the rapid accumulation of data supporting the historicity of the patriarchal tradition....
>
> Numerous recent excavations in sites of this period in Palestine, supplemented by finds made in Egypt and Syria, give us a remarkably precise idea of patriarchal Palestine, fitting well into the picture handed down in Genesis.

Correspondingly, in his work *Canaanite Israel During the Period of Israeli Occupation*, Dr. Yohanan Aharoni writes:[11]

> Recent archaeological discoveries have decisively changed the entire approach of Bible critics. They now appreciate the Torah (Bible) as a historical document of the highest caliber. The approach of Bible critics has...been drastically altered because parallel documents have been found which describe the same events, told in Biblical narratives, from the perspective of the Egyptians, the Assyrians, or ancient Canaanites. Their fundamental approach has undergone further alteration because the events described in Biblical narratives no longer exist in a historical vacuum. Today we are very familiar with populations and the political picture of the ancient world, and the geographical locations that staged the events of history. We are familiar with the customs and the laws that are described in Biblical narratives, as well as the names of the people and places which are mentioned. All of these are compatible with Biblical history. No author or editor(s) could have put together or invented these stories hundreds of years after they happened. No serious Bible scholar remains who can argue with the fact that these historical events were transmitted with incredible historical accuracy from generation to generation, until our time.

The Ipuwer Papyrus   IN LIGHT OF the anti-Jewish analysis above, which depicts the Jews' sojourn in Egypt as an archetype for subsequent anti-Jewish epochs, the following evidence bears mention. A papyrus consisting of the words of an ancient Egyptian named Ipuwer was acquired in 1828 by the Leiden Museum of the Netherlands.

According to its first possessor (Anastasi), it was discovered in Memphis, Egypt. (The papyrus is presently listed in the museum's catalogue as *Leiden* 344.) The papyrus has writing on both sides, with Ipuwer's story on the face and a hymn to some deity on the back. The text of Ipuwer was folded into a book of seventeen pages. Of the first page only a third is preserved, pages 9 to 16 are in bad condition, and only part of the first two lines of the last page remains.[12]

Since its discovery many attempts have been made to translate the text. In 1909 the papyrus, newly translated, was published by Alan H. Gardiner entitled: *The Admonitions of an Egyptian Sage from a Hieratic Papyrus in Leiden.* The papyrus was considered then to have been written around 1500 B.C.E., during the Egyptian Middle Kingdom, over two hundred years before the Hebrew Exodus. This date fell nicely into the larger context of the then-accepted history of ancient Egypt.

In light of the alleged time divergence between the papyrus and Biblical narratives, little attention was paid to the text. In addition, because the Bible was then not accepted as a valid historical document, and because its dating system was seemingly so divergent from accepted theories of the time, the relationship between the Ipuwer text and the "legendary" Hebrew Exodus received little attention. However, Professor Immanuel Velikovsky did discern the relationship between the contents of the papyrus and Biblical narratives. He analyzed the papyrus and compared the list of catastrophes and lamentations described by the Egyptian Ipuwer with the Egyptian plagues recorded in the Bible, and a significant correspondence was revealed.[13]

The Ipuwer papyrus is a text of lamentations, a listing of fear and destruction.

For example:

◆ Forsooth, the land turns around as does a potter's wheel. (Papyrus 2:8)

◆ The towns are destroyed... (ibid. 2:11)

◆ All is ruin! (ibid. 3:13)

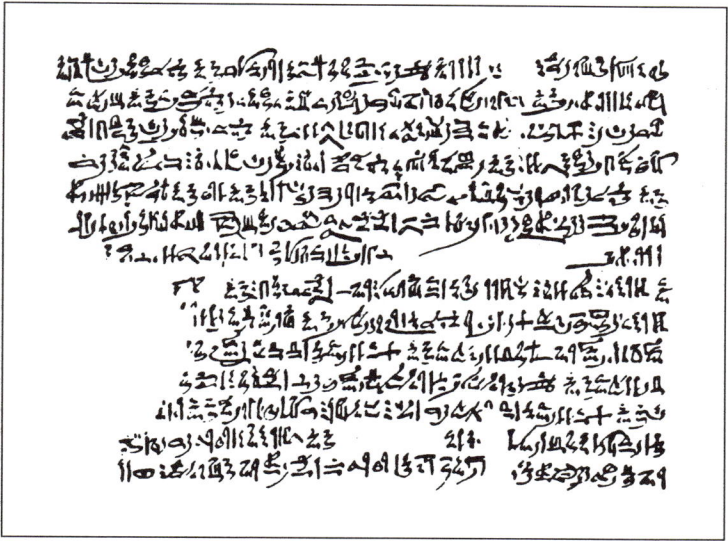

A page from the Ipuwer Papyrus[14]

In the words of Professor Velikovsky:[15]

> The Leiden Papyrus Ipuwer is a record of some catastrophe followed by a social upheaval; in the description of the catastrophe we recognized many details of the disturbances that accompanied the Exodus as narrated in Scripture. In addition, the inscription on the shrine from el-Arish contains another version of the cataclysm, accompanied by a hurricane and nine days' darkness; and there we found also

a description of the march of the Pharaoh and his army towards the eastern frontier of his kingdom, where he was engulfed in a whirlpool. The name of the Pharaoh is given in a royal cartouche which proves that the text was not regarded by its writer as mythical.

From the style of the papyrus it is clear that Ipuwer is not writing a song of prophecy concerning future events. It is a picture of events he had witnessed. Correspondingly, in accordance with Professor Velikovsky's dating approach of Egyptian dynasties, the papyrus is associated in time with the traditional Jewish date of approximately 1250 B.C.E. In short, the Ipuwer Papyrus is an Egyptian eyewitness account of events which correspond closely to those recorded in the book of Exodus.[16] The following are samples from the papyrus with corresponding Biblical narratives as presented in *Pathways to the Torah* (by the Arachim Staff, Jerusalem, 1985).

The Plague of the Blood

Exodus 7:21 There was blood throughout all the land of Egypt.

Papyrus 2:5-6 Plague is throughout the land. Blood is everywhere.

Exodus 7:20 All the water that was in the river was turned to blood.

Papyrus 2:10 The river is blood.

Exodus 7:21 And the river stank, and Egypt could not drink of the water of the river.

Papyrus 2:10 Men shrink from tasting—and thirst after water.

Exodus 7:24 And all the Egyptians dug round about the river for water to drink, but they could not drink of the water of the river.

Papyrus 3:10–13 That is our water! This is our happiness! What shall we do in respect thereof? All is ruin!

The Plague of Hail and Fire

Exodus 9:23–24 The fire ran upon the ground...there was hail and fire mingled within the hail, very grievous.

Papyrus 2:10 Forsooth, gates, columns and walls are consumed by fire.

Exodus 9:19–20 Gather your cattle, and all that you have in the field...he who feared the word of God among Pharaoh's servants...made his cattle flee into the houses. And he who disregarded God's word left his...cattle in the field.

Papyrus 9:2–3 Behold, cattle are left to stray, and there is none to gather them together. Each man fetches for himself those that are branded with his name.

Exodus 9:25 The hail smote every plant in the field and broke every tree of the field.

Papyrus 4:14 Trees are destroyed.

Papyrus 6:1 No fruit nor herbs are found...

The Plague of Pestilence

Exodus 9:3 The hand of the Lord is upon your cattle which is in the field, upon the horses, upon the asses, upon the camels, upon the oxen, and upon the sheep.

Papyrus 5:5 All animals, their hearts weep, cattle moan...

The Plague of Locusts

Exodus 10:15 There remained not any green thing in the trees or in the herbs in the fields throughout all the land of Egypt.

Papyrus 5:12 The land is left over to its weariness like the cutting of flax.

Papyrus 6:1 No fruit nor herbs are found...hunger.

Papyrus 6:3 Forsooth, grain has perished on every side.

Death of All First-Born Egyptians

Exodus 12:27 [The Lord] passed over the houses of the Children of Israel in Egypt, when he smote the Egyptians, and delivered our houses.

Papyrus 4:3 Forsooth, the children of princes are dashed against the wall.

Papyrus 6:12 Forsooth, the children of princes are cast out in the streets.

Exodus 12:29 And it came to pass, that at midnight the Lord smote all the firstborn in the land of Egypt, from the firstborn of Pharaoh who sat on his throne to the firstborn of the captive who was in the dungeon.

Papyrus 6:3 The prison is ruined and in uproar.

Exodus 12:30 And Pharaoh rose up in the night, he, and his servants, and all the Egyptians; and there was a great cry in Egypt: for there was not a house where there was not one dead.

Papyrus 2:13 He who places his brother in the ground is everywhere.

Papyrus 3:14 It is groaning that is throughout the land, mingled with lamentations.

Refuting Biblical Criticism IN ADDITION TO the archaeological finds made over the last century, which appear to uproot both the historical and philosophical foundations of Biblical Criticism, the literary basis has also come under significant attack. This attack has come from the field of technology: the computer.

Biblical critics in the nineteenth century attempted to reconstruct the Bible's literary history to accompany its alleged mythical character. For example, the Book of Genesis was interpreted as having at least three authors. Nineteenth-century critics theorized that there once existed a

Judahite history, which commenced well before the Hebrew Patriarchs and preserved the tradition of calling God's Name YHWH (referred to as the "J" source). Later on, they concluded, an Ephraimite historical sequel appeared, which began with the first Jewish Patriarch Abraham, and used a second term denoting God's Name, Elokim (the "E" source). They posited a third source of priestly origin (thus called the "P" source), and claimed it was added centuries after sources "J" and "E." Each source was said to have its own literary style, and supposedly displayed its own distinctive religious outlook. This general reapportionment of the Book of Genesis is better known as the *Classical Three-Source Hypothesis* of the Graf-Wellhausen School of Biblical Criticism.[17]

However, the Israel Institute of Technology (the Technion) has presented data which critically damage the above perspective. The goal was to create an objective approach from which to evaluate the basic literary postulates of classical Biblical Criticism. The approach became possible with the advent of the computer and the combined expertise of four disciplines (Bible, Linguistics, Statistics and Computer Science).

Biblical portions ascribed by the Graf-Wellhausen school of Biblical Criticism to the "J" (YHWH) source and the "E" (Elokim) source were extracted and compared with each other. After taking fifty-four literary variables (consistent with Biblical Criticism) into consideration, the computer concluded that the probability that these two sources resulted from the same author was eighty-two percent. The significance of this percentage is more fully appreciated when compared with the probability that the eighteenth-century German philosopher Kant or the nineteenth-century

German poet Goethe had, in actuality, written their own literary works. According to the computer program, the probabilities that Kant had independently written Kant, or that Goethe had written Goethe were eight and twenty-two percent, respectively.[18]

In assessing the above findings, the conclusions appear to be: (1) Either the computer is correct and the literary basis of Biblical Criticism — like its already defunct philosophical and historical foundations — has been proven highly inaccurate, or (2) the multiple literary variables are, in fact, invalid measurements, implying that the "critical" method (based on these variables) is so unreliable (after two centuries of refinement) as to make the "science" of Biblical Criticism functionally useless.

Correspondingly, Biblical scholar Dr. Moshe Katz and computer expert Dr. Menachem Weiner, also of the Israel Institute of Technology, researched the hypothesis that relevant words are concealed in the Hebrew text of the Pentateuch (the Five Books of Moses) and may be reproduced by separating out letters at fixed intervals. Using this approach, hundreds of words and concepts, revealed throughout the Pentateuch, have been found that relate to the text at hand (see examples on pp. 158–159).[19]

Dr. Katz, explaining his findings to journalists, stated that the empirical evidence dispels the belief that the Bible is a collection of various documents composed and edited by different people at different times. "The patterns of letters," he said, "repeated throughout the text, dismiss the theory of Biblical Criticism in light of the fantastic statistical probability of such patterns occurring wholly by chance, at times reaching 1:3,000,000."[20]

In effect, the pseudo-science of Biblical Criticism — as

espoused by its German proponents — should be a thing of the past. Philosophically, Germany was not the apex of civilization. Historically, the multitude of archaeological discoveries over the past century not only fail to invalidate Biblical narratives but can be interpreted to significantly support them. And from a literary perspective, the computer has struck Biblical Criticism a seemingly fatal blow. (Ironically, however, Biblical Criticism is still taught and disseminated in both American and European academia as the higher form of Biblical interpretation!)

In conclusion, the view of Werner Keller in his classic *The Bible as History* bears repeating:[21]

> In view of the overwhelming mass of authentic and well-attested evidence now available, as I thought of the skeptical criticism which from the eighteenth century onward would fain (i.e., happily) have demolished the Bible altogether, there kept hammering in my brain this one sentence: "The Bible is right after all!"

The Hidden Agenda of Biblical Critics

THE BIBLICAL "WORK of genius" by Wellhausen and his followers was actually much less objective than its proponents would like to admit. How much did Wellhausen's own biased view of the Bible, which in his own words, "robbed Israel of its old natural heathenism, and put in its stead gloom, Puritanism and self-righteousness, deadening the conscience and taking the soul out of religion,"[22] affect his allegedly clear and objective analysis of the same?

Over the past century and a half, Biblical critics seem to have been more interested in denying Biblical authenticity than in actually uncovering the real truth.

Other names in the field, such as Einhorn and Gabler, had an obsessive distrust of Jews as eyewitnesses. They believed that Jews, in particular, were unable to relate true facts without mixing them with biased interpretation. Another so-called Biblical scholar and critic, Franz Delitzsch held Jews responsible for Germany's loss in World War I, and cited "proof" that the Jewish religion fostered ritual murder. His initial attitude towards Judaism as "the Great Deception" was shared by Harnack, Kittel, Duhm, and other well-known Biblical critics in nineteenth- and twentieth-century Germany. Accordingly, German Biblical critics — such as Kittel and Hirsch — were Hitler's leading theological interpreters, and appeared to have played a significant role in the German Churches' silence during the systematic massacre of six million Jews.[23]

Another early name in this branch of scholarship was the nineteenth-century German-born Reform rabbi, Abraham Geiger. Geiger is often considered the most important early proponent of Reform Judaism. Geiger denied the Divine origin of the Pentateuch, scoffed at Jewish dietary laws, and called for the abolition of circumcision. In his essay, *The Uselessness and Evil Consequences of Religious Formalism,* he attacked Jewish tradition and maintained that in modern times they undermine deep religious consciousness and moral development. Geiger's hatred of Jewish tradition reached such heights that he contended that Jews who cling to their traditions are not worthy of civil emancipation. It is little wonder that this paragon of Jewish liberalism concluded that Jewish history be broken into four separate epochs, of which the fourth and most advanced was the scholarly Biblical Criticism of nineteenth-century Germany.[24]

Science and Religion

IN CONTRAST TO Biblical Criticism, many of the greatest scientists were of the opinion that science and religion are not mutually exclusive — and, in fact, complement each other. For example, Max Planck, recipient of the Nobel Prize in Physics and former professor at the University of Berlin, declared:[25]

> There can never be any real opposition between religion and science; for the one is the complement of the other. Every serious and reflective person realizes...that the religious element in his nature must be recognized and cultivated if all the powers of the human soul are to act together in perfect balance and harmony. And indeed it was not by accident that the greatest thinkers of all ages were deeply religious souls.... Science enhances the moral values of life...because every advance in knowledge brings us face to face with the mystery of our own being.

Professor A. Charniovsky, in *Between Science and Religion*, reflected likewise:[26]

> The astonishing progress in the natural sciences and their applications in the last hundred years has brought many broad sectors of scholars to the opinion that religion and science not only have no common ground, but by their very natures contradict and are inimical to one another.... An extreme expression of this philosophical position is the absolute rejection of religion as expendable, even dangerous; religion is deemed a remnant of the distant past, suitable only to a lower level of human culture....
>
> However, upon deeper examination it becomes clear that the negation of religion has not been founded upon scientific data, but rather on conclusions whose character goes beyond the limits of the scientific method.

These conclusions are not proven or logically well-founded and very often are rash generalizations at best. Accordingly, the negation of religion is not, as is generally thought, the result of scientific investigation.... Metaphysical speculations are presented as conclusive scientific evidence, with the premeditated intention of opposing and effectively vanquishing any claims of religion.

An academic community that bases itself on the scientific method and yet blatantly avoids the ramifications of religious validity is itself dogmatic.

Accordingly, Sir Isaac Newton, the famous seventeenth-century scientist, made it clear that the natural world is predicated on a metaphysical Source above and beyond the power of our senses. He writes:[27]

Whence is it that nature doth nothing in vain, and whence arises all that Order and Beauty which we see in the world? ...whence is it that planets move all one and the same way...what hinders the fixed stars from falling upon one another? How come the bodies of animals to be contrived with so much Art.... Was the eye contrived without skill in opticks and the ear without knowledge of sounds? How do the motions of the body follow from the will, and whence is the instinct in animals? ... These things being rightly dispatched, does it not appear from Phenomena that there is a Being incorporeal, living, intelligent, omnipresent, who in infinite space, as it were in his Sensory, sees the things themselves intimately, and thoroughly perceives them, and comprehends them wholly by their immediate presence to himself.

Albert Einstein, some three hundred years later, similarly declared:[28]

> The most beautiful experience that we are capable of feeling is that of the mystery of the cosmos. This is the source of true art and science. A human being to whom this experience is foreign, who is incapable of feeling this astonishment and of standing in excitement and awe in the face of ultimate mystery, must be considered dead. His eyes are sealed! It is imperative to know that that which lies beyond our grasp is nevertheless truly real. The mystery of reality is revealed in a supernal wisdom and sublime beauty that shines so exceedingly bright that our impoverished faculties can only comprehend it in the most primitive fashion.

The noted author Aldous Huxley was of the opinion that the negation of a Divine Being was in fact a rationalization not borne of true intellectual honesty. Towards the end of his life, he wrote:[29]

> I had reasons not to want the world to have meaning and, as a result, I assumed the world had no meaning, and I was readily able to find satisfactory grounds for this assumption. ... For me, as it undoubtedly was for most of my generation, the philosophy of meaninglessness was an instrument of liberation from a certain moral system.

In effect, the technological achievements of the nineteenth century created a misplaced faith in the omnipotence and omniscience of science, and everything "non-scientific" was considered, at best, expendable. Scholars who doubted the power of contemporary science were labeled religionists. Consequently, a supreme value was conferred upon science, and an almost religious ideology developed to promote certain theories, without concern for ever-mounting opposing data.[30]

Professor Charniovsky spoke of this type of mind-set; he wrote:[31]

> Faith in the omnipotence of the natural sciences gave rise likewise to the certainty that they were capable of replacing all other achievements of the human spirit, and among them the place of religion. In the place of religious theology, a theology of natural science was formulated.

In conclusion, it is interesting to note that the ideology of evolution — which depicts man as a zoological specimen — helped to foster the rise and popularity of Nazism.[32] Hitler, in *Mein Kampf*, summarized the relationship as follows: [33]

> In nature there is no pity for the lesser creatures when they are destroyed so that the fittest may survive. Going against nature brings ruin to man.... It is only Jewish impudence to demand that we overcome nature!

Examples Which Demonstrate Biblical Authenticity

ACCORDING TO THE discipline of logic, in order to discredit evidence, its implausibility must outweigh its plausibility. In other words, the objective researcher must weigh the strengths of an argument against its weaknesses.

Much of what we believe is not through direct experience, but through the accumulation of evidence, which leads us to conclude that a given phenomenon is indeed real. For example, do people know for a fact that the earth is round? The answer, for most of us at least, is no. We conclude the earth is round, not by direct experience but vicariously through multiple pictures, measurements and scientific authority. From the perspective of a skeptic, the pictures we see may be forged, the measurements and laws a hoax, and the scientific community may be misleading us. Although possible, we reject the skeptic's claim, for we have too much evidence suggesting the contrary.

In like fashion, do we know there is a land called Russia? Most Americans were never there to testify to its authenticity. What we see on television may be a media canard, and people claiming to have visited may be hallucinating! Who is right? Is there a Russia or not? Again, most of us must rely on the evidence from sources other than our own senses, to conclude that there truly is a land called Russia.

We, not unlike the objective researcher, weigh the evidence for and against the existence of a Russia, and based on the evidence decide whether Russia does or does not exist.

Moreover, does one know through direct experience who his or her real mother and father are? We do not, but we rely on the facts that hospitals do not usually make mistakes, that our parents are not lying to us, and that the physical similarities between ourselves and our parents are not accidental.

However, despite our seeming expertise at drawing accurate conclusions from the evidence, we do, at times, fail. This is particularly striking in the area of religion. In this area our usually good logic and decision-making processes falter, and our personal biases tend to cloud our thinking.

The objective thinker must weigh the evidence, and less probable hypotheses should defer to more probable ones. Anyone can play devil's advocate, but one who is truly seeking truth will analyze the facts in a logical and unbiased manner.

(The following discussion has been adapted from *Pathways to the Torah* by the Arachim Staff, Jerusalem, 1985.)

SIX HUNDRED THOUSAND
ADULT, MALE WITNESSES

The revelation at Mount Sinai, as recorded in the Bible, occurred in a manner entirely different from the alleged prophetic revelations described by other religions. For example, both Christianity and Islam claim some sort of Divine revelation via one or a few individuals. However, at Mount Sinai, the entire Jewish nation was present. It is difficult to believe that an event attested to by an entire nation is fictitious. Moses himself stressed this point: "With us (i.e., the Revelation was with all of us) who are all here alive this day."[34]

It is illogical to suggest that one person (or even a group of people) was able to brainwash an entire nation to believe they had witnessed an event that had actually never occurred — in particular a phenomenon which changed the lifestyle of a nation and eventually the world. And by the laws of logic, that which is perceived and attested to by the greater number of people has the greater historical validity. The Bible itself states:[35]

> For ask now of the days past, which were before you, since the day that God created man upon the earth, and from one end of Heaven to the other, whether there has ever been any great thing as this great thing? ...
>
> Did ever a people hear the voice of God speaking out of the midst of the fire, as you have heard? ... To you (the Jewish People) it was shown, that you might know that the Lord, He is God; there is no one else but Him.

Has any other nation made such a claim? It is highly improbable that a man (even of the stature of Moses) could have contrived phenomena that would be believed by an entire nation. In fact, we find that despite Moses' superior qualities, the Children of Israel never followed him blindly.

For example, after the Jewish People's Exodus from Egypt and as soon as they encamped by the Red Sea, they began speaking against Moses: "Were there no graves in Egypt that you have taken us away to die in the wilderness?"[36]

Later on, it states: "The whole congregation of the Children of Israel murmured against Moses and Aaron in the wilderness,"[37] and the nation's dissatisfaction intensified to such an extent that Moses himself cried out to God saying: "They are almost ready to stone me!"[38]

Even after the abortive rebellion of Korach and his followers, the Israelites' independent nature remained remarkably unchanged. Later we are told: "On the morrow, all the congregation of the Children of Israel murmured against Moses and Aaron saying, 'You have killed the people of the Lord (i.e., the rebellious Korach and his followers).'"[39]

From the above and other passages it becomes clear that the Israelites never followed Moses nor any Jewish leader blindly. Jewish leaders throughout history were, in fact, the object of acrimonious criticism by their own people.

However, despite their independent and rebellious nature, nowhere throughout the Bible did this rebellious and skeptical Jewish People ever deny Biblically recorded events.

On the contrary, Biblical history was oftentimes invoked to collectively rebuke and humble this "stiff-necked" nation.

UNFLATTERING LANGUAGE
SUGGESTS AUTHENTICITY

In P. Biberfield's work, *Universal Jewish History*, he writes:[40]

> It may be said that Biblical sources possess an objectivity and impartiality never matched by human documents. Nowhere on earth do we find the mistakes and blunders of kings so clearly described and condemned as those of the kings of Israel. No other nation has given such unbiased reports of its defects and of the tributes paid to foreign conquerors. The Egyptian historiographers avoided carefully the reports of any humiliating fact. The same was true with the otherwise more reliable Assyrian annals.

As mentioned above, the Hebrew Bible repeatedly talks in highly unflattering terms about the Jewish People. In their own national history book, they are consistently portrayed as a stiff-necked, stubborn people who have a penchant for rebelling against authority. They also openly admit that their national beginnings derive from Egyptian slavery. Is there another official national constitution and/or national history book which describes its people in such denigrating terms? Other national histories cover up their blemishes while aggrandizing, romanticizing, and even fabricating their deeds, heroism and prideful national origins. The fact that the Bible took the opposite approach in detailing the Jewish nation's faults and blunders bespeaks objectivity.

Correspondingly, the Bible openly records the sins of its greatest leader, Moses.[41] Logically, no leader should have had to detail his own sins and inadequacies so conscientiously. Honesty of this sort undermines credibility, and invites disrespect and rebellion — all the more so when this leader rebukes, punishes and criticizes the people as Moses did. In effect, he would be setting himself up for disqualification on the grounds that he himself is as culpable.[42]

This unwillingness to conceal Jewish shortcomings pervades Jewish Biblical history. The *New World Encyclopedia* likewise states:[43]

> Jewish historiography is unique in its objectivity. It does not deal in flattery or propaganda for the sake of the monarchy. Due to the objectivity of the authors of the Old Testament, an accurate description of the character of King David has been preserved which relates the very human faults which darken his otherwise extraordinary personality. No other national-historical document faintly compares to the Bible in the honest and uncensored exposé of the sins that stained David's personal life, the rebellions that endangered his monarchy, the isolationist tendencies which continued to exist throughout his reign, and the intrigues that accompanied the coronation of his successor, Solomon. No attempt was made to beautify, hide or obliterate condemning facts, as was common in the courts of all the rulers of the ancient East.

THE COMMANDMENTS TO REMEMBER

The Jewish nation is repeatedly commanded in the Bible to remember events they themselves supposedly witnessed. In several places the Bible emphatically commands: *You shall remember!* It is highly illogical that any nation would bind itself to remember what it allegedly saw and experienced had these events not occurred—especially the independently spirited Jewish People. Only when it becomes evident that the Bible was not written at a later date or dates, but at the time the events occurred, is it conceivable that the Jewish People would accept the responsibility to remember, for all time. For example, the Jewish People are commanded to remember:

◆ *The Exodus*: "...in order that you shall remember the day of your leaving the land of Egypt all the days of your life."[44]

◆ *Receiving the Torah at Mount Sinai*: "Only take utmost care and watch yourselves scrupulously so that you do not forget the things you saw with your own eyes and so that they do not fade from your mind as long as you live. The day you stood before your God at Sinai, when God said to me, 'Gather the people to Me that I may let them hear My words, in order that they may learn to revere Me as long as they live on earth and may so teach their children.'"[45]

◆ *Slavery in Egypt*: "And you shall remember that you were a slave in Egypt..."[46]

◆ *Their rebelliousness*: "Remember, never forget, how you provoked God to anger in the wilderness from the day you left the land of Egypt until you reached this place, you have been rebellious against the Lord."[47]

◆ *Amalek*: "Remember what Amalek did to you on your journey from Egypt, how he came upon you on the way, struck you in your hind parts, the weak ones following at the rear, and you were tired and exhausted and he was undeterred by the fear of God. Do not forget!"[48]

◆ *The Redemption from Egypt*: "When, in time to come, your son asks you, 'What do the testimonies and the laws and the legal regulations mean that God has commanded you?,' and that you may say to your son, 'We were slaves to Pharaoh in Egypt and God freed us from Egypt with a mighty hand and outstretched arm.'"[49]

◆ *The Ten Plagues*: "Be not afraid of them (i.e., the nations of Canaan). You have but to bear in mind what God did to Pharaoh and to all Egypt: The wondrous acts that you saw with your own eyes, the signs and the wonders, the mighty hand and the outstretched arm by which God liberated you."[50]

◈ *Miriam's leprosy*: "Remember what God did to Miriam on the journey after you left Egypt."[51]

◈ *The journey in the wilderness*: "Remember the entire journey that God has made you travel in the wilderness these past forty years in order to subject you to hardship, to test you and make known what was in your hearts, whether you would keep His commandments or not."[52]

THE BIBLE'S ANACHRONISTIC NATURE

A. Malamot, in his *A History of the Jewish People*, writes of the anachronistic nature of Biblical transmission. He states:[53]

> The early history of every nation is shrouded in mystery. Only faint memories of minimal historical value have succeeded in reaching us through the corridors of history. The Nation of Israel is unique among all the nations of the ancient east in its preserving a complex organic transmission, contained in the books of the Pentateuch and Joshua, concerning its origins and development before it emerged onto the horizon of history as a defined national entity. The possibility exists that among those nations that settled in close proximity to Israel there were records preserved from the countries of their origins; however, detailed information of origins or uninterrupted historical records of no other nation of the Biblical period has reached us which compares to that of the Biblical account of the Patriarchs, the Exodus or the conquering of the Land.

The Jewish scholar, philosopher and poet Rabbi Yehuda HaLevi, in his classic work *The Kuzari*, also argues that the authenticity of the Bible is attested to by its incongruity with the era of its birth, its unique and unborrowed nature, and the suddenness with which it came about in an era of violence and superstition among the other nations of the world.[54]

Many of the Biblical commandments represent a gaping departure from the lifestyle and philosophy of the time. For example:

- To rest and refrain from work one day each week (i.e., the Sabbath day) was unacceptable in ancient society.

- The rights of slaves, almost equivalent to that of masters, sharply deviated from the prevailing custom which treated slaves as beasts of burden.

- Love for strangers was a significant deviation, since strangers were more likely to be oppressed during that period in history.

- Charitable obligations to the poor far exceeded those of other nations.

- The commandment to protect and provide special care for the orphan and widow was in stark contrast to the exploitation of unfortunates then in vogue.

In short, Biblical laws were totally incompatible with the times: Monotheism, which espouses one God with no physical form, as opposed to the prevalent idolatries of the time, justice and ethics in place of enslavement and tyrannical oppression, and the sublimation of one's instincts in opposition to hedonism.[55]

PROMISES THAT DEFY HUMAN LOGIC

Several promises are made in the Bible which, according to the laws of nature, have zero probability of occurring. Moreover, these promises have to do with this world and not the next (i.e., after one dies). Their validity, or lack thereof, can be publicly observed. Other religions make supernatural promises but these promises deal with life after death (Heaven/Hell) or with future happenings — phenomena impossible to prove or support. In contrast, the Bible promises things that may be tested and observed, and thereby refuted if they fail to materialize. The fact that throughout hundreds of years of observation by the spirited and skeptical Jewish People these promises were never denied or refuted, suggests they did indeed occur.

Furthermore, it would be absurd and irrational for any leader to make supernatural promises that would be observed in the here and now, if the probability of them occurring naturally was zero. However, the Bible did make these types of promises, and to none other than the independently spirited Jewish People.

For example in the Book of Deuteronomy it states:[56]

> Moses then related to them (i.e., the Jews) the following commandment: "At the end of each seven year period, at a fixed time on the festival of Sukkot...when all [the people of] Israel come to present themselves before God your Lord in the place He will choose, you must read from this Torah (i.e., the Bible) before all Israel so that they will be able to hear it. You must gather together the people — the men, women, children and proselytes from your settlements — and let them hear it. They will thus learn to be in awe of God your Lord, carefully keeping all the words of this Torah."

Correspondingly, in the Book of Exodus we read:[57]

> Three times each year, all your males shall thus present
> themselves before God the Master, Lord of Israel. [And]
> when I expel the other nations before you and extend your
> boundaries, no one will be envious of your land when you
> go to be seen in God's Presence three times each year.

In brief, the above Biblical passages if, indeed, prescribed
by mortal man, propose a plan for national suicide. All males
were commanded to travel to Jerusalem three times yearly.
This commandment leaves all borders abandoned (while the
women and children remain in constant danger of attack). In
effect, they were commanded three times yearly to leave all
cities and their possessions open and accessible to enemies.

Why would a mortal lawmaker make an illogical and
potentially devastating law which portends national catastrophe?

How would this lawmaker be able to keep his promise
throughout history?

Has there ever been a similar promise promulgated by
other national leaders?

And how did this stiff-necked Jewish People accept and
follow this commandment for hundreds of years?

 · Another example: In the Book of Leviticus we find the
following passage:[58]

> The Lord spoke to Moses on Mount Sinai: Speak to the Isra-
> elite people and say to them: When you enter the land that
> I give you, the land shall observe a Sabbath of the Lord. Six
> years you may sow your field and six years you may prune
> your vineyard and gather in the yield. But in the seventh year
> the land shall have a Sabbath of complete rest...you shall
> not sow your field or prune your vineyard. You shall not

reap the after-growth of your harvest or gather the grapes of your untrimmed vines; it shall be a year of complete rest for the land. You shall observe My laws and faithfully keep My rules, that you may live upon the land in security; the land shall yield its fruit and you shall eat your fill, and you shall live upon it in security. And if you should ask, "What are we to eat in the seventh year, if we may neither sow nor gather in our crops?" I will ordain My blessing for you in the sixth year, so that it shall yield a crop sufficient for three years. When you sow in the eighth year, you will still be eating old grain of that crop; you will be eating the old until the ninth year, until its crops come in.

It is very difficult to understand the reasons for this commandment. An entire agricultural society is commanded to abandon its most important, if not only, source of livelihood — with no freezers, food preservatives or industry to soften the economic and social blow. In short, this commandment, as well, is a blueprint for national disaster.

What logic would explain a law that submits an entire people to the dangers of economic and physical demise? What human leader would introduce such laws, least of all to the highly spirited people of Israel? What ruler could guarantee his subjects' welfare, which only nature could provide? Who would promise a miraculous harvest every sixth year?

In effect, the command would de-legitimize the entire scheme of Torah observance. If the promise is not reliably kept for one or two seven-year cycles, the peoples' confidence in Jewish law would be lost.[59] Moreover, to endanger an entire nation's economy and food supply, in light of constant wars among rival nations, appears no less than insane if, indeed, promulgated by a mortal ruler.

In the Book of Numbers it reads:[60]

> God spoke to Moses telling him to speak to the Israelites
> and say to them: [This is the law] if any man's wife is sus-
> pected of committing adultery...[this is the case where] the
> man [had previously] expressed feelings of jealousy against
> his wife, and she then [may have been] defiled. [However,]
> he may have expressed such feelings of jealousy against his
> wife. and she [may not have been] defiled. [The law is] that
> the man must bring [his wife] to the priest (*kohen*). In the
> priest's hand shall be the curse-bearing bitter water. The
> priest shall administer an oath to the woman, saying to her,
> "If a man has not lain with you, and you have not com-
> mitted adultery so as to be defiled to your husband, you
> shall be unharmed by this curse-bearing water.... He shall
> then make the woman drink the bitter curse-bearing water.
> When the woman drinks the water, if she has been defiled
> and untrue to her husband, the curse-bearing water will en-
> ter her body to poison her, causing her belly to blow up and
> her sexual organs to rupture. However, if the woman is pure
> and has not been defiled, she will remain unharmed and will
> subsequently become pregnant [as compensation for being
> wrongly accused].

What mortal leader would stake his reputation and the
obedience of his people on supernatural occurrences which
could be openly refuted? And, what type of nation would
blindly accept such legislation when it could be proven
otherwise? And yet, one of the most capable leaders in history, Moses, did present the Jewish People with this law and
promise. Moreover, over centuries of its implementation, the
proverbial stiff-necked Israelites never questioned authority
or validity.

TEXTUAL CORROBORATION
VIA THE COMPUTER

Jewish tradition has always claimed that the Bible, as a God-given instrument, was made to be interpreted on several levels — from its revealed, simple interpretation to its hidden meaning.

According to Ramban (Moses Nachmanides [1194–1270]) the full depth and wisdom of the Bible "is hidden from the eyes of all living,"[61] and is "broader than the sea."[62] The same theme is expressed in the Talmud: "Ben Bag Bag said, 'Turn it over, and [continue to] turn it over, for everything is in it.'"[63]

In our time, some of the Bible's hidden esoteric knowledge seems to be increasingly accessible via the computer. As discussed above, in the beginning of this chapter, a computer program was devised to scan the entire Bible and mathematically decode words in the original Hebrew language. Its ability to survey the Bible, in almost any conceivable pattern, was impossible only a generation ago. In Israel, in particular, the investigation of Biblical code words is proceeding steadily. Significant code words are being found throughout the original Hebrew text.

Furthermore, the same procedures implemented on other books and literary classics fail to reveal any consistent or intelligible coding, let alone coding which is traditionally and logically connected to the text at hand.[64] No other book, past or present, has been found with similar characteristics.

Scientists from Israel's Institute of Technology, Dr. Moshe Katz and Dr. Menachem Weiner, state that the remarkable aspect of the research is not necessarily that words are uncovered by stringing together letters at regular intervals, but that the revealed word also bears relevance to the text in which it is found.[65]

Using the above-mentioned method, these scientists say that their evidence "strongly suggests" that the Bible could not have been composed by human intelligence. In the words of Dr. Weiner:[66]

> Such a phenomenon cannot be explained rationally, so we need a non-rational explanation. And ours is that the Bible was written by God, through the hand of Moses. Clearly, we have not scientifically proven this, but the preponderance of occurrences certainly point to it.

The following examples represent one type of data being generated. The computer was programmed to derive words from Biblical passages, based on an equal number of skips between letters from the original Hebrew text.

Is it possible that the Bible, thousands of years prior, knew that there would be a Nazi Holocaust? In the Book of Deuteronomy it reads:[67]

> God said to Moses: "When you go and lie with your ancestors, this nation shall rise up and stray after the alien gods of the land into which they are coming. They will abandon Me and violate the covenant that I have made with them. I will then display anger against them and abandon them. I will hide My face from them and they will be [their enemies'] prey. Beset by many evils and troubles, they will say, 'It is because our God is not in our midst that these evils have befallen us.' Yet on that day I will keep my countenance hidden, because of all the evil that they have done in turning to alien Gods. Therefore, write down this song and teach it to the people of Israel. Make them memorize it, so that it will be a witness for the Israelites."

Correspondingly, the following is a death-camp description by one World War II survivor:[68]

> The Holocaust stands at the center of the events of our generation and in many ways at the center of Jewish history in its entirety. The quintessential element that distinguishes this event was the search for God. Every Jew who remained in the ghettos and the camps remembers the God syndrome that shrouded everything there. From morning till night we cried out for a sign that God was still with us. From the depths of our tragedy, in the face of the piles of dead bodies of our brethren, and the gas chambers, in the face of the most inconceivable wickedness ever perpetrated, we screamed: "Almighty God! Merciful Compassionate God! Where are You?" We sought Him, but we did not find Him. We were always accompanied by the crushing and unsettling feeling that God had disappeared from our midst.

Utilizing the computer's capabilities, one is able to see that the aforementioned Biblical passage contains more than it openly reveals. Beginning from the third Hebrew letter *hei* (ה) in the passage and counting four sets of fifty letters downward, the fiftieth letter of each set — together with the first *hei* — produces the Hebrew letters *hei* (ה), *shin* (ש), *vav* (ו), *alef* (א) and *hei* (ה), spelling out the word השואה, *HaShoah*, which in English means "the Holocaust." The number fifty is also significant, for in Jewish tradition it represents, among other things, the number of days between the Exodus from Egypt and the giving of the Torah on Mount Sinai.

Moreover, the letters that comprise the word "Nazi" (in Hebrew: *nun* [נ], *tzadi* [צ] and *yud* [י]) appear in equal intervals of forty-nine letters (forty-nine is 7 x 7; seven and

multiples of seven are also traditionally significant) in the
Biblical passage dealing with rebuke and punishment for failing to observe the Torah.[69]

The following are additional examples of decoded words
that appear in the Bible; the context and number of equal
spacing between letters are also described:

The word תורה ("Torah") appears at an equal spacing of
fifty letters in the passage concerning the Creation of the
world.[70] Jewish tradition relates that God created the world
through the blueprint of Torah.

The word תורה ("Torah") appears at an equal spacing of
fifty letters in the passage concerning the boundaries of the
new land (i.e., the Land of Israel) the Jews were about to
enter.[71] This corresponds to Biblical passages which state
that Jewish occupation and survival, in their own land, are
dependent on Torah observance.[72]

The word שבת ("Sabbath") appears twice at an equal
spacing of fifty letters in the passage concerning Moses' in-
struction, as related to him by God, to keep the Sabbath day
holy.[73]

The word נפש ("soul") appears at an equal spacing of
thirty-nine letters in the passage concerning the prohibition
of doing work and eating on Yom Kippur.[74] According to Talmudic literature, there are thirty-nine major forms of work
prohibited on Yom Kippur which if performed intentionally,
while being cognizant of the law, will effect an excision of
the soul.

The word כבוד ("honor") appears at an equal spacing of
fifty-one letters in the passage concerning God's furnish-
ing dress for the first man Adam and his wife Eve, and then
sending them out to work the land.[75] The Talmud relates that
clothing bestow honor on the individual.

The word ברכה ("blessing") appears twice at an equal spacing of thirteen and fifteen letters regarding Jacob's final blessing to his son Joseph, who previously received a double inheritance.[76]

The word תורה ("Torah") appears at an equal spacing of fifty letters in the passage concerning Moses' praise of God, and his concluding instructions to the Israelites to keep the Torah.[77]

The words לאה ("Leah") and רחל ("Rachel"), Jacob's two wives, appear at an equal spacing of fifty letters in the passage concerning Isaac's instructions to his son Jacob to take a wife from his mother's family.[78]

The word משה ("Moses") appears at an equal spacing of fifty letters in the passage concerning Joseph's last words to his brothers, that God would eventually redeem the Israelites from Egypt.[79] (Moses was the agent of Egyptian redemption.)

THE FULFILLMENT OF BIBLICAL PROPHECIES

The fulfillment of Biblical prophecies is discussed in detail in the next chapter. However, it is fitting to end this chapter by mentioning that the realization of ancient Jewish prophecy concerning the Jewish People, the Land of Israel, the Torah and the relationship of the Jewish People to the nations of the world, is without precedent. Simcha Meiri, a leading Israeli educator, suggested the following analogy:[80]

> Try to imagine how amazed we would be if we were to uncover an ancient papyrus thousands of years old which describes events which actually occurred generations later, or even in modern times. Yet it would be that much more astounding if these events were of an extraordinary

nature, as were those recorded in Jewish history. But such a manuscript does exist, in fact several do — the books of the Scriptures, which are unquestionably older than the events they describe, and ... these events could not have been anticipated as they run counter to all accepted laws of history.

NOTES TO CHAPTER 10

1. Numbers 2:32.
2. E.g., Exodus 16:3 and Numbers 14:22.
3. Miller, A., *Behold a People* (New York: Balshon, 1968).
4. Feldman, E., "Changing Patterns in Biblical Criticism," in A. Carmel and C. Domb (eds.), *Challenge: Torah Views on Science and Its Problems* (Jerusalem: Feldheim, 1978).
5. Ganor, N. R., "Who Were the Phoenicians?" Sutton, A., and Arachim Staff (eds.), *Pathways to the Torah* (Jerusalem: Arachim, 1985).
6. Kaufman, Y., *The Religion of Israel: From Its Beginnings to the Babylonian Exile* (Chicago: University of Chicago Press, 1960).
7. E.g., Keller, W., *The Bible as History* (New York: Wm. Morrow, 1956); Negev, A., *Archaeological Encyclopedia of the Holy Land* (New York: Putnam, 1972); Ryan W., Pitman, W., "Noah's Flood: The New Scientific Discoveries about the Event that Changed the World" (New York; Simon and Schuster, 1999); Pheiffer, C.F. (ed.), "Wycliffe Dictionary of Biblical Archaeology" (Peabody, MA: Hendrickson Publishers Inc., 2000).
8. Albright, W.F., *Archaeology and the Religion of Israel* (New York: Anchor Books, 1969), p. 96.
9. In Keller, pp. 117–118.
10. Albright, W. F., *The Biblical Period* (New York: Harper & Row, 1963), pp. 1–3.
11. In Sutton et al., p. G1.
12. Ibid.
13. Ibid.

14. Ibid.
15. Ibid.
16. Ibid.
17. *Encyclopaedia Judaica* (Jerusalem: Keter, 1973).
18. Radday, Y.T., Shore, H., Pollatschek, M.A., & Wickman, D., *Genesis, Wellhausen and the Computer*, in Sutton et al.
19. Ibid.
20. Krosney & Schmueloff, *The National Jewish Ledger* (April, 1986).
21. Keller, end of Introduction.
22. Abelson, C.M., *Bias and the Bible*, in Carmell et al.
23. Ibid.
24. Ibid.
25. Planck, M., *Where Is Science Going?* (Woodbridge: Ox Bow Press, 1981), pp. 168–69.
26. Charniovsky, A., *Between Science and Religion* (Tel Aviv: Joshua Chachik Publishing, 1965).
27. Newton, I., *Opticks* (New York: Dover, 1952), pp. 369–370.
28. Einstein, A., *Comment Je Vois Le Monde* (New York: Philosophical Library, 1949), pp. 12–13.
29. Sutton et al., p. I12.
30. Ibid.
31. Charniovsky, A.
32. Bergman, S.H., "Can Transgression Have an Agent?" *Yad Vashem Studies*, 1963, pp. 7–15.
33. Sutton et al., p. I16.
34. Deuteronomy 5:2–3.
35. Ibid. 4:32–35.
36. Exodus 14:11.
37. Ibid. 16:2.
38. Ibid. 17:4.
39. Numbers 17:6.
40. Biberfeld, P., *Universal Jewish History* (New York: Feldheim, 1962), vol. 1.
41. Exodus 4:10–14.
42. Sutton et al., p. E8.
43. Ibid.

44. Deuteronomy 16:3.

45. Ibid. 4:9–10.

46. Ibid. 5:15, 16:12, 24:18.

47. Ibid. 9:7.

48. Ibid. 25:17–19.

49. Ibid. 6:20–21.

50. Ibid. 8:18–19.

51. Ibid. 24:9.

52. Ibid. 8:2.

53. Malamot, A., *A History of the Jewish People* (Cambridge, MA: Harvard University Press, 1976), p. 33.

54. HaLevi, J., *The Kuzari* (New York: Schocken Books, 1964).

55. Cohen, S., "Divine Origin of the Torah," in D. Kiel (ed.), *Return to the Source* (New York: Feldheim, 1984).

56. Deuteronomy 31:10–12.

57. Exodus 34:23–24.

58. Leviticus 25:1–5,18–22.

59. Sutton et al.

60. Numbers 5:11–30.

61. Job 28:21.

62. Ibid. 11:9.

63. Mishnah *Avos* 5:26 (Jerusalem: Ortsel, 1960).

64. Sutton et al.

65. Krosney et al.

66. Ibid.

67. Deuteronomy 31:16–19.

68. I.B.M. Machshavot, in Sutton et al., p. C41.

69. Deuteronomy 28:63–64.

70. Genesis 1:1–5.

71. Numbers 34:9–12.

72. E.g., Leviticus 26:3–43.

73. Exodus 34:35; 35: 1–5.

74. Leviticus 23:29–30.

75. Genesis 3:21–24.

76. Ibid. 49:25.

77. Deuteronomy 32:3–7.

78. Genesis 28:2–7.

79. Ibid. 50:24–25.

80. Meiri, S., "Burden of Proof," in Kiel (ed.), *Return to the Source* (New York: Feldheim, 1984), p. 104.

11 | Jewish Prophecy

*Remember days gone by, ponder
the years of each generation.*
(Deuteronomy 32:7)

THE BIBLE WARNS THAT IF THE JEWISH PEOPLE DISREGARD THE
laws of the Torah, the Temple and the land will be destroyed, and mass exile from the Land of Israel will
occur.[1] Prophecies which warn of the Temple's destruction
and of exile appear primarily in two places — in Leviticus,
ch. 26, and in Deuteronomy, ch. 28 — and, curiously, the
Jewish People were sent into exile twice; first, following the
destruction of the First Temple, and then again following the
destruction of the Second Temple.

The following are prophecies that appear in the Bible, with
appended historical corroboration (adapted from *Pathways to
the Torah* by the Arachim Staff, Jerusalem, 1985).

PROPHECIES CONCERNING THE
DESTRUCTION OF THE SECOND TEMPLE AND THE EXILE

PROPHECY: The prophecy that Jewish corpses would not
be allowed burial: "Your carcasses shall be-
come food for all the birds of the sky and all the beasts of the
earth, with none to frighten them" (Deuteronomy 28:26).

HISTORY: The noted historian Josephus, some 1,300 years later, writes:[3] "Dead bodies were heaped up high along all the main roads...."

HISTORY: The Talmud tells us:[4] "The Roman Emperor Hadrian had a vineyard eighteen miles by eighteen miles, equal to the distance from Tiberias to Tzippori. And he surrounded the vineyard with a great wall two-and-a-half meters high, made from the bodies of Jews whom he had slaughtered at Betar. He decreed that they not be buried, but rather rot."

*   *   *

PROPHECY: Oppression and extortion: "You will betroth a bride, but another man will lie with her. You will build a house, but you shall not live in it. You will plant a vineyard, but you will not harvest it. Your ox will be slaughtered before your eyes, but you will not eat of it; your donkey will be seized in front of you, and it will not be returned to you; your flock will be delivered to your enemies, with none to help you.... A people you do not know will eat up the produce of your soil and all your gains; you will be abused and downtrodden continually until you are driven mad by what your eyes behold" (Deuteronomy 28:30–34).

HISTORY: Josephus writes:[5] "Gessius (the Roman high commissioner) paraded the wrongs he did to the [Jewish] nation openly and indulged in every form of robbery and violence. ... To make a profit out of individuals seemed to him too petty; he plundered whole cities, ruined whole communities, and virtually announced to the entire country that everyone might become a bandit if he chose, as long as he [Gessius] himself received a share of the spoils.

The result of his avarice was desolation upon all the cities; many people deserted their ancestral homes and sought refuge in foreign provinces."

*   *   *

PROPHECY: Abduction of children: "Your sons and daughters shall be delivered to another people, while you look on; and your eyes shall strain for them constantly, but you shall be helpless." (Deuteronomy 28:32)

HISTORY: Again Josephus describes:[6] "Caesar picked out the tallest and most handsome of the lot and reserved them for the triumph. Of the rest, those that were over seventeen he put in chains and sent to hard labor in Egypt, while great numbers were presented by Titus to the provinces to perish in the theaters by sword or by wild beasts; those under seventeen were sold."

*   *   *

PROPHECY: "The alien among you will rise higher and higher, while you will descend lower and lower. He will become the master, while you the vassal." (Deuteronomy 28:43–44)

HISTORY: "First, the [Jewish] plaintiffs were given permission to state their case [before the Roman authorities] and began by enumerating Herod's crimes. 'He was not a king whom they had to bear with (for he was a non-Jewish slave, the son of Antipater the Idumean) but the most savage tyrant who ever lived. Many had been executed by him, and the survivors had suffered so much that they envied the dead. Not only had he tortured individual subjects, but whole cities; he had crippled his own towns and embellished those of other people; he had shed the life blood of Judah to gratify foreigners. Depriving them of their old prosperity and their ancestral laws, he had reduced the people to poverty and utter lawlessness.' The fact was that in the course of a few years the Jews had endured more calamities at Herod's hands than their ancestors had endured since they left Babylon to return to their country in the reign of Xerxes."[7]

*   *   *

PROPHECY: The strange Eagle from afar: "God will bring upon you a nation from afar, from the edge of the earth, swooping down as an eagle. It will be a nation whose language you do not understand..." (Deuteronomy 28:49–50).

HISTORY: Josephus writes:[8] "After Vespasian came the cavalry, the infantry, the cohort commanders and tribunes, with an escort of picked troops. Next the standards surrounding the eagle, which in the Roman army precedes every legion, because it is the king and the most fearless of all birds. They regard this as the symbol of their empire and the portent of victory, whomever may be their adversary."

HISTORY: "The great eagle was one of the common symbols of the Roman government, it being found on the totem of every Roman Legion. These 'eagles' were more than insignias. They served as the representation of the deity of each legion, and as a result, the eagle became the symbol of divine Rome and her army."[9]

HISTORY: "The rise of the Romans and their language (Latin) upon the stage of history was, in those days, a relatively new phenomenon. Their language was unknown in the East until they appeared as conquerors."[10]

*   *   *

PROPHECY: There will be famine: "He who is most tender and fastidious among you shall begrudge his brother and the wife of his bosom and the children he has spared to share with any of them...because he has nothing else left as a result of the desperate straits to which your enemy shall reduce you in all your towns" (Deuteronomy 28:54–55).

HISTORY: Again Josephus relates:[11] "Pitiful was the fare and worthy of tears the spectacle.... All human emotions yield to hunger, but of nothing is it so destructive as of shame; what at other times would claim respect is, in the time of famine, treated with contempt. Thus it was that wives snatched food from their husbands, children from fathers, and — most pitiful of all — mothers out of the very mouths of their infants; while their dearest ones were dying in their arms, they did not hesitate to deprive them of the life-giving morsels."

*   *   *

PROPHECY: "And it shall come to pass, that as the Lord rejoiced over you to do good, and to multiply you; so the Lord will rejoice over you to destroy and annihilate you, and you will be torn from the land which you are about to occupy." (Deuteronomy 28:63)

PROPHECY: "God will bring you back to Egypt in ships, along the way of which I spoke to you, that you should never see again. You will [try to] sell yourselves as slaves and maids, but no one will want to buy you." (Deuteronomy 28:68)

HISTORY: "And at that time approximately one hundred thousand Jews were taken from the land of the Jews to Egypt.... And the remaining masses of Jews — those who were too old or too young, as well as the women — were taken into servitude."[12]

HISTORY: "Now that Betar had been captured, everything came under Roman control, while Jerusalem was reduced to a desolate mound. Captives were sold into slavery in numbers too great to count.... Each slave was sold for the price of a horse. Those captives not sold were brought to the market place in Azza which was called the market place of Hadrian because of the great multitude of slaves who were sold there. Those who could not be disposed of there were herded into ships and taken to Egypt. Many died in transit, whether by starvation or by shipwreck, while others were killed by cruel masters."[13]

*   *   *

PROPHECY: "You will betroth a bride, but another man will lie with her." (Deuteronomy 28:30)

HISTORY: Before Jewish marriages were consummated, brides were forced to have relations with Roman officials first.[14]

THE JEWISH PEOPLE'S STATUS AMONG THE NATIONS

PROPHECY: "You will be an object of horror, a byword and an abject lesson among all the nations where God will lead you." (Deuteronomy 28:37)

HISTORY: The bowed Jew, up to the creation of the modern state of Israel, was for millennia a symbol of humiliation and persecution throughout Christendom and the Middle East. The famous Jewish commentator Rashi (Rabbi Shlomo ben Yitzchaki, 1040–1105) explained the phrase "a byword" to mean that the nations of the world will speak of the Jewish People "again and again." This appears to be an accurate description even till the present. For instance, in modern times, despite the fact that Jews represent significantly less than one-half of one percent of the world's population, how many headlines are devoted to issues on Jews, Judaism or Israel? And how many sessions at the United Nations concern Jews and/or Israel?[15]

HISTORY: "…But as I researched more deeply into the history of this people the feeling of dread and oppressiveness magnified within me at the sight of the willfully evil acts of violence that were perpetrated against them at every time in history and in almost every place in the world. The persecutions, the expulsions, the atrocities, the degradations, the countless murders that we find on these pages are part and parcel of the story of the Jewish People."[16]

HISTORY: "Of all the extreme fanaticism that plays havoc in man's nature, there's not one as traditional as anti-Semitism. The Jews cannot vindicate themselves in the eyes of these fanatics. If Jews are rich, they're victims of theft. If they're poor, they're victims of ridicule. If they take sides in a war, it is because they wish to gain advantage from the spilling of non-Jewish blood. If they espouse peace, it is because they're scared by their nature or traitors. If the Jew dwells in a foreign land, he is persecuted and expelled. If he wishes to return to his own land, he is prevented from doing so."[17]

HISTORY: "The Jews have been objects of hatred in pagan, religious, and secular societies. Fascists have accused them of being Communists, and Communists have branded them Capitalists. Jews who live in non-Jewish societies have been accused of having dual loyalties and Jews who live in the Jewish state have been condemned as racists. Poor Jews are bullied, and rich Jews are resented. Jews have been branded as both rootless cosmopolitans and ethnic chauvinists. Jews who assimilate are often called a fifth column, while those who stay together often spark hatred for remaining different. Literally hundreds of millions of people have believed that Jews drink the blood of non-Jews, that they cause plagues and poison wells, and that they plan to conquer the world."[18]

DISPERSION AMONG THE NATIONS

PROPHECY: "God will scatter you among the nations from one end of the earth to the other." (Deuteronomy 28:64)

PROPHECY: "God will then scatter you among the nations." (Deuteronomy 4:27)

PROPHECY: "I will scatter you among the nations, and disperse you in the countries." (Ezekiel 22:15)

HISTORY: "The dispersion of the Jewish People over the face of the earth is a completely unique phenomenon in the history of the world. In the course of their long and pain-filled wanderings, and while preserving their national identity, willingly or not, this people has established residence in almost every inhabited land on earth."[19]

HISTORY: For 1,900 years from the destruction of the
                  Second Temple (70 C.E.) to the establishment
of the modern State of Israel (1948), the Jewish People have
wandered literally around the world. This wandering was
usually precipitated by intolerable spiritual and/or physical
persecution. The scope of the Jews' nineteen-hundred-year
exile is reflected in the lands from which they were expelled
en masse. For example, in the third century (C.E.) they were
expelled from Carthage (North Africa); in the fourth century from Alexandria (Egypt); in the sixth from provinces in
France; and in the seventh from the Visigothic empire. In the
ninth century they were expelled from Italy; in the eleventh
from Mayence (Germany); in the twelfth from France; in the
thirteenth from England; the fourteenth from France, Swit-
zerland, Hungary and Germany; and in the fifteenth from
Austria, Spain, Lithuania, Portugal and Germany. In the sixteenth and seventeenth centuries Jewish populations were
expelled from Bohemia, Austria, Papal States, the Netherlands, the Ukraine, Lithuania, and Oran (North Africa). In
the eighteenth and nineteenth centuries they were expelled
from Russia, Warsaw (Poland), and Galatz (Romania). In the
twentieth century all Jews living in Nazi controlled lands
were relocated, and from 1948 to 1952 hundreds of thousands of Jews managed to escape from the lands of Egypt,
Lebanon, Syria and Iraq.[20]

FEAR AND INSECURITY IN THE EXILE

PROPHECY: "And upon those of you who will be left alive,
                   I will send a faintness into their hearts in the
lands of their enemies; and the sound of a shaken leaf shall
chase them; and they shall flee, as fleeing from a sword, and

they shall fall when none pursues. And they shall fall one upon another, as it were before a sword, when none pursues; and you shall have no power to stand before your enemies" (Leviticus 26:36–37).

PROPHECY: "Yet even among those nations you shall find no peace, nor shall your foot find a place to rest. The Lord will give you there an anguished heart and eyes that pine and a despondent spirit. The life you face shall be precarious; you shall be in terror, night and day, with no assurance of survival. In the morning you shall say, 'If only it were evening!' and in the evening you shall say, 'If only it were morning!' — because of what your heart shall dread and your eyes shall see." (Deuteronomy 28:65–67)

HISTORY: For an account of Jewish suffering in the Diaspora, refer back to Chapters 2 and 3.

HISTORY: The mark of fear was engraved upon the face of the wandering Jew throughout millennia of persecution. The Jewish People's suffering and bondage at the hands of ruthless and tyrannical despots imprinted a characteristic fear in their very being.[21]

HISTORY: "The Torah [Bible] said: 'The Lord shall give you a trembling heart, and failing of eyes, and sorrow of mind. And you shall fear day and night, and shall have no assurance of your life.' There could be no clearer picture of the bitter fate and lack of peace of mind of the Jew in the Diaspora.... Even when Jews prospered, they lived in constant fear. The history of the Jewish nation in the Diaspora is a tale of bloodshed. We left the Land of Israel at the point of a sword, and that sword has never been sheathed."[22]

THE LAND OF ISRAEL

When the Land of Israel was inhabited by Jews (i.e., from approximately 1250 B.C.E. to 423 B.C.E., and then again from 353 B.C.E. to 70 C.E. — a combined total of approximately 1,200 years) the Land of Israel was considered "the beauty of all lands" (Ezekiel 20:6,15). Accordingly, in the book of Exodus (3:8) it states: "I have come down to rescue them from the Egyptians and to bring them out of that land (Egypt) to a good and spacious land, a land flowing with milk and honey." The Land was further described in the book of Deuteronomy (8:7–9):

> For the Lord...is bringing you into a good land, a land with streams and springs and fountains issuing from plain and hill; a land of wheat and barley, of vines, figs and pomegranates, of olive trees and honey; a land where you may eat food without stint, where you will lack nothing; a land whose rocks are iron and from whose hills you can mine copper.

Some twelve hundred years later, immediately preceding the second exile, the historian Josephus also described the beauty and bounty of the land thus:[23]

> For the whole area is excellent for crops or pasturage and rich in trees of every kind, so that by its fertility it invites even those least inclined to work on the land. In fact, every inch of it has been cultivated by the inhabitants and not a parcel goes to waste. It is thickly covered with towns, and thanks to the natural abundance of the soil, the many villages are so densely populated that the smallest of them has more than fifteen thousand inhabitants.

In light of the above scenarios, the following excerpts take on greater significance.

PROPHECY: "And I will bring the land into desolation; and your enemies who dwell in it shall be astonished at it. I will scatter you among the nations...and your land shall be desolate, and your cities waste." (Leviticus 26:32–33)

PROPHECY: "And later generations will ask — the children who succeed you, and foreigners who come from distant lands — when they see the plagues and diseases that the Lord inflicted upon the land, all its soil devastated by sulfur and salt, beyond sowing and producing, no grass growing in it just like the upheaval of Sodom and Amora, Admah and Zeboiim, which the Lord overthrew in His fierce anger — all nations will ask, 'Why did the Lord do thus to this land?'" (Deuteronomy 29:21–23)

PROPHECY: "I will make the land a desolate waste, and her proud glory will cease; and the mountains of Israel will be desolate." (Ezekiel 33:28)

PROPHECY: "For the mountains, I take up weeping and wailing. For the pastures in the wilderness, a dirge. ... I will turn Jerusalem into rubble, into dens for foxes. And I will make the towns of Judah a desolation without inhabitants." (Jeremiah 9:9–10)

HISTORY: The Land of Israel is located in the center of the Fertile Crescent, and forms the meeting ground for three continents. While inhabited by the Jews it was heavily populated and developed. However, once the Jewish People were exiled, it was left in ruins and remained that way for over eighteen hundred years. Following the Jewish exile, many a people (e.g., Romans, Crusaders, Mamelukes, Arabs and Turks) conquered the land, and numerous wars were fought for its possession. However, all efforts to settle the land or cause its desolate wastes to blossom were in vain. It remained a barren wasteland until the Jewish People began returning, en masse, in the twentieth century.

HISTORY: In 1260, the Jewish Talmudist, Moses Nachmanides, while in the Land of Israel, wrote to his son: "What shall I tell you about the land? There are so many forsaken places, and the desolation is great. It comes down to this: the more sacred the place, the more it has suffered. Jerusalem is most desolate, Judea more so than the Galilee."[24]

HISTORY: Similarly, Mark Twain, visiting the Land in 1867, described it as: "...[a] desolate country whose soil is rich enough, but is given over wholly to weeds — a silent mournful expanse.... A desolation is here that not even imagination can grace with the pomp of life and action. We never saw a human being on the whole route. The Land of Israel dwells in sackcloth and ashes. The spell of a curse hovers over her which has blighted her fields and imprisoned her mighty potential with shackles. The Land of Israel is a wasteland, devoid of delight. It is no longer to be considered a part of the world. It is reserved for poetry and legend — a land of dreams."[25]

HISTORY: In 1888, Professor Sir John William Dawson wrote: "Up until today no people has succeeded in establishing national control in the Land of Israel.... No national unity or spirit of nationalism has acquired any hold there. The mixed multitude of itinerant tribes that managed to settle there did so only as temporary residents. It seems indeed that they, too, were awaiting the return of the permanent residents to the land."[26]

HISTORY: As late as the early twentieth century, the Palestine Royal Commission described the land thus: "The road leading from Gaza to the north was only a summer track suitable for transport by camels and carts...no orange groves, orchards or vineyards were to be seen until one reached Yabna village. The western part, towards the sea, was almost a desert.... The villages in this area were few and thinly populated. Many ruins of villages were scattered over the area, as owing to the prevalence of malaria, many villages were deserted by their inhabitants."[27]

HISTORY: Correspondingly, Moses Nachmanides (thirteenth century) in his commentary on the book of Leviticus explained: "...that which He stated here, 'and your enemies that shall dwell therein shall be desolate in it' constitutes a good tiding, proclaiming that during all our exiles, our land will not accept our enemies. This also is an assurance to us, for in the whole inhabited part of the world one cannot find such a good land which was always lived in and yet is as ruined as it is today; for since the time that we left it, it has not accepted any nation or people. They all try to settle it, but to no avail."[28]

*   *   *

PROPHECY: "But you, O mountains of Israel, shall yield your produce and bear your fruit for My people Israel, for their return is near. For I will care for you: I will turn to you, and you shall be tilled and sown. I will settle a large population on you, the whole House of Israel; the towns shall be resettled, and the ruined sites rebuilt. I will multiply men and beasts upon you, and they shall increase and be fertile, and I will resettle you as you were formerly, and will make you more prosperous than you were at first. And you shall know that I am the Lord" (Ezekiel 36:8–11).

PROPHECY: There is no surer sign for the subsequent (Messianic) Redemption than when the Land of Israel becomes fertile again for the Jewish People (Talmud, *Sanhedrin* 98a).

PROPHECY: "As long as Israel does not dwell on its land, the land will not give her fruit as she is accustomed. When she will begin to re-flourish, however, and give of her fruit, this is a clear sign that the end — the time of redemption — is approaching, when all of Israel will subsequently return to the Land" (Rabbi Samuel Eliezer [the Maharsha], 1630).

HISTORY: We ourselves are witness today to the fact that in a relatively short period of time the Land of Israel has undergone a remarkable transformation into a green and blossoming land, after thousands of years of desolation. Perhaps it may be inferred that the Land, by giving of its fruits again, is preparing for the arrival of the entire Jewish nation.[29]

RETURNING TO THE LAND OF ISRAEL

PROPHECY: "God will then bring back your remnants and have mercy on you. God your Lord will gather you from among the nations where He scattered you. Even if your dispersal is to the ends of the heavens, God your Lord will gather you up from there and He will take you back. God your Lord will then bring you to the land that

your ancestors occupied, and you will occupy it" (Deuteronomy 30:3–5).

HISTORY: Despite the fact that over sixty percent of the
                     Jewish People today reside outside the Land
of Israel, over the last hundred years Jewish immigration has
been extraordinary. Since the establishment of the State of
Israel in 1948 until 2005, the Jewish People's striking return
to the Land of Israel can be seen in the following immigration statistics:[30]

AFRICA		EUROPE	
140,365	Morocco	1,155,012	Former USSR
184,413	Algeria	168,533	Poland
14,703	Tunisia	260,188	Romania
35,778	Libya	39,887	Bulgaria
30,002	Egypt & Sudan	15,649	Germany
21,555	South Africa	23,459	Czechoslovakia
74,307	Ethiopia	28,175	Hungary
10,566	Rest of Africa	33,646	United Kingdom
		75,325	France
		37,009	Rest of Europe

AMERICA, OCEANIA		ASIA	
118,618	USA, Canada	60,136	Turkey
66,664	Argentina	129,497	Iraq
25,260	Rest of Latin America and Oceania	46,411	Yemen
		69,755	Iran
		24,789	India, Pakistan
		26,644	Rest of Asia

A RETURN TO JEWISH TRADITION

PROPHECY: "And it shall come to pass, when all these things come upon you — all the words of blessing and curse that I have presented to you... you will then return to God your Lord, and will obey His voice, doing everything that I am commanding you today. You and your children [will repent] with all your heart and with all your soul." (Deuteronomy 30:1–2)

HISTORY: Though the number of non-observant (non-Orthodox) Jews today greatly exceeds that of observant Jews, the fact that adherence to traditional Torah Judaism is steadily increasing suggests that the above prophecy is materializing. Simcha Meiri describes this phenomenon thus:[31] "'Realistic' projections thirty or forty years ago envisioned the number of religious Jews as slowly but surely fading away. Observant Jews were to become a thing of the past within a generation or two. Not only has this prediction proven false, not only have religious institutions not emptied of their scholars, but, on the contrary, their numbers have increased. We are witnessing a great and gratifying spiritual rebirth which, although contrary to all human expectations, was specifically foretold in the Torah: 'And it shall come to pass, when all these things come upon you... you will then return to God your Lord, and will obey His voice...'[32] No one could have anticipated that the number of observant Jews would increase daily, and even today we still do not grasp the full significance and extent of this welcome turn of events, yet knowledge of it was plainly imparted to the prophet Amos: 'Behold the days come, says the Lord God, that I will send a famine in the land, not a famine of bread, nor a thirst for water, but of hearing the words of the Lord.'"[33]

THE TEMPLE'S WESTERN WALL

PROPHECY: In the Biblical book Song of Songs (2:9) it states: "Behold, he stands behind our wall." The Midrash explains: "Behind the Western Wall of the [Jerusalem] Temple. Why [the Midrash asks, is God (figuratively) standing there]? For God has sworn that it will never be destroyed."[34]

HISTORY: "During two thousand years of exile, Jerusalem was the scene of multiple battles, and was razed and rebuilt no less than nine times. But although it was seized by nations who sought to erase any trace of its past glory, one thing remained intact. The Western Wall has miraculously stood to this very day. There were periods during which it was covered in dirt and rubbish, but it has never crumbled."[35]

THE CITY OF BABYLON

PROPHECY: "And Jeremiah said to Seraya: 'When you come to Babylon and will see, and will read all these words, then will you say, "O Lord, You have spoken against this place, to cut it off, that none will remain in it, neither man nor beast, but that it will be desolate forever." And it will be, when you have finished reading this book, bind a stone to it, and cast it into the midst of the Euphrates, and say: "Thus will Babylon sink and not rise...."'" (Jeremiah 51:61–64)

PROPHECY: "And Babylon the glory of kingdoms, the beauty of the pride of the Kasdim, shall be as when God overthrew Sodom and Amora. It shall never again be inhabited, neither shall it be dwelt in from generation to generation, neither shall the Arabs pitch tent there, neither shall the shepherds make their flock lie down there. But wild beasts of the desert shall lie there, and their houses shall be full of owls; and ostriches shall dwell there, and owls shall live there. And jackals shall cry in their castles, and wild dogs in their pleasant palaces." (Isaiah 13:19–22)

PROPHECY: "And I will pay back to Babylon and to all the inhabitants of Kasdim all their evil that they have done in Zion (Jerusalem) in your sight, says the Lord… and I will stretch out My hand upon you, and roll you down from the rocks, and will make you a burnt mountain…for you shall be desolate forever." (Jeremiah 51:24–26)

HISTORY: "The city of Babylon was the capital of the old Babylonian empire from about 2000 B.C.E. It was the metropolis of antiquity, the center of Oriental civilization. Nebuchadnezar restored it in the middle of the sixth century (B.C.E.). After the reign of Cyrus, Babylon still continued to be an important city, remaining one of the capitals of the Persian empire. But gradually the city became more and more deserted. Alexander the Great intended to make it the center of his world empire, but his early death prevented this. And Babylon eventually passed from the scene. It was reduced to rubble and has remained in this condition until our time."[36]

HISTORY: "Why did the prophets endanger their credibility with a long-range prophecy which would extend till the end of history? The demise of an empire and the destruction of a city are natural occurrences, but all the great cities of the ancient Near East were destroyed and rebuilt numerous times until the modern period. Damascus, Rabat Amon, Jericho, Jerusalem and Alexandria were all repeatedly rebuilt and are standing today on the ruins of their past. Why then was Babylon, the greatest and most glorious city of old, standing at the economic hub of empires that arose around her one after the other, transformed into an eternal desolation?"[37]

THE INDUSTRIAL REVOLUTION

It is hard to imagine how some five million Jews, in a country as small and geographically indefensible as Israel (particularly before 1967) could consistently prevail over more than one hundred million Arabs in adjacent and surrounding lands. Naturally speaking, this could only have occurred with to-day's technology. However, from a historical perspective, this technological boon, beginning (for all practical purposes) in the early nineteenth century, did not slowly and progressively evolve, but rather broke into history as a radical departure from the past.

Correspondingly, the Zohar, which is the primary classic of Jewish mysticism (the Kabbalah) attributed to the school of Rabbi Shimon bar Yochai (circa 120 C.E.) predicted that in the six-hundredth year of the sixth millennium of the Hebrew calendar (corresponding to the nineteenth century C.E.) unprecedented "knowledge" breakthroughs would occur.

PROPHECY: The Zohar reads:[38] "Every sixty years of the sixth millennium the gates of lower wisdom will be strengthened and rise up gradually to become stronger. Then, at the end of ten complete stages of sixty years each — i.e., at the end of six hundred years into the sixth millennium (nineteenth century C.E.) — the gates of supernal knowledge will open above, along with the wellsprings of knowledge below (secular). This will begin the process whereby the world will prepare to enter the seventh millennium. This is symbolized by Israel who start preparing themselves on the afternoon of the sixth day for the Sabbath. In the same manner, the sixth millennium parallels Friday which is the sixth day of the week. Towards afternoon of the sixth millennium everything is accelerated and all the preparations are readied for the Great Sabbath."

HISTORY: Accordingly, at the turn of the nineteenth century, a revolution commenced in all areas of applied secular science. The following is a partial list of scientific discoveries:[39]

1805	Dalton's Atomic Theory
1823	Ampere, electricity
1825	Laplace, formulas
1831	Joseph Henry, telegraph
1833	K. F. Gauss, electromagnetism
1834	Faraday, theory of electro-chemistry
1842	H. Joule, 2nd Law of Thermodynamics, Conservation of energy
1842	Doppler effect
1842	Radio
1845	Boolean algebra, basis for modern computer languages
1857	Louis Pasteur, breakthrough in discovery of microbes and immunization
1859	Bunsen and Kurchoff, spectroscopy
1864	Alfred Nobel, dynamite
1865	Mendel, laws of genetic inheritance
1869	Mendeleev, periodic table of elements
1873	Maxwell's formulas (electromagnetic)

HISTORY: "In one generation (from 1801 to 1840) more
                progress was made in all branches of science
than in the thousands of years that passed since man first
contemplated the stars and asked himself, 'Where is all this
from?'"[40]

HISTORY: "The nineteenth century reached a greater
                degree of progress than all previous cen-
turies put together in the understanding of nature and its
laws. Important riddles of the universe were solved which
were considered impossible to unravel at the beginning of
the century. The veil was removed from science and from
man's awareness of new frontiers whose existence was never
suspected less than a hundred years ago."[41]

THE JEWISH NATION BEING FEW IN NUMBER

PROPHECY: "I will draw out a sword after you...and you
                shall perish among the nations, and the land
of your enemies shall eat you up." (Leviticus 26:33–38)

PROPHECY: "And you shall be left few in number among
                the nations...." (Deuteronomy 4:27)

HISTORY: Present-day demographers claim that the Jews
                would number several hundred million (as
opposed to approximately thirteen million today) were it not
for periodic physical persecution and annihilation.[42]

CONTINUITY OF THE TORAH AND THE JEWISH NATION

PROPHECY: "When they are then beset by many evils and
                troubles, this song (i.e., the Torah) shall tes-
tify for them like a witness, since it will not be forgotten by
their descendants." (Deuteronomy 31:21)

PROPHECY: "As for Me, this is My covenant with them, says the Lord...My words which I have put in your mouth, shall not depart out of your mouth, nor out of the mouth of your seed, nor out of the mouth of your seed's seed, says the Lord, from henceforth and forever." (Isaiah 59:21)

HISTORY: "We were...assured that the Torah would live forever in the nation. For a nation that lived so long among other peoples, encountering alien cultures, this is nothing if not unnatural.... The Torah faced many ordeals in its exile from the Land of Israel together with the nation. But whenever a center of Torah study was destroyed, others immediately took its place.... In every generation there were those who attempted to exterminate us or bring us, in various ways, to abandon our Torah.... The physical survival of the Jewish nation and its continued observance of the Torah are among the most astounding phenomena in human history. They are unparalleled in the annals of any other nation. Despite our contact with other cultures, the Torah was preserved unaltered in its original form. Even today, the daily routine and cultural life of observant [Orthodox] Jews the world over, whether shoemaker or famous scientist, is essentially the same as that of our forefathers some three thousand years ago."[43]

*   *   *

PROPHECY: "And yet for all that, when they be in the land of their enemies, I will not cast them away...to destroy them utterly, and to break My Covenant with them." (Leviticus 26:44)

HISTORY: World Jewry, 2007.

NOTES TO CHAPTER 11

1. E.g., Leviticus 26:14–32; Deuteronomy 2:16–17.

2. See Kings II, ch. 25.

3. Josephus, *The Jewish Wars* 4:6:3.

4. Jerusalem Talmud, *Ta'anit* 84–85 (Jerusalem: Torah Mitzion, 1968).

5. Josephus 2:14:2.

6. Ibid. 6:9:2.

7. Ibid. 2:6:2.

8. Ibid. 3:6:2.

9. Ganor, N. R., "Who Were the Phoenicians?" Sutton, A., and Arachim Staff (eds.), *Pathways to the Torah* (Jerusalem: Arachim, 1985).

10. Ibid.

11. Josephus 5:10:3.

12. In Sutton et al., p. B38.

13. Munter the Historian, in Sutton et al., p. B38.

14. Talmud *Ketubot* 3b (Jerusalem: Ortsel, 1960).

15. Meiri, S., "Burden of Proof," J.D. Kiel (ed.), *Return to the Source* (New York: Feldheim, 1984).

16. Gilbert, M., *Atlas of Jewish History* (New York: Dorset Press, 1985), in Preface.

17. Lloyd George (1923), in Sutton et al., p. B43.

18. Prager, D. & Telushkin, J., *Why the Jews? The Reason for Anti-Semitism* (New York: Simon & Schuster, 1983), p. 17.

19. Leschzinsky, "The Jewish Dispersion," in Sutton et al., p. B47.

20. Grosser, P.E. & Halperin E.G., *The Causes and Effects of Anti-Semitism* (New York: Philosophical Library, 1978).

21. Sutton et al.

22. Meiri, pp. 107–108.

23. Josephus 3:3:2.

24. Nachmanides, M., "Epistle to his Son Nachman," in *Kitvei Ramban* (Jerusalem: Mossad HaRav Kook, 1964), vol. 1, pp. 367–68.

25. Twain, M., *The Innocents Abroad*, in Sutton et al., p. B67.

26. Cited in Sutton et al., p. B67.

27. In Davis, L.J., *Myths and Facts 1985: A Concise Record of the Arab-Israeli Conflict* (Washington, D.C.: Near East Research, Inc., 1984), p. 10.

28. Nachmanides, M., in *Mikraot Gedolot*, Leviticus 26:32 (New York: Pardes, 1951).

29. Sutton et al.

30. Israel Aliyah Center, Chicago, 2005.

31. Meiri, pp. 112–113.

32. Deuteronomy 30:1–2.

33. Amos 8:11.

34. *Shir HaShirim Rabbah*, in *Midrash Rabbah* (Jerusalem: Levin-Epstein, 1965).

35. Meiri, p. 111.

36. Biberfeld, P., *Universal Jewish History* (New York: Spero Foundation, 1948), vol. 1, p. 22.

37. Sutton et al., p. B91.

38. Zohar, *Parshat Vayera* (Jerusalem: Mossad HaRav Kook, 1964).

39. Sutton et al., p. B84.

40. VaLoon, H.W., *The Story of Mankind* (New York: Liveright, 1984), p. 21.

41. Chakiovsky, A., *Between Science and Religion* (Tel Aviv: Joshua Chachik Publishing, 1965).

42. Meiri, pp. 107–108.

43. Ibid. pp. 109–110.

12 | Historical Consequences of Torah Observance

Your destroyers and those who lay
you waste will come from you.
(Isaiah 49:17)

T HE RELATIONSHIP BETWEEN THE JEWISH PEOPLE'S COLLECTIVE behavior and subsequent oppression— or conversely prosperity and security — can be seen throughout Jewish history. Examples of this are evidenced over a period of almost nine hundred years — as recorded in the five Books of Moses, the Prophets and in the Holy Writings.

This seeming cause-and-effect relationship began with the creation of an independent Jewish nation some 3,300 years ago. The Jewish People had been miraculously emancipated from Egyptian exile some ninety days prior. The nation had witnessed the wonders and plagues in Egypt, the redemption therefrom, the splitting of the sea, manna from heaven and God Himself speaking to the entire Jewish nation.

However, when Moses ascended Mount Sinai for forty days and nights and failed to return when expected, part of the nation became impatient and worshiped before the

Golden Calf. This transgression brought upon the nation three thousand fatalities and afterwards a fatal plague (see Exodus, ch. 32). Accordingly, the following delineates chronologically the eras of Joshua, the Judges and the ruling Jewish (Davidic) monarchy — with the events that took place under their leadership that seem to highlight the above relationship. (The dating system used in this chapter is based on information culled from *Legacy of Sinai*, by Rabbi Zechariah Fendel, and the dates in parentheses represent the time periods during which they ruled.)

JOSHUA SON OF NUN (1272–1244 B.C.E.)

THE JEWISH NATION FOLLOWS GOD'S LAW ⮕ SUCCESS IN WAR ⮕ SECURITY AND PROSPERITY

During this twenty-eight-year period, Joshua son of Nun, Moses' successor, presided over the Jewish nation. In the book of Joshua (24:31), it reads:

> Israel served God throughout Joshua's lifetime and during the lifetime of the elders who survived Joshua, and who knew everything that God had done for Israel.

The effect or correlation between the collective behavior of the Jewish nation, as just mentioned, and national success is also found in the book of Joshua (21:41–43):

> God gave Israel the entire land which He had sworn to their forefathers that He would give them. They took possession of it and settled in it. God gave them rest on all sides, as He had sworn to their forefathers. None of their enemies withstood them. God delivered all their enemies into their hands. Not one of the good things God had promised the House of Israel failed; everything was fulfilled.

In short, the historical account of the Jewish nation, who collectively observed the precepts of the Torah, as related in the Book of Joshua, correlates with an era of security and prosperity.

THE PERIOD OF THE JUDGES

OTHNIEL SON OF KENAZ (1244–1204 B.C.E.)

THE JEWISH PEOPLE TRANSGRESS ⇝ SUBJUGATION AND PERSECUTION ⇝ COLLECTIVE REPENTANCE ⇝ VICTORY IN WAR ⇝ NATIONAL SECURITY AND TRANQUILITY

During the following forty-year-period the Jewish People began to breach Torah law, and subjugation followed in its wake. In the Biblical book of Judges (3:5–11), it reads:

> The Israelites lived among the Canaanites, the Hittites, the Amorites, the Perizzites, the Hivvites and the Jebusites. They took their daughters in marriage and [the Canaanites] gave their daughters to [the Israelites'] sons. The Israelites did what was offensive to God; they forgot God their Lord and worshiped Baal and the Asherahs. God's anger blazed against Israel, and He delivered them into the hands of King Kushan Rishathayim of Aram Nahara'im.
>
> The Israelites served Kushan Rishathayim for eight years. Then the Israelites cried out to God (i.e., they repented). He appointed a savior for the Israelites to rescue them — Othniel son of Kenaz, Caleb's younger brother. God's spirit rested on him, and he judged Israel.
>
> He went out to war, and God delivered King Kushan Rishathayim of Aram into his hands. [Othniel] prevailed over Kushan Rishathayim and the land had peace for forty years, until Othniel son of Kenaz died.

The above historical process appears clear; transgression of the Torah was followed by subjugation and oppression. Only after collective repentance did national sovereignty and security return.

EHUD SON OF GERA (1204–1124 B.C.E.)

JEWISH BACKSLIDING ↪ SUBJUGATION AND OPPRESSION ↪ COLLECTIVE REPENTANCE ↪ VICTORY IN WAR ↪ NATIONAL SECURITY AND PEACE

With the demise of Othniel son of Kenaz the Israelites regressed. The correlation of events during this time period are related in the book of Judges (3:12–15,27–30). It reads:

> The Israelites again did what was offensive to God, so God had King Eglon of Moab prevail over Israel.... Eglon summoned the Ammonites and Amalek, who went and attacked Israel and took possession of the City of Palms. The Israelites served King Eglon of Moab for eighteen years. Then the Israelites cried out to God (they repented), and He appointed a savior for them, Ehud son of Gera the Benjaminite. ... When he [Ehud] reached the hill country of Ephraim, he blew the shofar, and the Israelites came down with him from the hills. He said to them, "Follow me, because God has delivered your enemies, Moab, into your hands!" They followed him and captured the Jordan's crossings into Moab.... At that time they struck down about ten thousand of Moab's men, all robust and brave; not one escaped. On that day Moab surrendered to Israel, and the land had peace for eighty years.

The historical process is repeated: A backsliding from Torah precepts is followed by foreign subjugation and persecution. This, in turn, was followed by mass repentance which brought both victory and security for the Jewish nation.

DEBORAH THE PROPHETESS (1124-1084 B.C.E.)

JEWISH BACKSLIDING → SUBJUGATION AND OPPRESSION
→ JEWISH REPENTANCE → MILITARY VICTORY →
NATIONAL LIBERATION AND PEACE

The next forty year period is also described in Judges (4:1–7,
23–24; 5:31). The passage states:

> The Israelites again did what was offensive to God after Ehud
> died, so God delivered them into the hands of King Jabin of
> Canaan, who ruled in Hazor. The commander of his army
> was Sisera. The Israelites cried out (repented) to God, for
> [Jabin].... had oppressed [the Israelites] harshly for twenty
> years. Deborah, Lappidoth's wife, was a prophetess; she
> judged Israel at that time. She sat beneath Deborah's Palm,
> between Ramah and Bethel in the hill country of Ephraim.
> The Israelites went to her for judgment. She summoned
> Barak son of Abinoam from Kedesh Naphtali, and said to
> him, "God, Lord of Israel, had commanded, 'Go take ten
> thousand Naphtalites and Zevulunites with you, and lead
> them to Mount Tabor. I will draw Sisera, the commander of
> Jabin's army, his chariots and his troops over to you at Wadi
> Kishon, and I will deliver him into your hands.'" ...
>
> On that day God subdued King Jabin of Canaan before
> the Israelites. The Israelites' hand bore harder and harder
> against King Jabin of Canaan, until they destroyed him....
> And the land had peace for forty years.

The recurring process is evident. As in the time of Othniel and Ehud, so too in the time of the prophetess and judge
Deborah, a collective spiritual decline is followed by subjugation and oppression. Only after the Jewish People repented
and cried out to the God of their forefathers, did victory and
extended peace result.

GIDEON (1084–1037 B.C.E.)

THE JEWS RELAPSE ↪ SUBJUGATION ↪ MASS
REPENTANCE ↪ PROPHETIC REBUKE ↪ SALVATION AND
MILITARY SUCCESS

The next forty-seven years (1084–1037 B.C.E.) as recorded in
Judges (6:1–16; 8:22,23,28) witnessed a similar process, with
minor variations. It states:

> The Israelites did what was offensive to God, and God de-
> livered them into Midian's hands for seven years. Midian
> prevailed against Israel... After Israel had sowed, Midian,
> Amalek and the Easterners would come up and raid them.
> They attacked them and destroyed the produce of the land
> all the way to Gaza, leaving no food for Israel.... They in-
> vaded the land to destroy it. Israel was impoverished by
> Midian and the Israelites cried out to God. When the Is-
> raelites cried out to God because of Midian, God sent a
> prophet to Israel, who told them, "God, Lord of Israel says:
> 'I brought you out of Egypt and took you out of the house
> of bondage. I saved you from the Egyptians, from all your
> oppressors; I drove them out before you and gave you their
> land. I said to you: I am God your Lord; do not worship the
> gods of the Amorites in whose land you live. But you did
> not obey Me.'" An angel of God came to Ophrah and sat
> under the terebinth of Joash the Aviezrite. His son Gideon
> was beating wheat in the winepress to hide from Midian.
> The angel of God appeared to him and said to him, "God
> be with you, mighty warrior!" "Please, sir," Gideon answered
> him, "If God is among us, why has all this happened to us?
> Where are all His wonders of which our fathers told us? ...
> For God has abandoned us now and delivered us into the
> hands of Midian!" God then turned to him and said: "Go
> with this strength of yours and save Israel from Midian, I

have sent you!" Gideon said to Him, "Please, God, how can I save Israel? My family is the poorest in Menasseh, and I am the youngest in my father's house!" God answered him, "I will be with you, and you will strike Midian down as if they were a single man!" ... The men of Israel said to Gideon (after he had defeated Midian) "Rule over us, you, your son and your grandson — for you have saved us from Midian." "I will not rule over you, nor will my son rule," Gideon responded. "God will rule over you." ... Midian submitted to the Israelites and did not raise its head again. The land had peace for forty years during Gideon's time.

An already common theme, the Jewish People relapse and transgress. Subjugation and oppression follow, which in turn is followed by mass repentance. However, this time immediate help is not forthcoming. Rather, a prophet is sent to rebuke the Israelites for failing again to keep the commandments. Only afterwards is a judge (Gideon) sent, who subsequently leads them to victory. Peace and security follow.

JEPHTAH (990–941 B.C.E.)

TRANSGRESSION ↪ SUBJUGATION AND PERSECUTION ↪
NATIONAL REPENTANCE ↪ HEAVENLY REBUKE ↪
THE JEWS PERSIST IN THEIR REPENTANCE ↪
MILITARY SUCCESS

The subsequent period describes a similar historical pattern but with important variations. In Judges (10:6–16; 11:29,32,33) the narrative reads:

The Israelites continued to offend God. They worshiped the Baals and the Ashtores and the gods of Aram, Sidon, Moab, the Ammonites, and the Philistines. ...

> God delivered them into the hands of the Philistines and
> the Ammonites, who oppressed and persecuted the Isra-
> elites...for eighteen years...in the land of the Amorites in
> Gilead. The Ammonites also crossed the Jordan to make
> war against Judah, Benjamin and the House of Ephraim, and
> they troubled Israel greatly. The Israelites cried out to God,
> "We have sinned against You, for we have abandoned our
> God and worshiped the Baals."
>
> God said to the Israelites. "Didn't I save you from Egypt,
> from the Amorites, from the Ammonites and from the Phi-
> listines? The Sidonians, Amalek and Moab oppressed you;
> you cried out to Me, and I saved you from them. But you
> abandoned Me and worshiped other gods. Therefore, I shall
> no longer save you. Go and cry out to the gods you have
> chosen; let them save you when you are in trouble!"
>
> "We have sinned," the Israelites declared to God. "Do to
> us as You see fit, but please save us today!" They removed
> the foreign gods from their midst and worshiped God, until
> He could not bear Israel's distress....
>
> God's spirit (then) rested on Jephtah.... Jephtah crossed
> over to the Ammonites to make war with them, and God
> delivered them into his hands. He defeated them from
> Aroer up to Minnith, twenty towns, to Avel Keramim — a
> very great defeat. The Ammonites surrendered to the Isra-
> elites.

Backsliding and sin are followed by subjugation and
oppression, which in turn is followed by mass repentance.
However, this time God rebukes the Jewish nation for being disloyal and refuses to help in light of their cumulative
transgressions. Only after the Jews persevere in heartfelt
repentance is a leader (Jephtah) sent, who leads them to
military victory.

THE PERIOD OF THE JEWISH KINGS

THE NEXT 450 years of Biblical history — the period of the Jewish kings — are different than the preceding four hundred years. During the previous four-hundred-year period of the Judges there was no central government. The Torah was the nation's sole constitution and legislation (which resulted in a historically unprecedented self-government) without king or president to coerce. Notwithstanding the episodes of subjugation and oppression, the years of peace and security were actually much more numerous. The period of Biblical Judges was a remarkable time, an experiment of self-government based on Torah legislation, without a central government to enforce the law. This successful and even miraculous social experiment for approximately four hundred years was never duplicated, up to our present time, by any other nation.

However, when the Jewish nation became overly influenced, at the end of this remarkable period, by the naturalistic ways of the nations, they adamantly requested a Jewish king to rule over them. A king, they hoped, would unite them in a more natural manner against their enemies. Through this request, however, they unwittingly placed themselves in a precarious situation, which would endanger the future of Jewish existence in the Land of Israel. When the king was a righteous David, Jehoshaphat or Hezekiah, life would be secure, but when the kingship fell to the likes of a Jehoram, Ahaz or Menasseh, ruination would ensue.

The Jewish king (like other ancient monarchs) had almost absolute power. He was subservient to no mortal but to God alone. The power and influence the Jewish king had over the nation is aptly described in the Biblical book of Samuel I (8:10–20). After the Israelites had requested a king from the prophet Samuel, the prophet (who was the Jewish leader at the time) attempts to explain to the erstwhile Jewish People the downside of having a king. The prophet Samuel explains:

> "This is what will happen when a king reigns over you; he will take your sons and place them before his chariot as horsemen to run before his chariot; [he will] appoint officers of thousands and officers of fifties to plow for him and harvest for him, to manufacture his arms and his cavalry equipment. He will take your choice fields, vineyards and olive groves and give them to his servants. He will tithe your seed and your vineyards and give it to his servants. He will take your servants, your maidservants, your fine young men and your donkeys to do his work. He will tithe your sheep, and you will be his slaves. And when you cry out because of the king you chose for yourselves, God will not answer you on that day." But the people refused to listen to Samuel. They said, "No! We must have a king over us! We (are determined) to be like all the other nations; our king will govern us, and go out before us and fight our wars!"

It becomes evident from the above narrative that with the advent of a Jewish king, some four hundred years after the nation had entered the Land of Israel, the king would wield enormous power and would have the greatest influence on the Jewish body politic. Perforce, the nation would follow the ways of the king whether voluntarily or conversely through coercion. Therefore, when the king was the pious David, or those who followed in his footsteps, all went well for the Jewish nation, but when kings like Menasseh and Ahaz ruled, the destruction of the people and their land would result. Hence, over the next 450 years, the collective behavior of the Jewish nation can, to a significant extent, be reflected in the behavior and activities of their kings. In short, the king would lead and the masses, in general, would characteristically follow.

KING DAVID (876–836 B.C.E.)

RIGHTEOUS BEHAVIOR ⇝ MILITARY AND DOMESTIC SUCCESS

The correlation between the righteousness of King David and the success of the nation is found in the Biblical book of Chronicles I (18:13–14). It concisely states: "And the Lord made David victorious wherever he went. And David reigned over all Israel, and he administered justice and charity for all his people."

KING REHOBOAM (794–777 B.C.E.)

ABANDONMENT OF THE LAW ⇝ MILITARY DEFEAT

During the seventeen-year rule of King David's grandson, Rehoboam, a correlation is also visible. However this relationship is less than favorable.

In Chronicles II (12:1,2,4,5,9) it reads:

> Now it came to pass when Rehoboam's kingdom was established and when he became strong, he abandoned the Law of God and all Israel with him. And it came to pass in the fifth year of King Rehoboam, that Shishak, the king of Egypt, marched against Jerusalem, for they had betrayed God.... And he (Shishak) seized Judah's (a few years prior, the Jewish People had broken into two Jewish nations — the land of Judah being the southern nation) fortified cities, and he came until Jerusalem. And Shemaiah the prophet came to Rehoboam and the princes of Judah who had gathered to

Jerusalem because of Shishak, and he said to them, "So said the Lord: You have forsaken Me; so I, too, have forsaken you in the hand of Shishak".... And Shishak, the king of Egypt, marched against Jerusalem, and he took the treasures of the king's palace; everything he took.

KING ASA (774–733 B.C.E.)

FOLLOWS GOD'S LAWS ➺ MILITARY SUCCESS AND NATIONAL SECURITY

King Asa, son of Abijah, ruled over the Jewish nation of Judah for the next forty-one years. The nature of his success follows a similar pattern. In Chronicles II (14:1,3,5,8–13) it reads:

Now (King) Asa did what was good and proper in the eyes of the Lord his God.... And he commanded Judah to seek God, the God of their forefathers and to implement the Law and the commandments.... And he built fortified cities in Judah, because the land was tranquil, and there was no war with him in these years, because God gave him peace...[then] Zerah the Cushite came out against them with an army of a million.... And Asa came out before him, and they set the battle in the valley of Zephath at Mareshah. And Asa called out to the Lord his God, and he said: "O God, there is no difference to You to help either the great or the powerless; help us, O Lord our God, for we have relied on You, and we have come with Your Name upon this multitude. You are the Lord our God; let no man rule against You." And God smote the Cushites before Asa and before Judah, and the Cushites fled. And Asa and the people who were with him pursued them all the way to Gerar, and there fell the Cushites until they had no life, for they were broken before the Lord and before His camp. And they smote all the cities around Gerar, because the fear of God was upon them.

KING JEHOSHAPHAT (733–708 B.C.E.)

FOLLOWS TORAH LAW ⇢ MIRACULOUS VICTORY ⇢
NATIONAL SECURITY AND TRANQUILITY

King Jehoshaphat ruled over the Jewish nation of Judah for the next twenty-five years. In Chronicles II (17:3,4,9,10; 20:1–32) we find the following:

> And God was with Jehoshaphat because he went in the ways of (King) David...he inquired of the God of his father, and he went in His commandments.... And they taught in Judah, and with them was the scroll of the Law of God and they went around throughout all the cities of Judah, and they taught among the people. And the fear of God was upon all the kingdoms of the lands that were around Judah, and they would not wage war with Jehoshaphat.... And it came to pass afterwards that the sons of Moab and the sons of Ammon... came to Jehoshaphat to wage war. And they came and told Jehoshaphat, saying, "A great multitude has come upon you from across the sea".... And Jehoshaphat was frightened and he set his face to seek God, and he proclaimed a fast over all Judah. And the Judeans gathered to seek help from God.... And he (Jehoshaphat) said, "O Lord, God of our fathers, is it not so that You are God in heaven, and that You rule over all the kingdoms of the nations, and in Your hand is strength and might, and no one can stand against You? Have You, our God, not driven out the inhabitants of this land from before Your people Israel and given it to the seed of Abraham, who loved You, forever? And they dwelt therein and therein they built You a sanctuary for Your Name, saying: 'Should evil come upon us, whether sword, pestilence or famine, we shall stand before this House and before You, for Your name is in this House, and we shall cry out to You from our distress,

and You will hear and save.... For we have no strength before this great multitude that is coming upon us, and we know not what to do, but our eyes are upon You...."

And Jahaziel the son of Zachariah the son of Benaiah the son of Jeiel the son of Mattaniah the Levite of the sons of Asaph, the spirit of God was upon him in the midst of the assembly. And he said, "Hearken, all Judeans, inhabitants of Jerusalem, and King Jehoshaphat, so said God to you: You shall not fear, neither shall you be dismayed because of this great multitude, for the war is not yours but God's.... It is not for you to fight in this war; set yourselves, stand and see the salvation of God with you, O Judah and Jerusalem; fear not and be not dismayed. Tomorrow, go forth before them, and God will be with you...." And they arose early in the morning and went forth to the desert of Tekoa, and when they went forth, Jehoshaphat stood and said, "Hear me, O Judeans and inhabitants of Jerusalem. Believe in the Lord our God ...believe in His prophets, and you will prosper".... And the sons of Ammon and Moab rose up against the inhabitants of Mount Seir (their previous allies) to destroy and annihilate, and when they finished with the inhabitants of Seir, each one helped to destroy his own friend. And the Judeans came upon the place overlooking the desert, and they turned to the multitude (their enemies), and behold they were corpses on the ground, with no survivors.... And all the men of Judah and Jerusalem returned with Jehoshaphat at their head, to return to Jerusalem with joy, because God had given them joy from their enemies.... And the fright of God was upon all the kingdoms of the lands when they heard that God had fought with Israel's enemies. And Jehoshaphat's kingdom was tranquil, and God granted him peace from round about.... And he went in the way of his father Asa and did not turn away from it, and did what was right in the eyes of God.

KING JEHORAM (708–703 B.C.E.)

TRANSGRESSES TORAH LAW → MILITARY DEFEAT

Jehoram ruled after Jehoshaphat. In Chronicles II (21:4,6,8, 10–19) it reads:

And Jehoram rose upon the kingdom of his father...and assassinated all his brothers with the sword, and also of the chieftains of Israel.... And he went in the ways of the kings of Israel (that is, the northern Jewish kingdom that was continuously riddled by idolatry and corruption and was eventually destroyed in 527 B.C.E.)...and he did that which was evil in God's eyes. ...in his days, Edom rebelled from under the yoke of Judah.... And Edom rebelled from under the yoke of Judah to this day; then Libnah rebelled at that time....because he had forsaken God, the God of his forefathers. He made high places (a Torah prohibition) in the mountains of Judah, and led the inhabitants of Jerusalem astray and led Judah astray. And a letter came to him from Elijah the prophet, saying, "So said the Lord, the God of David your father: Because you did not go in the ways of Jehoshaphat your father and in the ways of Asa, the king of Judah.... And you led Judah and the inhabitants of Jerusalem astray, and you assassinated your brothers of your father's house, who were better than you. Behold, God will smite your people with a great plague, and your sons and your wives and all your possessions. And you will have many illnesses with the illness of your bowels, until your bowels come out because of the illness, days upon days." And God stirred up against Jehoram the spirit of the Philistines and the Arabians who dwell alongside the Cushites. And they marched upon Judah and split it, and they captured all the possessions found belonging to the king's house, and also his sons and his wives, and no son was left to him except Jehoahaz the youngest of his sons. And after all this, God plagued him in his bowels with an incurable illness. And it was in the passing of time, at the end of two years, his bowels came out by reason of his illness and he died with a malignant illness.

KING JEHOASH (702–662 B.C.E.)

INITIALLY FOLLOWS TORAH LAW ⤳ NATIONAL SECURITY ⤳ THEN TRANSGRESSES ⤳ MILITARY DEFEAT

The following historical relationship is found in Chronicles II (24:2,17–24). King Jehoash is described as having a checkered career. During the lifetime of his uncle and mentor, the high priest Jehoyada, he followed Torah law, but with Jehoyada's demise he became corrupt. The relationship between King Jehoash's newly corrupt ways and the nation's lack of success is recorded in the following Biblical passage. It reads:

And after the death of Jehoyada, the princes of Judah came and prostrated themselves to the king; then the king hearkened to them. And they forsook the House of the Lord, the God of their fathers, and they worshiped the Asherahs and the idols, and there was wrath upon Judah and Jerusalem because of this. And He sent prophets among them, to return them to God and they warned them, but they did not incline their ears. And the spirit of God enveloped Zachariah the son of Jehoyada the priest, and he stood above the people and said to them, "So said God: Why do you transgress the commandments of God? You will not succeed because you have forsaken God.... And it came to pass at the turn of the year that the army of Aram marched against him (Jehoash) and they came to Judah and Jerusalem and they destroyed all the princes...with few men the army of Aram came, and

God delivered into their hands an exceedingly large army (the Judeans) for they had forsaken the Lord, the God of their fathers; and they dealt out punishment to Jehoash.

KING AMATZIAH (662–633 B.C.E.)

FOLLOWS TORAH LAW ↪ MILITARY SUCCESS
↪ THEN TRANSGRESSES ↪ MILITARY DEFEAT

The next king of Judah, Amatziah, also had a mixed career. In the beginning of his rule he followed the commandments of Jewish law and was successful. Afterwards, however, he imitated the customs of his non-Jewish pagan neighbors. Tragedy then resulted for him and the entire Jewish nation. The historical narrative is related in Chronicles II (25:1,2,11–12,14–16,21–23). It states:

When he was twenty-five years old, Amatziah became king, and he reigned twenty-nine years in Jerusalem.... He did what was right in the eyes of God.... And Amatziah strengthened himself and led his people, and he went to the Valley of Salt, and he smote the sons of Seir, ten thousand. And the sons of Judah captured ten thousand alive.... And it was, after Amatziah had come from smiting the Edomites, that he brought the gods of the sons of Seir with him and set them up for gods, and he prostrated himself before them and burned incense to them. And God became angry with Amatziah, and He sent him a prophet and he said to him, "Why have you sought the gods of the people who did not save their people from your hand?"...

"I know that God has given counsel to destroy you, because you have done this, and you have not heeded my counsel." ...and Judah was beaten before (the northern kingdom) Israel, and they fled each man to his tent.

KING UZIAH (633–595 B.C.E.)

SEEKS GOD ⟶ SUCCESS IN WAR

In the narrative of Chronicles II (26:1,4–8) it reads:

> And the entire people of Judah took Uziah...and they made
> him king in place of his father Amatziah.... And he did what
> was right in the eyes of God....
>
> And it was his custom to seek God in the days of Zacha-
> riah, who understood the visions of God, and when he
> sought the Lord, God caused him to prosper. And he went
> forth and waged war with the Philistines.... And God helped
> him against the Philistines and against the Arabs....
>
> And the Ammonites paid Uziah tribute, and his name
> became well known until Egypt for he had become exceed-
> ingly successful.

KING JOTHAM (595–580 B.C.E.)

TORAH OBSERVANCE ⟶ SUCCESS IN WAR

In Chronicles II (27:1,2,5,6) the historical narrative reads:

> Jotham was twenty-five years old when he became king...he
> did what was proper in the eyes of God, as all that his father
> Uziah had done....
>
> And he fought with the king of the sons of Ammon and
> he overpowered them, and the sons of Ammon gave him in
> that year a hundred talents of silver and ten thousand mea-
> sures of wheat and ten thousand of barley; this, the children
> of Ammon returned to him, and in the second year and the
> third.
>
> And Jotham became powerful, because he prepared his
> ways before the Lord his God.

KING AHAZ (580–564 B.C.E.)

TRANSGRESSES JEWISH LAW → MILITARY DEFEAT

In Chronicles II (28:1–3,5,6) it states:

> Ahaz was twenty years old when he became king, and reigned for sixteen years in Jerusalem and he did not do what was proper in the eyes of God...and he also made molten images for the Baals (idolatry). And he burnt incense in the valley of Ben Hinnom, and he burnt his son in fire, like the abominations of the nations whom God had driven out from before the Children of Israel.... And the Lord his God delivered him into the hand of the king of Aram, and they smote him and captured from him a great captivity, and they brought them to Damascus....

KING HEZEKIAH (564–535 B.C.E.)

FOLLOWS TORAH LAW → STRENGTHENS JEWISH OBSERVANCE → MIRACULOUS SALVATION FROM SENNACHERIB

Chronicles II (29:1–2; 30:6–8; 32:1,6–8,20,21) relates:

> Hezekiah became king at the age of twenty-five and he reigned twenty-nine years in Jerusalem.... And he did that which was proper in the eyes of God, as all that his forefather David had done.... The couriers then went with the letters from the hand of the king and his officers throughout all Israel and Judah, and according to the king's command, saying: "Children of Israel, return to the Lord, the God of Abraham, Isaac and Israel, so that He may return to the remnant that has escaped from the clutches of the kings of Assyria. And do not be like your fathers or like your brothers (i.e., the northern Jewish kingdom which was already destroyed by

Assyria) who acted treacherously against the Lord, the God
of their Fathers, and He made them a desolation, as you see.
Now, do not be stiff necked like your fathers...and worship
the Lord your God, so that His burning wrath returns from
you.... After these deeds of integrity, Sennacherib the king
of Assyria came, and he entered into Judah and encamped
against the fortified cities and he planned to make a breach
therein for himself.... And he (Hezekiah) appointed officers
of war over the people, and he gathered them to him to the
square of the city...saying: "Be strong and of good courage,
do not fear and do not be dismayed because of the king of
Assyria and because of all the multitude that is with him,
because He Who is with us is greater than those with him.
With him is an arm of flesh, and with us is the Lord our God
to help us and to wage our wars, and the people relied on
the words of Hezekiah, king of Judah. ... And King Hezekiah
and the prophet Isaiah, the son of Amoz, prayed concerning
this, and they cried out to Heaven. And God sent an angel,
and he destroyed every mighty warrior and ruler and officer
in the camp of the king of Assyria and he (Sennacherib) returned shamefacedly to his land.

KING MENASSEH (535–480 B.C.E.)

ABANDONS TORAH LAW ➞ SUBJUGATION
AND PERSECUTION

In Chronicles II (33:1–6, 9–13) it reads:

Menasseh was twelve years old when he became king, and
he reigned in Jerusalem for fifty-five years. And he did that
which was evil in the eyes of God, like the abominations of
the nations that God had driven out from before the children
of Israel.... And he built altars to the entire host of heavens
in the two courts of the House of God. And he passed his

sons through fire...he practiced sooth-saying, divination, and sorcery, and he consulted necromancers...; he did much that was evil in the eyes of God to provoke Him.... And Menasseh led Judah and the inhabitants of Jerusalem astray to do what was evil, even more than the nations whom God had destroyed from before the Children of Israel.... And God brought upon them the generals of the king of Assyria, and they seized Menasseh with hooks and bound him with copper chains and brought him to Babylon.

KING JOSIAH (478–447 B.C.E.)

FOLLOWS TORAH LAW ↪ FOREBODING PROPHECY
↪ REPRIEVE OF PEACE FOR THIRTY YEARS

Chronicles II (34:2,22–28,33) relates:

And he (Josiah) did that which was right in the eyes of God, and he walked in the ways of David his forefather, and turned aside neither to the right nor to the left.... And Hilkiah and those whom the King sent went to Huldah the prophetess.... And she said to them, "So has the Lord God of Israel said...behold I bring calamity upon this place and upon its inhabitants — all the curses that are written in this Scroll...because they have forsaken Me and have burned incense to pagan deities, in order to provoke Me with all the deeds of their hands. My wrath is poured down upon this place, and it shall not be quenched." And concerning the king of Judah, who has sent you to inquire of the Lord, so shall you say to him: So has the Lord God of Israel said, "Since your heart has become soft, and you have humbled yourself before God when you heard His words about this place and about its inhabitants...and rent your garments and wept before Me, I, too, have heard it," says God. Therefore, behold I gather you to your forefathers, and you shall be

gathered to your graves in peace, and your eyes shall not
see any of the calamity that I am bringing upon this place
and upon its inhabitants. ... And Josiah removed all the
abominations from the land of the Children of Israel, and
he caused all those found in Israel to serve the Lord, their
God; all his days they did not turn away from following the
God of their forefathers.

KING JEHOIAKIM (447–436 B.C.E.)

TRANSGRESSES→MILITARY DEFEAT AND SUBJUGATION

In Chronicles II (36: 5–7) it states:

Jehoiakim was twenty-five years old when he became king,
and he reigned eleven years in Jerusalem; and he did that
which was evil in the eyes of the Lord his God. Nebuchadnezzar the king of Babylon advanced upon him, and bound
him in copper chains and brought him to Babylon.

*   *   *

In summary, as depicted in the above scenarios, which
span close to nine hundred years of recorded Jewish history, when the Jewish nation adhered to Jewish Law, they
were blessed with victory and security. However, when they
transgressed, they were invariably met with oppression and
subjugation.

13 | Primary Target Areas of Anti-Jewish Hostility

They have said, "Come and let us wipe them out as a nation — that the name of Israel be remembered no more."

(Psalms 83:4)

A S DESCRIBED IN CHAPTERS 2 AND 3, A PRIMARY CAUSE OF anti-Jewish hostility appears to be the intimidating nature of Jewish distinctiveness. It has posed a psychological threat to both nations and religions, whose objective to dominate ran counter and collided with Jewish separatism. To win the world over to their way of thinking, these national and international entities seemed pressured to crush all forms of Jewish resistance.

The Jewish nation, with its ancient ideology and lifestyle, was unlike other nations and refused to disappear. In fact, throughout its nineteen-hundred-year history of exile, it has continued to prosper on an intellectual, spiritual and, sometimes, even material level. As long as the Jewish presence existed, the declared supremacy of these national/

international movements was brought into question, and absolute domination was perforce withheld. To create a sense of political security and unity, the leaders of these movements attempted to eliminate the source of anything Jewish. The Jewish threat was that the Jewish People did not completely merge into the dominant culture, and appeared to ignore the historical law of nations (i.e., "when in Rome do as the Romans") by maintaining a separate identity.

However, this analysis is incomplete; for group differences need not lead to inter-group hostility. For example, ideological opposites like the Soviet Union and the United States were allies during World War II. Accordingly, the racist Nazis allied themselves with the Japanese and Arabs.

Why was it different with the Jewish nation? Why did the Jews fail to build, on the basis of similarities and necessity, an infrastructure of peaceful coexistence? Why, concerning the Jewish nation, have differences been accentuated? Have not Jews, throughout history, benefited the many nations in areas as diverse as the arts, sciences, commerce and politics? Could not their productivity be used to create, at worst, a tolerant inter-group atmosphere? How much more so when Judaism itself demands tolerance, civil obedience and even prayers for the ruling government — irrespective of time and place.

Why, then, have Jews, historically, been depicted as strangers from a strange land instead of fellow countrymen? And why were gentile leaders so compelled to uproot the Jewish presence?

In response, to admit imperfection was seemingly unbearable for these totalitarian-type governments and/or ideologies. The need to dominate was best displaced on some out-group whose "heretical" nature posed a fateful threat.

Attacking Jews and Judaism was rationalized as something positive and, in fact, fostered national/international unity. In order to bring the world over to their way of thinking, they were driven to crush all dissidents. However, the Jewish nation, unlike others, would not significantly change or disappear. As long as the Jewish presence existed, their supremacy was compromised. Consequently, Jews were portrayed as undermining society at large, and for these movements to truly dominate, the subjugation or elimination of Jews appeared imperative.

**Areas of
Anti-Jewish
Focus**   AS DELINEATED IN previous chapters, hostility towards the Jewish nation appears not to be against the Jews per se, but against their unnatural connectedness to the foundations of their faith. Historically, attacks against Jews were attempts to uproot (1) the Jewish People's relationship to their Land (Jewish nationalism), (2) the Jewish People's relationship to their Law (Jewish spirit), and/or (3) the Jewish collective body. Anti-Jewish movements appeared pressured to eradicate the Jewish presence by attacking one or more of these sources. Jewish nationalism was usually the first to be attacked. When this failed, the Jewish spirit was assailed via book-burning and prohibitions against teaching or observing Jewish Law. And as the Jewish entity inexplicably remained (more or less) intact, physical persecution and total annihilation became the logical and "final solution."

Why did subjugation result in spiritual and physical oppression? Why did expulsion and physical onslaught often follow? What is the significance of these three target areas that anti-Jewish movements, throughout history, have so assiduously attempted to destroy? In essence, the above three areas can be understood to represent the Jewish People's relationship to their God. Anti-Jewish powers, throughout history, have seemed to attack the areas above, not necessarily to annihilate Jews, but to eradicate the relationship it represented. It appears it was this relationship between the Jewish nation and their God which produced and maintained the intimidating nature of Jewish distinctiveness.

When this relationship between the Jewish People and their God was perceived, conflict and tension resulted. The means of dealing with this threat was to eradicate the mechanisms involved. The first strategy was usually to suppress Jewish independence. This was accomplished by expelling the Jews from the Land of Israel, by prohibiting their return, and by denying them the civil liberties granted to others. By denying civil liberties, they were, in effect, relegated to vassal status — far removed from independent nationalists — and a seemingly easy prey for assimilation. When this failed, the Jewish spirit was targeted via religious persecutions. When this proved inadequate, total annihilation was proposed.

The following paragraphs attempt to describe the source and significance of Jewish nationalism, the Jewish spirit, and the Jewish collective body — which anti-Jewish leaders, nations and movements, throughout history, have so attempted to eradicate.

JEWISH NATIONALISM

Jewish nationalism represents the relationship between the Land of Israel and the Jewish People, as Biblically bestowed to them by God Himself. The following represents a sample of this relationship, which gentile nations and religions have so feverishly attempted to sever. As said earlier, this is usually the first objective of anti-Jewish movements.

❖ A land [the Land of Israel] which the Lord your God cares for; the eyes of the Lord your God are always upon it. (Deuteronomy 11:12)

❖ For the Lord has chosen Zion; He has desired it for His habitation. (Psalms 132:13)

❖ If I forget you, O Jerusalem, let my right hand forget her cunning. Let my tongue cleave to the roof of my mouth if I do not remember you, if I do not set Jerusalem above my highest joy. (Psalms 137:5–6)

We find in the Talmud:

❖ Every Jew who lives in the Land of Israel is similar to one who has a God, and one who dwells elsewhere is similar to one who hasn't,[1] as is written: "To give to you (i.e., the Jewish People) the Land of Canaan, to be God for you" (Leviticus 25:38).

❖ Even after one dies it is important to be buried in the Land of Israel because of its holiness. To be buried in the Land of Israel is analogous to being buried under the Altar of the Temple in Jerusalem.[2]

The traditional Midrashic commentary on the Biblical books of Numbers and Deuteronomy, the *Sifrei* (composed in the third century C.E.) relates:[3]

> The story of Rabbi Yehuda son of Betayra, Rabbi Matya son of Cheresh, and Rabbi Chanina son of the brother of Rabbi Yehoshua and Rabbi Yonatan who ventured outside the Land of Israel. They reached the Paltom and remembered the land. They picked up their eyes, cried bitterly and tore their clothing [as a sign of mourning] and recited the Biblical verse: "When God excises the nations to which you

are coming, and drives them away before you, you shall expel them and live therein" (Deuteronomy 12:29). They then
returned, reciting: "Living in the Land of Israel is equal to
all the commandments of the Torah."

The architects of the Talmud, who lived during the third
to fifth century C.E., expressed their affection thus:[3]

Rabbi Abba would kiss the cliffs of Akko (a city on the
northern coast of Israel). Rabbi Chanina would repair its
roads.... Rabbi Chiyya the son of Gamda would roll himself
in its dust, for the Bible states (Psalms 52:15): "Your servants
take pleasure in her stones, and love her dust!"

A leading Talmudic scholar of the thirteenth century,
Moses Nachmanides (Ramban), wrote in his *Hosafot l'Sefer
HaMitzvot*:[4]

The commandment is that we should inherit the land given
by God, exalted be He, to our forefathers Abraham, Isaac
and Jacob, and that we should neither let it fall to any of
the other nations nor let it grow into a wasteland.... This
is a positive commandment for all time until eternity. It is
obligatory on each and every one of us, even in times of
exile and dispersion, as evident from many places in the
Talmud.

Even in exile, the Jewish People's active relationship to the
Land bears testimony to this attachment. Whether they lived
in neighboring Persia, or in warm Italy or Spain, whether
they settled in cold Eastern Europe, found their way to North
America, or came to live in the southern hemisphere where
the seasons are reversed, Jews have always celebrated the Land
of Israel's seasonal change. They pray for dew in May and for
rain in October. On Passover, they celebrate their liberation

from Egyptian bondage, the beginning of Jewish nationalism in the Promised Land. They pray three times daily facing the Land, and request in each prayer to be brought back to the Land with all the Jewish exiles. After eating bread they pray for the rebuilding of Jerusalem, and during weddings as well as deaths make explicit mention of their exile, their hope, and their belief in their eventual return.

In conclusion, Israel is the only country today which is inhabited by the same nation, with the same religious culture and language, that inhabited it thirty-two hundred years ago — despite having been exiled twice, where the latter lasted almost nineteen hundred years.

THE JEWISH SPIRIT

Jewish spirit represents the Jewish People's attachment to their traditional God-given Torah (which denotes both the Written and Oral Law), and has created extreme animosity among our enemies. This relationship is depicted in the following Biblical and Oral Law sources.

The Talmud relates:

◆ God's purpose in Creation required that Israel accept the Torah. If not, all creation would lose its reason for being and would cease to exist.[5]

◆ Each law is nourishment for the soul, strengthening it and increasing a person's spiritual fortitude.[6]

◆ The Revelation of the Torah at Mount Sinai was final, and would never be abrogated or altered by any succeeding prophet.[7]

◆ The Torah sets limits through which a Jew can fulfill God's purpose while living in a materialistic world.

Through the Torah, the Jew learns to be part of the world, and at the same time, dedicated to the spiritual.[8]

The Torah is considered the only means through which a Jew can fulfill God's purpose in Creation (Rabbi Yehuda HaLevi).[9] The immediate benefit of following the Torah is spiritual, bringing a person closer to God (Zohar).[10] Moreover, the many laws associated with daily life are to teach the Jewish People self-discipline (Maimonides).[11]

The Talmud asserts: "When Israel is occupied with the study and practice of Torah, they master their desires, and are not mastered by them."[12]

Similarly in Numbers (15:39) it states: "You shall remember all God's commandments and keep them, and not stray after your heart or after your eyes, by which you are led astray."

Torah law acts as a survival mechanism, enabling the Jewish People to endure even the harshest of persecutions,[13] while a single generation's lapse leads to major spiritual debilitation.[14]

The following narrative is found in the Midrash:[15]

> God said to the people of Israel. "If you accept My Torah and observe My laws, I will give you a thing most precious." "And what," asked Israel, "is that precious thing?" God replied, "The World to Come."

Similarly, when Moses entreated God to enter the land of Canaan, the following reply was given:[16]

> Moses, my son, much honor has been stored up for you in the future world...which I have created for every pious man, that through love of Me devoted himself to the [study and fulfillment of the] Torah.

The following Midrashic conversation between the non-Jewish prophet Bilaam and the gentile nations of the world relates:[17]

> The nations asked Bilaam: "Why did God command Israel, and not us, to bring sacrifices?" He replied: "The purpose of sacrifices is to establish peace; but peace without Torah is impossible, and the Israelites accepted the Torah."

The Midrash relates that when God instructed Moses to teach the Torah to Israel, Moses asked that it be written down in full. God replied:[18]

> Gladly I would give them the whole in writing, but I know that the nations of the world will, at a later date, read the Torah translated into Greek (the Septuagint) and will say: "We are the true Israel; we are the chosen children of God." Then I shall say to the nations: "You claim to be My chosen children, but are you not aware that My chosen children are those who received My Oral teachings as well?" God then said to the Jewish People: "Before you accepted the Torah, you were like all other nations, but for the Torah's sake alone I have lifted you above all others. Even your king, Moses, owes the distinction he enjoys in this world and in the World to Come to the Torah alone."

Another *midrash* relates the following dialogue between God and Moses: "Moses said: 'Lord of the world, had we worshiped the stars and planets, the Midianites would not have hated us; they hate us only because of the Torah that You have given us.'"[19]

Similarly, when the Persian prime minister Haman delivered his indictment of the Jews, the angel Michael spoke to God, saying: "Lord of the world, You know that the Jews are not accused of idolatry, nor of immoral conduct, nor of shedding blood. They are accused only of observing Your Torah." God then placated Michael by saying: "As you live, I have never completely abandoned them. I will not abandon them."[20]

THE JEWISH COLLECTIVE BODY

Once the Jewish People were exiled from their land and distanced from the Torah through assimilation, the various enemies of the Jewish People (e.g., Haman, Hitler) were still unable to find respite. They, incredulously, remained intimidated by the Jewish collective presence alone. However, unlike the above two relationships, the only way to sever this attachment between God and the Jewish People was through physical annihilation. A description of this relationship is represented in the following:

- ❖ You shall be My treasure from among the nations, for all the earth is Mine; and you shall be to Me a kingdom of priests and a holy nation. (Exodus 19:5–6)

- ❖ I am God your Lord Who has separated you out from among all the nations. (Leviticus 20:24)

- ❖ You shall be holy to Me, for I, God, am holy, and I have separated you from among the nations to be Mine. (Ibid. 20:26)

- ❖ You are a nation consecrated to God your Lord. God your Lord chose you to be His special people among all the nations on the face of the earth. It was not because you had greater numbers than all the nations that God embraced you; you are among the smallest of all the nations. It was because of God's love for you, and because of the oath He made to your forefathers. (Deuteronomy 7:6–8)

❖ God's portion is His people. (Deuteronomy 33:9)

❖ You have avouched the Lord this day to be your God, and to walk in His ways…and the Lord has avouched you this day to be a people for His own possession, as He promised you, and that you may be a holy people to the Lord your God as He has spoken. (Deuteronomy 26:17–19)

❖ Israel is holy to the Lord; the first fruits of His increase. (Jeremiah 2:3)

❖ The Lord has chosen Jacob to Himself. (Psalms 135:4)

The Jewish People are seen as having the mission of proclaiming God's teachings to the world (not through proselytization, but through example) as is portrayed in the following verses:

❖ I, God, have called you in righteousness… and have set you up as a covenant of the people, for a light unto the nations." (Isaiah 42:6)

❖ The Jewish People are depicted as having a mission to bear witness to God's existence: "You are My witnesses… and My servant whom I have chosen." (Ibid. 43:10)

❖ I have put My words in your mouth, and I have covered you in the shadow of My hand, that I may plant the heavens and lay the foundation of the earth, and say to Zion: "You are My people." (Ibid. 51:16)

The Jewish nation is portrayed as the means through which God's essence becomes more revealed in the world,[21] as is written: "[To] give strength to God is the duty of Israel

His pride" (Psalms 68:35). According to the Jerusalem Talmud, the Jewish People are to represent God's Presence in the world.[22]

In the Midrash, "Rabbi Shimon bar Yochai said: God said to the people of Israel, 'I am God of the entire world, but I did not designate My Name on any nation but you. I am not called the God of all the nations, but only the God of Israel.'"[23]

Similarly, the Zohar, which is the primary classic of Jewish mysticism, attributed to the traditions of Rabbi Shimon bar Yochai (circa 120 C.E.), reads: "And the people of Israel are holy; pleasant is their portion in this world and the next, for God did not give them over to any other power but He Himself holds them for His special portion."[24]

THE CONCEPT OF
"THE CHOSEN PEOPLE"

In today's liberal society the concept of "the chosen people" has very negative connotations. However, the Jewish concept of chosen-ness is different from that of others. In light of the concept's generally unfavorable description, the Jewish meaning requires clarification.

In brief, the Jewish meaning of "chosen" has more to do with obligations than benefits. According to the Bible, man was created to emulate God's righteousness. Originally, all mankind was chosen for this task but early man failed, and allowed corruption and violence to predominate over justice and kindness. Thereafter, punishment for failure was to be on a national rather than universal scale. As the Bible relates, God chose one nation to act as a model, whose purpose was to demonstrate, in practice, the desired society.[25]

The people chosen for this task were the descendants of

Abraham, Isaac and Jacob. Abraham's covenant with God guaranteed that his descendants would receive Divine favor provided they follow God's teachings. The covenant required that Jews meet obligations not required of others. They were expected to maintain a higher level of morality, and their self-control and devotion to a spiritual end would be severely tested. If the Jewish nation did not live up to the standards set by the Written and Oral Law, they would cause a lessening of God in the eyes of mankind, and would be held accountable.[26]

As is evident, the traditional Jewish concept of "chosen" is radically different from that of others. The term "chosen," concerning other groups, usually denotes superiority, freedom to act with impunity, exclusive salvation and/or the right to dominate. In Judaism, rights are replaced by obligations.

Historically, anti-Jewish movements seemed to have recognized and attacked this concept of Jewish chosenness. Even when the Jewish People themselves denied or were unaware of their "chosen nation" status (e.g., during the Russian revolution and in Nazi Germany), their detractors were not.

In Summary   THE HEIGHTENED ANIMOSITY and obsession to break the Jewish nation's attachment to their God is manifested through the attempted destruction of Jewish nationalism, the Jewish Torah spirit and the Jewish collective body. In the mind of hostile demagogues, the attachment between the Jewish People and God seems to be palpable and highly intimidating. In essence, the focus of national and international anti-Jewish hostility appears not to be directed towards the Jewish People themselves, but rather towards a Power which transcends the temporal, and calls into question their supremacy and imagined immortality. In short, their attack appears to be against God Himself.

NOTES TO CHAPTER 13

1. Talmud *Ketubot* 110b (Jerusalem: Ortsel, 1960).
2. *Ketubot* 111a.
3. *Sifrei* (*Parshat Re'eh*).
4. Jaakobi, S. "Land of Israel," in D. Kiel (ed.), *Return to the Source* (New York: Feldheim, 1984), pp. 47–48.
5. Talmud *Shabbos* 88a (Jerusalem: Ortsel, 1960).
6. Talmud *Yoma* 39a (Jerusalem: Ortsel, 1960).
7. Talmud *Temurah* 16a (Jerusalem: Ortsel, 1960).
8. Talmud *Berachot* 35b (Jerusalem: Ortsel, 1960).
9. HaLevi, Y. (twelfth century C.E.), *The Kuzari* (New York: Schocken Books, 1964).
10. Zohar (*Acharei Mot*) (Jerusalem: Ortsel, 1960).
11. Maimonides (twelfth century C.E.) in A. Kaplan, *Handbook of Jewish Thought* (New York: Moznaim, 1979).
12. Talmud *Avodah Zarah* 5b (Jerusalem: Ortsel, 1960).
13. HaLevi.
14. Kaplan.
15. *Bereshit Rabbah* (Jerusalem: Vaharmon, 1965).
16. Talmud *Sanhedrin* 100a (Jerusalem: Ortsel, 1960).
17. *Tanchuma HaKadum V'HaYashan* (3:6), in *Midrash Tanchuma* (New York: Sefer, 1946).
18. *Shemos Rabbah* 47:1–4, in *Midrash Rabbah* (Jerusalem: Levin-Epstein, 1965).
19. *Bemidbar Rabbah* 22:2, in *Midrash Rabbah* (Jerusalem: Levin-Epstein, 1965).
20. *Midrash Abba Gurion*, in A. Jellinek (ed.), *Beit HaMidrash* (Jerusalem: Wahrman-Books, 1967).
21. Kaplan.

22. Jerusalem Talmud, *Ta'anit* 2:6 (Jerusalem: Torah Mitzion, 1968).
23. *Shemos Rabbah.*
24. Zohar (*Parshat Ha'azinu*).
25. Gevirtz, E., *Lehavin U'lehaskil: A Guide to Torah Hashkafah. Questions and Answers on Judaism* (New York: Feldheim, 1980).
26. Ibid.

14 | The Traditional Jewish Perspective

And who is like Your People, Israel,
a unique nation on earth.
(I Chronicles 17:21)

A NTI-JEWISH HOSTILITY SEEMED TO CULMINATE IN WORLD War II, when over six million Jews were massacred. Immediately thereafter, the defamation and oppression of Jews was superficially condemned.

However, the respite from discrimination and persecution has ended. Jews, today, are targets of Muslim and Neo-Nazi propaganda and terrorism. The United Nations has become a breeding ground for disseminating venomous anti-Jewish and anti-Israel slander, and in the West the reactionary Right and radical Left attack both Jews and Israel.

In addition, a belief that the United States will always come to the economic and military aid of Israel is naive. A downturn in the American economy, an increase in Arab terrorism or a change in American politics may radically alter American sympathy for the Jewish State — and Jews, in general. Sixty-five years ago Nazi atrocities were overlooked by the Western world, and the Jewish People were left, once again, to suffer the atrocities of an insane demagogue.[1] Are we so certain it could never happen again? What, then, are the Jewish People and Jewish State to do?

The Secret of Jewish Longevity
HISTORICALLY, OTHER ANCIENT nations retained their national and/or religious distinctiveness only as long as they were in the majority or in positions of power; once conquered or dispersed, it was not long before they were absorbed into the prevailing culture of their surroundings. Yet, the Jews not only remained distinct, but, amidst the most brutal persecutions and multiple expulsions over an extraordinary period of time, continued to maintain their separate identity and lifestyle, while oftentimes becoming an integral part of the larger non-Jewish culture.

In Chapter 8, we explained that Jewish longevity plays a major role in the intensity and extensiveness of anti-Jewish hostility. This longevity can be directly attributed to the Jewish People's bond with God, as seen from traditional Jewish literature. These sources, recorded thousands of years ago, may help to explain the Jews' seeming inability — whether voluntarily or involuntarily — to totally assimilate. For example:

- ❖ In the Bible, God promised that the descendants of Abraham, Isaac and Jacob would never be completely abandoned even if they transgress His Torah Law (see Exodus 32:13).

- ❖ I have set you apart from all other peoples. (Leviticus 20:26)

- ❖ And yet for all that, when they are in the land of their enemies, I will not cast them away, nor will I abhor them, to destroy them utterly, or to break My covenant with them. (Ibid. 26:44)

❖ They are a people who will dwell separately. (Numbers 23:9)

Despite the Jewish People's backslidings, God promised that they would continue, perforce, to exist as a nation, as we find in the following passages:

❖ The mountains may depart, and the hills may be removed, but My kindness will not depart from you, neither will My covenant of peace be removed. (Isaiah 54:10)

❖ No weapon that is raised against you shall be successful. (Isaiah 54:17)

❖ Lo, I will bring a nation upon you from afar, O house of Israel, says the Lord: it is a mighty nation, it is an ancient nation, a nation whose language you know not, neither do you understand what they say. And they shall eat up your harvest, and your bread, what your sons and daughters should eat: they shall eat up your flocks and herds; they shall eat up your vines and fig trees; they shall batter your fortified cities, wherein you trust, with the sword. Nevertheless also in those days, says the Lord, you will not be totally consumed. (Jeremiah 5:8–14)

❖ Thus said the Lord Who established the sun for light by day, the moon and stars for light by night, Who stirs up the sea into roaring waves, Whose name is Lord of Hosts: If these (natural) laws should ever be annulled by Me — declares the Lord — only then would the offspring of Israel cease to be a nation before Me for all time. (Jeremiah 32:35–36)

❖ And that which comes into your (i.e., Israel's) mind will
  never come about, that you say, "We will be like the other
  nations...." As I live, says the Lord God, surely with a
  mighty hand, an out-stretched arm and with out-poured
  anger, will I be King over you. (Ezekiel 20:32–34)

❖ For I am the Lord, I do not change; therefore, you, children of Jacob, are not consumed. (Malachi 3:6)

❖ Let Israel now declare, since my youth they [the nations]
  have assailed me, but they never prevailed (in light of
  God's providence). (Psalms 129:1–2)

In the Jerusalem Talmud it states that Jacob's offspring
would always survive as a distinctive people.[2] We find many
places throughout the Midrash, as well, where God vows to
the Jewish People that He would never exchange them for
another people or nation, and that He would never permit
them to dwell permanently in any land other than the Land
of Israel.[3] Another *midrash* explains that during Jacob's prophetic dream, God promised him that his seed would be like
the dust of the earth; and just as the earth survives all things,
so will Jacob's seed survive all the nations of the world. However, just as the earth is trodden upon by all, so will Jacob's
seed be trodden upon.[4] The following excerpts are taken from
Midrash Rabbah (redacted over 1,500 years ago):

❖ When [the people of] Israel stood at Mount Sinai and
  received the Torah, God said to the Angel of Death:
  "On all the nations of the world you have permission to
  eventually destroy but on this nation [Israel] you have no
  jurisdiction."[5]

❖ Hadrian, the emperor of Rome (circa 150 C.E.) asked the
  Jewish sage Rabbi Yehoshua: "Is the sheep (i.e., Israel)

stronger than the seventy wolves (i.e., the nations of the world) it stands among?" He replied: "No. However, great is the Shepherd Who rescues, guards and destroys on behalf of the sheep!"[6]

The Biblical book of Lamentations (1:3) states: "[When] she [Israel] dwells among the nations, she finds no rest." The Midrash explains the reason for this:[7]

> Rabbi Judan the son of Rabbi Nechemya, in the name of Rabbi Shimon son of Lakish, said: "If she [Israel] found rest she would never return [to her indigenous culture and land] and similarly you find in the Book of Deuteronomy (28:65); 'And among the nations you [Israel] will find no ease, neither shall the sole of your foot have rest.'"

Another *midrash* compares the nation of Israel to sand, and anti-Jewish powers to the ocean:[8]

> The first wave [of the ocean] says, "Now I'm going to flood the entire earth," but when it reaches the sand it becomes impotent to go any further and dies out. Shouldn't the second [wave] have learned from the first? Likewise, Pharaoh [Egypt] arrogantly came against Israel and was destroyed by God. Shouldn't the Amalekites have learned from the Egyptians? And shouldn't the mighty kings Sichon and Og have learned from the Amalekites?

Yet they, too, came to fight against the Jewish People and were miraculously uprooted.

Modern Thinkers

CORRESPONDINGLY, OVER THE past two hundred years, more contemporary thinkers have likewise pondered the metaphysics of Jewish survival. They appear to marvel at this phenomenon.

For example, Leo Tolstoy in his *What is the Jew?* wrote:[9]

What is the Jew? This is not as strange a question as it would first appear to be. Come let us contemplate what kind of unique creature is this whom all the rulers and all the nations of the world have disgraced and crushed and expelled and destroyed; persecuted, burned and drowned, and who, despite their anger and their fury, continues to live and flourish. What is this Jew, whom they have never succeeded in enticing with all the enticements in the world, whose oppressors and persecutors only suggested that he deny [and disown] his religion and cast aside the faithfulness of his ancestors?! The Jew is the symbol of eternity. He is the one whom they were never able to destroy, neither bloodbath nor afflictions, neither the fire nor the sword succeeded in annihilating him. He is the one who for so long has guarded the prophetic message and transmitted it to all mankind. A people such as this can never disappear. The Jew is eternal. He is the embodiment of eternity.

In his book, *The Ancient World,* Professor T.R. Glover similarly wrote: [10]

No ancient people has had a stranger history than the Jews.... The history of no ancient people should be so valuable, if we could only recover it and understand it.... Stranger still, the ancient religion of the Jews survives, when all the religions of every ancient race of the pre-Christian world have disappeared. Again it is strange that the living religions of the world all build on the religious ideas derived from the Jews.... This, then, is the problem offered by the Jews to the historian. The great matter is not, "What happened?" but "Why did it happen?" Why does this race continue? Why does Judaism live? How did it really begin? Why did it come out so?

Professor Nicholas Berdkilaev, of the Moscow Academy of Spiritual Culture, in his book *The Meaning of History* commented thus: [11]

> The Jews have played an all-important role in history. They are pre-eminently a historical people and their destiny reflects indestructibility...their destiny is too imbued with the metaphysical to be...explained either in material or positive-historical terms. I remember how the materialist interpretation of history, when I attempted in my youth to verify it by applying to it the destinies of peoples, broke down in the case of the Jews, where destiny seemed absolutely inexplicable from the materialistic standpoint. And, indeed, according to the materialistic and positivist criterion, this people ought to have perished long ago. Its survival is a mysterious and wonderful phenomenon demonstrating that the life of this people is governed by a special predetermination, transcending the process of adaptation expounded by the materialistic interpretation of history. The survival of the Jews, their resistance to destruction, their endurance under absolutely peculiar conditions and the fateful role played by them in history, all these point to the particular and mysterious foundations of their destiny.

The eighteenth-century Talmudic scholar, Rabbi Jonathan Eibeschutz, commented:[12]

> Will the atheist not be embarrassed when he reflects on Jewish history? We, an exiled people scattered sheep from antiquity, have endured brutal persecution over thousands of years. There is no nation or people pursued as we. Many and powerful are those who aspired to totally destroy us but they never prevailed. How will the wise philosopher respond? Is this extraordinary phenomenon truly by chance?

Dr. Isaac Breuer wrote:[13]

> The "People of the Book" among the nations is the most
> fantastic miracle of all, and the history of this people is lit-
> erally one of miracles. And one who sees this ancient people
> today, after thousands of years among the nations of the
> world, when he reads the Scriptures and finds that they
> prophetically relate clearly and simply the ever-transpiring
> Jewish phenomenon, and does not fall on his face and ex-
> claim "God, the Lord of Israel, He is God," then no other
> miracle will help him. For, in truth, this individual has no
> heart to understand, no eye to discern, and no ear to hear.

The French author Jon DeBileda, during the latter part of
the nineteenth century (i.e., before the Russian Revolution,
Nazi Germany and the modern Jewish State) described the
situation thusly:[14]

> In essence the Jewish People chuckle at all forms of anti-
> Semitism. Think all you want and you will not be able to find
> one form of brutality or strategy that has not been used in
> warfare against the Jewish People. I cannot be defeated, says
> Judaism. All that you attempt to do to me today has been
> attempted 3,200 years prior, in Egypt. Then tried the Babylo-
> nians and Persians. Afterwards tried the Romans and then
> others and others.... There is no question that the Jews will
> outlive us all. This is an eternal people.... They cannot be de-
> feated, understand this! Every war with them is a vain waste
> of time and manpower. Conversely, it is wise to sign a mutual
> covenant with them. How trustworthy and profitable they are
> as allies. Look at their patriotism, their commercial benefit,
> and their ambition and success in science, the arts and poli-
> tics. Be their friend and they will pay you back in friendship
> one-hundred fold. This is an exalted and chosen people.

A more modern-day example of the Jewish People's survival mechanism was interestingly described in the secular Israeli newspaper *Maariv* (April 17, 1983) concerning the Jewish State's War of Independence in 1948:[15]

> Is this how things really happened? Just as they are told in the history books? And 650,000 Jews who escaped from the horrors of the Second World War and from the cruel struggle with the oppressive British — did they really build up this whole infantry on their own efforts? Six hundred and fifty thousand who created a nation-state from emptiness and desolation? And they stood in bitter warfare against the organized armies of five Arab countries? Five percent of the Jewish People, and not only did they strike a blow against every enemy that stood up against them, but absorbed hundreds of thousands of refugees from the remnants of European and Middle East Jewry. By all logic, and by all human reason, everything that happened in 1948 is in the category of the impossible. It was impossible with the limited arms that the Jews possessed, with the rudimentary international support they managed to gather, with the limited resources that were available to them, to do all that they did. To bring a system of public services into operation from nothing. To establish a military industry from its beginning. To sustain supplies and minimal services, and to run a war that had no clear delineated front or rear lines, no organized lines of defense, no organized reserves of ammunition, and no expert commanders to lead its battalions!

Jewish Suffering

IF THE JEWISH nation is so intimately connected to God (as expressed above in both Biblical and Oral Law literature) then why were Jews subjugated, persecuted, exiled, tortured and slaughtered throughout history? Why would God allow this?

The traditional source for understanding Jewish suffering is again the Bible. In the Pentateuch, the concept of Jewish suffering plays a prominent role and is predicted and elaborated on in the Biblical books of Leviticus and Deuteronomy and throughout the Prophets and Holy Writings. Jewish suffering is explained as being contingent upon the Jewish People's collective actions — benedictions for following Torah Law, and maledictions for acting to the contrary. God's covenant with the Jewish People is described as irreversible, obligating the Jewish nation to remain separate through adherence to the Torah; and if not, they will, perforce, remain separate via discrimination and oppression. In the third book of the Pentateuch, Leviticus (ch. 26), written more than 3,200 years ago, it states:

> If you follow My laws and are careful to keep My commandments, I will provide you with rain at the right time, so that the land will bear its crops and the trees of the field will provide fruit. You will have your fill of food, and [you will] live securely in the land. I will grant peace in the land so that you will sleep without fear. I will rid the land of dangerous animals, and the sword will not pass through your land. You will chase away your enemies, and they will fall before your sword. Five of you will be able to chase away a hundred, and a hundred of you will defeat ten thousand.
>
> [But this is what will happen] if you do not listen to Me. If you come to denigrate My decrees, and grow tired of My laws...I will then do the same to you. I will bring upon you feelings of anxiety, along with depression and excitement, destroying your outlook and making life hopeless.
>
> You will plant your crop in vain, because your enemies will eat it. I will direct My anger against you, so that you

will be defeated by your foes and your enemies will dominate you. You will flee even when no one is chasing you.

I will make the land so desolate that [even] your enemies
who live there will be astonished. I will scatter you among
the nations, and keep the sword drawn against you. Your
land will remain desolate and your cities in ruin.

The few of you who survive in your enemies' lands will
realize that your survival is threatened as a result of your
non-observance. [These few] will also [realize] that their
survival has been threatened because of the non-observance
of their fathers. But when the time finally comes that their
stubborn spirit is humbled, I will forgive their sin.

Thus, even when they are in their enemies' land, I will
not grow so disgusted with them nor so tired of them that I
would destroy them and break My covenant with them.

Likewise, in Deuteronomy (ch. 28–30) it reads:

If you obey God your Lord, carefully keeping all His commandments as I am prescribing them to you today, then
God will make you highest of all the nations on earth. As
long as you listen to God your Lord, all these blessings will
come to bear on you.

If you do not obey God your Lord and do not carefully
keep all His commandments and decrees as I am prescribing
them for you today, then all these curses will come to bear
on you. God will send misfortune, confusion and frustration
against you in all you undertake. God will make you panic
before your enemies. You will march out in one column,
but flee from them in seven. You will become a terrifying
example to all the world's kingdoms.

Your sons and daughters will be given to a foreign nation.
You will see it happening with your own eyes, and will long
for them all day long, but you will be powerless. A strange

nation will consume the fruit of your land and all your toil. You will be constantly cheated and crushed. You will go insane from what you will have to witness.... You will be an object of horror, a by-word and an abject lesson among all the nations where God will lead you. You will have sons and daughters, but they will not remain yours, since they will be taken into captivity.... [These curses] will be a sign and proof to you and your children forever. When you had plenty of everything, you would not serve God your Lord with happiness and a glad heart. You will therefore serve your enemies when God sends them against you, and it will be in hunger, thirst, nakedness and universal want. Your enemy will place an iron yoke on your neck so as to destroy you.

God will scatter you among the nations, from one end of the earth to the other. Among those nations you will feel insecure, and there will be no place for your foot to rest. There God will make you cowardly, destroying your outlook and making life hopeless. There shall come a time when you shall experience all the words of blessing and curse that I have presented to you. There, among the nations where God will have banished you, you will reflect on the situation.

This mandate that I am prescribing to you today is not too mysterious or remote from you. It is not in heaven, so that you should say, "Who shall go up to heaven and bring it to us so that we can hear it and keep it?" It is not over the sea so [that you should] say, "Who will cross the sea and get it for us, so that we will be able to hear it and keep it?" It is something that is very close to you....

See! Today I have set before you [a free choice] between life and good [on one side], and death and evil [on the other]. I have commanded you today to love God your Lord, to walk in His paths, and to keep His commandments, decrees and laws. You will then survive and flourish....

The prophet Amos (3:1–2) similarly declared: "Hear this word that the Lord has spoken against you, O Children of Israel...only you have I known of all the families of the earth, therefore I will punish you for all your iniquities."

The Jewish People are depicted as representing the word of God through following His Torah. Their actions, therefore, are to be judged differently from others. On this point, one of the leading Talmudists and Jewish mystics of the sixteenth century, the Maharal of Prague writes:[16]

> It behooves you to ask, why have the chosen people suffered so greatly, while other nations seemingly sin much more yet receive relatively little punishment?... Therefore, you should know that the great unprecedented suffering that Israel has endured is because they have acted contrary to what was expected of them. Punishment is meted out in respect to the nation's responsibility, and Israel's responsibility is greater than others. They [Israel], as opposed to other nations, must be exceedingly upright, and they, unlike others, are held responsible for even slight deviations.

In Conclusion   IF GOD DID, in fact, bestow the Torah with its multiple commandments upon the Jewish People, then by abandoning their responsibility — regardless of whether they remain Jewish in name or not — they are again creating misfortune for themselves and indirectly for all mankind (see Chapter 17).

From a contemporary perspective it is startling to imagine all the resources spent and lives destroyed over the past sixty years (from the inception of the modern State of Israel) in an attempt to appease Israel's enemies with little to no success. How much money, how many think-tanks, how many lives have been wasted with no tangible results of peace or security? How can Jewish leaders truly lead while being oblivious or worse yet, denying the historical source of Jewish individual and collective success and blessings, and hence true security and peace. If we would only appease our God — through the observance of Torah Law — instead of constantly trying to appease our enemies, how different contemporary life might be.

Just as thousands of years ago the prophet Elijah exclaimed: "How long will you waver between two opinions? If the Lord be God, follow Him; but if [you believe in] Baal, follow him" (I Kings 18:22), so, too, must Jews today demand of themselves. Past recurring history is clearly the best predictor of future events. Ancient and modern history have taught that attempts to break with tradition are but rationalizations, fraught with extremely deleterious effects for both the individual Jew and society at large. World Jewry cannot continue to straddle this issue and remain undisturbed, but must categorically decide and act.

Over three millenia ago, an era of benevolence for the Jewish People was prophesied — when the Jewish People return to traditional Torah Law, as described in the following Biblical passage (Deuteronomy, 30:1–9):

> There shall come a time when you shall experience all the words of blessing and curse that I have presented to you. There, among the nations where God will have banished you, you will reflect on the situation. You will then return to God your Lord, and you will obey Him, doing everything that I am commanding you today. You and your children (will repent) with all your heart and with all your soul. God will then bring back your remnants and have mercy on you.

> God your Lord will once again gather you from among all the nations where He scattered you. Even if your diaspora is at the ends of the heavens, God your Lord will gather you up from there and He will take you back. God your Lord will then bring you to the land that your ancestors occupied, and you too will occupy it. God will be good to you and make you flourish even more than your ancestors. God will remove the barriers from your hearts and from the hearts of your descendants, so that you will love God your Lord with all your heart and soul. Thus will you survive. God will then direct all these curses against your enemies and against the foes who pursued you. ... God will then grant you a good surplus in all the work of your hands, in the fruit of your womb, the fruit of your livestock, and the fruit of your land. God will once again rejoice in you for good, just as He rejoiced in your fathers.

Historically, when the Jews followed Torah Law they enjoyed peace and blessing (see Chapter 12). According to the Jewish perspective, fostering a return to tradition can, in effect, produce everlasting peace for the Jewish People and for the world at large (see Chapter 17). Therefore, it does not appear too bold or fanciful to assert that the Jewish People's collective implementation of Shabbos observance, Jewish dietary laws, and family purity laws — for starters — may well be the only true salvation, both physically and spiritually, for the individual Jew, the Jewish nation and, indirectly, for all mankind.

NOTES TO CHAPTER 14

1. E.g., Gilbert, M., *Auschwitz and the Allies* (New York: Holt, Rinehart, & Winston, 1981); Morse, A.D., *While Six Million Died* (New York: Random House, 1968); Wyman, D.S., *The Abandonment of the Jews* (New York: Pantheon Books, 1984).

2. Jerusalem Talmud, *Ta'anit* 2:6 (Jerusalem: Torah Mitzion, 1968).

3. *Midrash, Seder Eliyahu Rabbah* (18:141–147) (Jerusalem: Vaharmon, 1960).

4. *Midrash Bereshit Rabbah* (69:4–5) (Jerusalem: Vaharmon, 1965).

5. *Midrash Shemos Rabbah* (32), in *Midrash Rabbah* (Jerusalem: Levin-Epstein, 1965).

6. *Midrash Esther Rabbah* 10:2, in *Midrash Rabbah* (Bnei Brak: Tiferet Zion, 1963).

7. *Midrash Eichah Rabbah* (10), in *Midrash Rabbah* (Bnei Brak: Tiferet Zion, 1963).

8. *Midrash Yalkut Shimoni* (*Parshat Balak*) (Jerusalem).

9. Sutton, A. and Arachim Staff (eds.), *Pathways to the Torah* (Jerusalem: Arachim, 1985), p. A9.

10. Glover, T.R., *The Ancient World: A Beginning* (Westport, CN: Greenwood Press, 1979), pp. 184–187.

11. Berdkilaev, N., *The Meaning of History* (Cleveland: Meridian Books, 1962), pp. 86–87.

12. In Sutton et al., p. A7.

13. Schwartz, Y., *Am Segulah* (Jerusalem: Dvar Yerushalayim, 1981), pp. 120–121.

14. Ibid.

15. In Sutton et al., p. A7.

16. Maharal, *Netzach Yisrael* 80:12 (Warsaw: Freedberg, 1886).

15 | UnOrthodox Judaism and the Oral Law

Preceding the coming of the Messiah...
truth will be [conspicuously] lacking.
(Talmud, Tractate Sotah 49b)

THE SIGNIFICANCE OF THE NEXT TWO CHAPTERS DEPENDS UPON how seriously the reader has taken the previous chapters. If the Torah is true and its non-observance would therefore lead to dire consequences, then it is imperative to examine the present state of Judaism, in order not to repeat mistakes of the past.

The three main Jewish groups in America today are Reform, Conservative and Orthodox Judaism. A major problem for individuals seeking their Jewish roots is that all three groups claim to be authentic forms of Judaism and have their own criteria for determining what makes a "good Jew."

Reform and Conservative Judaism   THE REFORM MOVEMENT originated in Germany in the early nineteenth century, and was transported to America during the large German-Jewish immigration which began in the 1840s. By the second half of the nineteenth century it appeared that the future of Jews in America would be found in the Reform movement.[1]

The Conservative movement is more an American phenomenon, originating as a reaction to Reform Judaism which
it deemed "too reform."[2] Conservative Judaism achieved
primacy in America — in terms of number of constituents —
after World War II.

While espousing different religious philosophies, both
movements deny the binding (Divine) authority of the Oral
Torah (Law) and proclaimed at their inception the alleged
unadaptability of Orthodox Judaism, which they viewed as an
anachronism. They portrayed themselves as legitimate forms
of Judaism, whose destiny it was to succeed the antiquated
Orthodox tradition. They were to lead modern Jewry in the
liberal Western society of today. According to their leaders,
they were never attempting to sever the Jewish People's relationship to the Torah, but rather trying to save Judaism,
which allegedly could not adapt without an overhaul in observance and perspective. Although this was their claim, the
following points suggest that their leaders were more interested in breaking with Oral Law (Orthodox) tradition than
in providing American Jews with a meaningful and authentic
Jewish experience.

Firstly, their claim to legitimately succeed Orthodoxy was
based on the alleged inability of Oral Law Judaism to adjust
and adapt to the American way of life. However, in stark
contrast to their claim, the only Judaism to ever survive all
forms of cultures and societies, throughout history, was the
same Judaism known today as Orthodoxy. Therefore, either
Reform and Conservative leaders were unaware of Jewish
history, or their claim was specious — used to rationalize
their break with tradition.

Secondly, before abandoning the Judaism of their forefathers (that is, the Orthodox tradition) how much of an

effort and attempt was made to adapt the tenets of Orthodoxy to American society? How many generations of Jews in
America had passed before Reform and Conservative leaders
concluded that Orthodox Judaism was outdated?

The answer appears to be zero. Orthodox Judaism was
never given a chance by either movement. Evidence to support this claim is based on the number of Jews residing in
America around the turn of the century. In 1880 and 1900
the percentage of Jews in America was approximately five
and fifteen percent, respectively, of what it was in 1972. The
source of this growth rate was the mass immigration of Jews
from Eastern Europe during the turn of the century and
thereafter.[3] The language and mores of America were foreign
to these immigrants, whose primary concern was providing
food and shelter for their families. Their lifestyle was and
remained primarily Eastern European.

It was their children, the first generation of Jews born in
America (in significant number), who had the opportunity to
create a synthesis between traditional Orthodox Judaism and
American culture. However, this opportunity was never realized, for first-generation American Jews, who began raising
families immediately preceding and following World War II,
followed their Reform and Conservative leaders' claim concerning the inevitable need for change.

They were the first generation to truly test Orthodox
Judaism's resilience, but instead they accepted their men-
tors' ahistorical and non-empirical claims, concerning the
"dated" Judaism of their forebears. (It is important to note
that the number of Jews who arrived from Germany in the
1840s was insignificant in comparison with the number
of Eastern European Jews who arrived at the turn of the
century. Moreover, the German Jews brought with them

the traditions of Reform, and would therefore not have the knowledge or inclination to adapt the Orthodoxy of their forefathers.)

A third point is that Reform and Conservative Judaism are not too dissimilar from other Jewish sects in the past (e.g., Sadducees, Bitosim and Karaites) who also attempted to abolish the binding authority of the Oral Law. Both Reform and Conservative Judaism deny the Divinity of the Oral Law, and with regard to the Divinity of the Written Law (the Bible) a variance of opinion exists within the groups themselves — accepting parts while rejecting others. Denying the Divine nature of the Oral Torah (and to a lesser extent the Written Torah) should not be taken lightly, for it implies that:

(1) The redactors of the Talmud flagrantly lied when they declared that the Oral Torah was given by God,[4] and that some or most of the places throughout the Bible where it states "And God spoke to Moses" (and other introductions with the same expressed meaning) are outright fabrications. To suggest these statements are open to interpretation, like other more obscure passages in the Talmud or Bible, is to deny the possibility of direct prophecy.

(2) The literally millions of Jewish men, women and children who were exiled, pillaged, tortured and murdered because they believed that the Oral Torah, as an explanation of the Written Law, was God-given and therefore refused to deviate from its observance, were cruelly misled and mistaken.

(It is important to note that this discussion refers only to the Oral Law of Sinaitic origin — that which was conferred concomitantly with the Written Law. Oral Law legislation of Rabbinic origin came about at a later date.)

Oral Law Authenticity INTELLECTUAL HONESTY DICTATES that the Bible without Oral Torah explanation and deliniation is little more than an amorphous body of terse phraseology, which can easily be manipulated to represent various positions and ideologies. Moreover, it is impossible for any group of people to conduct themselves individually or collectively on the basis of the Bible alone. If we were honest with ourselves, we would admit that if there never was an accompanying body of legislation (that is, the Oral Torah) then the Bible itself could not possibly have been God-given. For a righteous God (and in Judaism there is no such thing as unrighteousness when pertaining to God) would never hold a people accountable for something which is impossible to clearly understand and apply.

For example, the commandment we call *tefillin* is spoken of no less than four times in the Bible, but like other commandments is totally incomprehensible without an accompanying body of legislation. The Biblical verses are:

❖ And it shall be for a sign for you upon your hand, and for a memorial between your eyes. (Exodus 13:9)

❖ And it shall be for a sign upon your hand, and for frontlets between your eyes. (Exodus 13:16)

❖ And You shall bind them for a sign upon your hand, and they shall be as frontlets between your eyes. (Deuteronomy 6:8)

❖ And bind them for a sign upon your hand, and they shall be as frontlets between your eyes. (Deuteronomy 11:18)

Who could explain, from the above verses, what a sign and frontlets are made of? What should they look like? Where on the hand should they be placed, and if "between the eyes" is to be taken literally, then why have Jews, throughout history, done otherwise? And must everyone put on *tefillin*, and at all times? These are only a small sample of the many questions needed to be addressed if the commandment is to be practically applied. It is illogical to assume that a God-given law was delivered so ambiguously as to depend on the arbitrary whim of each succeeding generation. In short, there are only two possibilities; either the Bible is a hoax, or there is indeed an accompanying body of interpreting legislation.

A further example is the commandment of *tzitzit* (fringes). In the Bible it states:

> And the Lord spoke to Moses, saying, "Speak to the children of Israel, and bid them that they make fringes on the corners of their garments throughout their generations, and that they put upon the fringe of each corner a thread of blue: and it shall be to you as a fringe." (Numbers 15:37–39)

Who could explain what a "fringe" looks like? What kind of material is it made from? Must it be attached to every piece of clothing such as one's undershirt and winter hat and must everyone wear fringes and at all times? The answers to these questions and other details concerning this commandment cannot be understood from the Biblical text itself.

Even the most seemingly explicit Biblical command, the commandment of circumcision, without Oral Law legislation is inexplicable. For example, in the book of Genesis it reads:

> Every male among you shall be circumcised. You shall cir-
> cumcise the flesh of your *orlah*.... Thus shall My covenant
> be marked in your flesh as an everlasting pact. And if any
> male who is uncircumcised fails to circumcise the flesh of
> his *orlah,* that soul shall be cut off from his people; he has
> broken My covenant. (Genesis 17:10–14)

In most Bibles the above word *orlah* is translated as foreskin, referring to part of the male genitals. However, based
strictly on the Biblical text, this is an arbitrary and forced
translation. In other places in the Bible the word *orlah* refers specifically to the mouth, the ear and the heart.[5] In fact,
nowhere in the Bible does the word *orlah* refer specifically to
the genitals. Contextually, it would be more logical that circumcision be done on the heart, as found in Deuteronomy
(10:16): "Circumcise therefore the *orlah* [foreskin] of your
heart." In other words, if decisions were based exclusively
on the Written text, we today would be performing heart
surgery on all male infants eight days of age and older.[6]

However, even if we do arbitrarily declare that *orlah*
means the foreskin of the genitals, other unanswerable
questions still need to be addressed. For instance, how is the
operation performed? What happens when the eighth day
falls on the Sabbath, during which operations, in general,
are prohibited? And what does it mean when it says that
one who refrains from performing this commandment will
be "cut off"?[7]

Another example pertains to slaughtering an animal (for
food purposes) of which it states:

> You need only slaughter your cattle and small animals that
> God will have given you in the manner that I have pre-
> scribed. (Deuteronomy 12:21)

However, nowhere in the Bible did God prescribe how the animal is to be slaughtered.[8]

The Bible, by itself, is even contradictory. For example Leviticus 23:6 states: "Seven days you shall eat unleavened bread," but in Deuteronomy (12:21) it states: "Six days you shall eat unleavened bread." In truth, these nebulous and contradictory statements are easily reconciled in the Oral Torah, but in and of themselves are unintelligible.

In fact, what has been shown regarding the commandments of *tefillin*, *tzitzit*, circumcision, ritual slaughter and the prohibition of eating unleavened bread (on Passover) is similarly seen with regard to all the many commandments mentioned ever so briefly in the Bible. To accept or partially accept the Divinity of the Written Torah without accepting the authority of an accompanying body of legislation is to make a mockery of the Bible and of Judaism itself.

Rabbi Samson Raphael Hirsch compared the relationship between the Written and the Oral Torah with the relationship between notes taken at a lecture and the lecture itself. The notes are clear to one who heard the lecture, but incomprehensible to one who did not. In other words, the Written Torah is consistent and logical to one guided by the Oral Torah, but objectively incomprehensible to one who is not.

Historical Transmission of the Oral Law   MAIMONIDES, IN HIS *Introduction to Mishneh Torah,* explains the historical transmission of the Oral Torah. He writes:[9]

> All the precepts which Moses received on Sinai (c. 3,250 years ago) were given together with their interpretation [the Oral Torah].... Moses taught the whole of it to his court (that is to say, the outstanding scholars of his generation).

The "mitzvah" — which is the explanation [and implementation] of the written Torah verse — was not written down, but was taught orally to the Elders, to Joshua (Moses' main disciple) and to all the people. (The Oral Torah was not to be commited to writing for public consumption, but each sage and student would write down his own private notes. The Oral tradition was transmitted from generation to generation as delineated below.)

The Sages mentioned below were the greatest scholars of the successive generations; some of them were heads of yeshivos, some exilarchs, and some were members of the great Sanhedrin (the Jewish Supreme Court); with them were thousands and tens of thousands of disciples and colleagues [in each and every generation].

Accordingly, Joshua, throughout his life, taught the Oral Torah. The Elders received the Oral Torah from Joshua. Eli received it from the Elders and from Phineas. Samuel, from Eli and his court. David, from Samuel and his court. Ahijah the Shilonite...received the Oral Torah from David and his court. Elijah received it from Ahijah and his court. Elisha, from Elijah and his court. Yehoyada the priest, from Elisha and his court. Zachariah, from Yehoyada and his court. Hosea, from Zachariah and his court. Amos, from Hosea and his court. Isaiah, from Amos and his court. Micah, from Isaiah and his court. Joel, from Micah and his court. Nahum, from Joel and his court. Habakkuk, from Nahum and his court. Zephaniah, from Habakkuk and his court. Jeremiah, from Zephaniah and his court. Baruch the son of Neriah, from Jeremiah and his court. Ezra and his court received it from Baruch and his court. The members of Ezra's court were called "The Men of the Great Assembly." They were Haggai, Zachariah, Malachi, Daniel, Chananiah, Mishael, Azariah, Nehemiah, Mordecai, Zerubabel and many other sages, numbering altogether one hundred and twenty elders. The last of them was Simon the Just. He received the Oral Torah from all of them....

Antigonos of Socho and his court received the Oral Torah from Simon the Just and his court. Jose the son of Jo'ezer of Zeredah, and Joseph the son of Jochanan of Jerusalem and their court, from Antigonos and his court. Joshua the son of Perahiah, and Nitai the Arbelite and their court, from Jose the son of Jo'ezer and Joseph the son of Jochanan and their court. Judah the son of Tabbai, and Simeon the son of Shetah and their court received from Joshua the son of Perahiah and Nitai the Arbelite and their court. Shemaiah and Abtalion, proselytes of righteousness, and their court received from Judah and Simon and their court. Hillel and Shammai and their court received from Shemaiah and Abtalion and their court. Rabban Jochanan the son of Zakkai, and Rabban Simeon the son of Hillel received from Hillel and his court.

Rabban Jochanan had five [outstanding] disciples who were the most distinguished among the scholars who received the Oral Torah from him. They were Rabbi Eliezer the Great, Rabbi Joshua, Rabbi Jose the Priest, Rabbi Simeon the son of Nathaniel, and Rabbi Elazar the son of Arach.

Rabbi Akiba the son of Joseph received the Oral Torah from Rabbi Eliezer the Great. Joseph, his father, was a proselyte of righteousness. Rabbi Ishmael and Rabbi Meir, the son of a proselyte of righteousness, received the Oral Torah from Rabbi Akiba. Rabbi Meir and his colleagues also received it from Rabbi Ishmael. The colleagues of Rabbi Meir were Rabbi Judah, Rabbi Jose, Rabbi Simeon, Rabbi Nehemiah, Rabbi Elazar the son of Shammua, Rabbi Jochanan, the sandal-maker, Simon the son of Azzai and Rabbi Hananiah the son of Teradion. Rabbi Akiba's colleagues received the Oral Torah from Rabbi Eliezer the Great. The colleagues of Rabbi Akiba were Rabbi Tarfon, the teacher of Rabbi Jose the Galilean, Rabbi Simeon the son of Elazar, and Rabbi Jochanan the son of Nuri.

Rabban Gamaliel the Elder received the Oral Torah from Rabban Simeon, his father, a son of Hillel the Elder. Rabban Simon his son, received it from him. Rabban Gamaliel his son, received it from him. Rabban Simeon his son, received it from him. Rabbi Judah the son of Rabban Simeon, called "Our Teacher, the Saint," received the Oral Torah from his father and from Rabbi Elazar the son of Shammua, and from Rabbi Simeon, his father's colleagues. Our Teacher, the Saint, compiled the Mishnah. From the time of Moses (circa 1250 B.C.E.) to that of Our Teacher the Saint (circa 180 C.E.) no [written] work had been composed from which the Oral Torah was publicly taught. In each generation, the head of the existing court, or the prophet at that time wrote down for his private use a memorandum of the traditions which he had heard from his teachers, and which he taught orally in public. So too, each student wrote down, according to his ability, the explanations of the Torah as he heard them....

Ravina and Rav Ashi were the last of the Talmudic sages. Rav Ashi compiled the Babylonian Talmud (circa 450 C.E.).

However, during the continued Jewish exile and dispersion, even the completed Talmud required further clarification. Therefore, the most erudite and authoritative Jewish scholars in each generation had the task of explaining Torah Law (the Talmud), based on the traditions of their predecessors. Medieval Torah giants (e.g., the Rif, the Rambam, the Rosh, Rabbi Jacob ben Asher, etc.) produced works which made the Oral Torah significantly more accessible. In 1565, Rabbi Joseph Karo produced the *Shulchan Aruch*, which was an Oral Torah compendium based on Talmudic and post-Talmudic sources.

Remarkably, today, in the early part of the twenty-first century, Orthodox Jews still live by the *Shulchan Aruch,* which is an unbroken chain of tradition from Moses to the Jewish People of today (some 3,250 years later).

The Kuzari IT IS INTERESTING to note a conversation between "the Rabbi" and the King of the Khazars, "Al Khazari," in the literary classic *The Kuzari,* by Rabbi Yehuda HaLevi (1074–1141). In the following conversation the Rabbi speaks of a particular Jewish sect, the Karaites, who accepted the Divinity of the Written Law, but (like Reform and Conservative Judaism) denied Oral Torah Divinity and hence, Oral Torah authority:[10]

> **The Rabbi:** The acknowledgment of tradition is therefore incumbent upon us as well as upon the Karaites, as upon anyone who admits that the Torah (the Pentateuch) as is read, is the Torah of Moses.
>
> **Al Khazari:** This is exactly what the Karaites say. But as they have the Written Torah, they consider the tradition [i.e., Oral Torah] superfluous.
>
> **The Rabbi:** Far from it. If the text of the Mosaic Book requires so many traditional classes of vowel signs, accents and divisions of sentences, how much more so for the comprehension of the same? The meaning of a word is more comprehensive than its pronunciation! When God revealed the verse: "This month shall be unto you the beginning of months" (Exodus 12:2), how was there no doubt whether He meant the calendar of the Copts — or rather the Egyptians among whom they lived — or that of the Chaldeans, who were Abraham's people in Ur-Kasdim; or solar or lunar

months, or lunar years which are made to agree with solar years...I wish the Karaites would give me a satisfactory answer to questions of this kind. I would not hesitate to adopt their view, as it pleases me to be enlightened. I further wish to be instructed on the question as to what makes an animal lawful for food; whether "slaughtering" means cutting its throat or any other mode of killing? ... Let them draw me the line between the fat which is lawful and that which is not, inasmuch as there is no difference visible. ... I desire an explanation of the lawful and unlawful birds, excepting the common ones, such as the pigeon and turtle dove. How do they know that the hen, goose, duck and partridge are not unclean birds? I further desire an explanation of the words: "Let no man go out of his place [on the seventh day]" (Exodus 16:29). Does this refer to the house or precincts, estate where he can have many houses — territory, district or country? For the word "place" can refer to all of these. I should, further, like to know where the prohibition of work on the Sabbath is detailed. Why pens and writing material are not admissible in the correction of a Scroll [on the Sabbath day] but lifting a heavy book, table or eatables, entertaining guests and all cares of hospitality should be permitted — although the guests would be resting and the host kept employed? This applies even more to servants, as it is written: "That your manservant and your maidservant rest as well as you" (Deuteronomy 5:14)! ... Then, again, I wish to see a Karaite give judgment between two parties according to the chapters in Exodus 21 and Deuteronomy 21. For that which appears plain in the Written Torah is yet obscure, and how much more so are the obscure passages, because the Oral supplement was always relied upon. I should wish to hear the deductions he draws from the case of the daughters of Zelofchad to questions of inheritance

> in general. I want to know the details of circumcision and
> fringes...why it is incumbent to say prayers; whence he
> derives his belief in reward and punishment in the world
> after death; how to deal with laws which interfere with each
> other, as circumcision or the paschal lamb with the Sabbath,
> which must yield to which, and other details too many to
> enumerate.

In summary, the written Torah (as a Divine document)
can only be understood and implemented when accompanied
by God-given instructions and explanations. Without the latter the former is reduced to a hoax and cruel bluff — hardly
worth dying, or even living, for.

Orthodox (Oral Law) Judaism has been the sole possessor of that Divine body of legislation, contiguously for
over thirty-two hundred years. Groups that deny Oral Law
Divinity are only detractors, attempting to build on the de-
molition of their millenia-old predecessor. Their brand of
Judaism cannot historically or even logically be considered
God-conferred. Yet they continue to seduce the masses of
uneducated American Jews into their man-made religions of
rationalization and convenience.

NOTES TO CHAPTER 15

1. Sklare, M. (ed.), *American Jews: A Reader* (New York: Behrman
House, 1983).
2. Liebman, C.S., "The Religion of American Jews," cited in Sklare.
3. Gartner, L.P., "Immigration and the Formation of American Jewry,"
1840–1925, cited in Sklare.
4. E.g., Talmud *Shabbat* 31a, Talmud *Berachot* 5a, Talmud *Gittin* 60b.
5. E.g., Exodus 6:12,30; Jeremiah 6:9; Ezekiel 44:9.

6. Sutton et al.

7. Ibid.

8. Schimmel, H.C., *The Oral Law* (Jerusalem: Feldheim, 1971).

9. Maimonides, M., *Mishneh Torah* (Jerusalem: Mossad HaRav Kook), pp. 5–11.

10. HaLevi, J., *The Kuzari* (New York: Schocken Books, 1964), 3:33–35.

16

The Study: A Breakdown of American Jewry

A FTER CITING SOME OF THE CONTRADICTIONS INHERENT IN Reform and Conservative Judaism, it was considered necessary to study these movements empirically. This was done by taking a random sample of over eight hundred Jewish adults from the city of Chicago (as part of the author's 1985 doctoral dissertation) and questioning them on issues of alleged importance to all Jewry. Groups representing Orthodox, Conservative, Reform and non-affiliated Jews were compared with respect to their positions on three vital issues. They were: assimilation, Jewish education and the State of Israel.

The study's objective was to investigate the groups' accomplishments, over the past generation, in relation to their claims made only a generation or two prior. The results presented below are a representation of the many statistics elicited throughout the study. Anyone interested in exploring further is encouraged to acquire the full panorama of statistics via University Microfilm International, Ann Arbor, Michigan. (Based on general observation, the following results appear as true today as they were twenty years ago.)

Participants   A RANDOM SAMPLE of 811 Jewish adults from Chicago proper participated in the study, which began in February of 1985. Three-quarters of the respondents were selected randomly from the Chicago telephone book on the basis of "distinctively Jewish names." This procedure is commonly used when conducting surveys on Jewish populations, and no significant differences have been found between Jews with common Jewish names and those without. To ensure a solid representation of Orthodox Jewry, who comprised less than ten percent of Chicago's Jewish population (in 1985) the remaining participants were drawn randomly from mailing lists of all major Orthodox organizations and day-schools in Chicago.

Procedure   DATA WERE COLLECTED at the Bernard Horwich Jewish Community Center of Chicago, where two rooms and ten telephones were obtained for a period of one month. The Jewish Federation of Metropolitan Chicago provided all the necessary equipment and twenty university students were employed to conduct the interviews. All participants were asked the same attitudinal, behavioral, demographic and general-knowledge questions dealing with religious affiliation, education, religious observance and Israel.

Religious Observance Data   PARTICIPANTS WERE ASKED what type of synagogue they belong to, and questions concerning religious activities and beliefs. The following is the questionnaire and responses obtained, according to group affiliation.

Participants affiliated with other Jewish religious movements (e.g., Reconstructionists) were not included in the study in light of their insignificant numbers. All percentages were rounded off to the nearest whole number.

JEWISH OBSERVANCE SCALE

	(N=322) Non-affiliated	(N=79) Reform	(N=114) Conservative	(N=231) Orthodox
1. Do you refrain from eating bread and bread products during Passover?				
Yes	37%	56%	75%	99%
No	63%	44%	25%	1%
2. Do you refrain from driving on Saturday?				
Yes	8%	1%	9%	91%
No	92%	99%	91%	9%
3. Do you keep Kosher?				
Yes	10%	5%	31%	96%
No	90%	95%	69%	4%
4. Do you believe in God?				
Yes	81%	92%	91%	100%
No	19%	8%	9%	0%
5. Do you fast on Yom Kippur?				
Yes	48%	69%	80%	99%
No	52%	31%	20%	1%
6. Do you eat pork?				
Yes	67%	61%	40%	1%
No	33%	39%	61%	99%
7. Do you fast on Tisha B'Av?				
Yes	5%	1%	8%	87%
No	95%	99%	92%	13%

	(N=322) Non-affiliated	(N=79) Reform	(N=114) Conservative	(N=231) Orthodox

8. Do you believe in a "World to Come" after death?

	Non-affiliated	Reform	Conservative	Orthodox
Yes	34%	16%	39%	92%
No	66%	84%	61%	8%

9. Do you believe that the Bible was given to the Jews by God?

	Non-affiliated	Reform	Conservative	Orthodox
Yes	46%	38%	70%	97%
No	54%	62%	30%	3%

10. Do you attend synagogue services weekly?

	Non-affiliated	Reform	Conservative	Orthodox
Yes	4%	21%	22%	73%
No	96%	79%	78%	27%

11. (For Men Only) Do you put on *tefillin* daily?

	(N=174)	(N=38)	(N=68)	(N=96)
Yes	6%	3%	6%	90%
No	94%	97%	94%	10%

12. (For Women Only) Do you light Sabbath candles?

	(N=148)	(N=42)	(N=47)	(N=135)
Yes	18%	48%	60%	99%
No	82%	52%	40%	1%

Jewish Identity Data

THE REFORM AND Conservative rationale for breaking with traditional Judaism was its alleged unadaptable and anachronistic nature. Therefore, according to their claims, Orthodox Judaism in 1985 (when the study was conducted) should have diminished significantly from the generation prior, and conversely the Reform and Conservative movements should have grown significantly over the past generation. This issue was therefore investigated. It was also important to study what type of religious background the non-affiliated Jews (i.e., non-affiliated with any synagogue) were coming from. Non-affiliated Jews, in general, were seen as representing a substantive loss of Jewish identity for the following four reasons:

(1) **Intermarriage:** Results showed that 42% of all married non-affiliated Jews between the ages of twenty-one and forty were currently married to gentiles (i.e., spouses that had not converted to any branch of Judaism). This rate of intermarriage was ten times greater than the rates within the other groups — Reform, Conservative and Orthodox. Correspondingly, Jews who were married to gentile spouses scored lowest, as a group, on all major Jewish indices.

(2) **Jewish Organization Affiliation:** Reform, Conservative and Orthodox Jews were two-and-a-half times more likely to be members of Jewish organizations (other than synagogue membership) than were the non-affiliated.

(3) **Marital Status:** Non-affiliated Jews (between the ages of thirty-five and fifty-five) were six times more likely never to have married than each of their Reform, Conservative and Orthodox counterparts.

(4) **Divorce Rate:** The divorce rate among the non-affiliated (between the ages of thirty-five and fifty-five) was more than three times that of each of the Reform, Conservative and Orthodox.

Religious Affiliation Data   AS STATED ABOVE, an objective of the study was to investigate Reform and Conservative claims concerning the unadaptability of Orthodoxy. According to their claims, the younger generation of Jews (in 1985) should have significantly abandoned

the Orthodoxy of their parents. In addition, Reform and
Conservative constituencies should, at the very least, be
maintaining their numbers.

All participants were asked their religious affiliation and
the religious affiliation of their parents. Participants with
children and/or grandchildren above the age of twenty were
asked the type of synagogue their children and/or grandchildren are presently affiliated with.

In order to determine the rate of increase over the previous generation, a comparison was made between the religious
affiliation of young adults (between the ages of twenty-one
and forty) and their parents. The following table represents
the differences in religious affiliation over one generation
(roughly 1955 to 1985).

PARENT/CHILDREN'S RELIGIOUS AFFILIATION

		Children's Affiliation				
		(N=408)	(N=67)	(N=120)	(N=293)	
		NA	R	C	O	Total
NA	(N=126)	81%	3%	3%	10%	97%
R	(N=167)	65%	22%	8%	3%	98%
C	(N=296)	49%	7%	31%	12%	99%
O	(N=303)	16%	2%	2%	76%	96%

(Parents' Affiliation)

The above table can be understood by the following example of parents who are or were (if deceased) affiliated
with Reform Judaism: 167 parents (who had children in
1985, between the ages of twenty-one and forty) were af-

filiated with the Reform movement. Of their young adult children (again, between the ages of twenty-one and forty) 65% were now non-affiliated, 22% were still affiliated with the Reform movement, 8% affiliated with the Conservative movement, and 3% affiliated with Orthodoxy. (The additional percent were affiliated with movements unspecified in the study.)

The maintenance of any group is not solely dependent upon its inter-generational drop-out or growth rate. It is also dependent on the birthrate of its members. Therefore the birthrate of the participants was also compared. When birthrate was taken into consideration the change over one generation was:

Non-affiliated	Reform	Conservative	Orthodox
+203%	−63%	−58%	+9%

In summary, the non-affiliated group increased by 203% over one generation, the Reform and Conservative groups decreased by 63% and 58% respectively, and Orthodox Judaism increased by 9%. In addition, it becomes clear from the data that the non-affiliated group (the group defined as representing a significant loss of Jewish identity) has been inflated by children leaving the Reform and Conservative movements of their parents. For example, 65% of all children whose parents were Reform were, in 1985, non-affiliated; for the Conservative movement, the figure was 49%.

Relationship to the Land of Israel   THE OFFICIAL PLATFORMS of both Reform and Conservative Judaism emphasize a positive relationship to the Land of Israel. For example, as early as 1937 the Reform movement's *Guiding Principles of Reform Judaism* declared that the Jewish People have a responsibility to build and recreate the Jewish homeland. Furthermore, in 1975, on the hundredth anniversary of the founding of the Hebrew Union College (the Reform movement's institution for training rabbis) their statement of principles, the *Centenary Perspective,* was issued. In it they proclaimed their relationship to the Land and State of Israel.

It reads:[1]

> We are privileged to live in an extraordinary time, one in which a third Jewish commonwealth has been established in our people's ancient homeland. We are bound to that land and to the newly reborn State of Israel by innumerable religious and ethnic ties. We have been enriched by its culture and ennobled by its indomitable spirit. We see it providing unique opportunities for Jewish self-expression. We have both a stake and a responsibility in building the State of Israel, assuring its security and defining its Jewish character. We encourage *aliyah* [immigration] for those who wish to find maximum personal fulfillment in the cause of Zion.

The Conservative movement also emphasizes a positive relationship to the Land of Israel. For example, one of its founding fathers, Solomon Schechter, was active in the Zionist Organization of America and was a delegate at several Zionist congresses and conventions. According to Conservative Judaism, "Dr. Schechter...made the JTS (i.e., The Jewish Theological Seminary, the institution which trains Conservative rabbis) an institution for the graduation not only of rabbis, but also of Zionists. Without exception, its rabbis...have carried the message of Zionism to all parts of America."[2]

Another of its main proponents, Rabbi Louis Ginzberg, proclaimed: "Jewish nationalism without religion would be a tree without fruit, Jewish religion without Jewish nationalism would be a tree without roots."[3]

As early as 1927, Rabbi Israel Goldstein reported that the Zionist Organization of America looks upon the Conservative rabbinate "as the rabbinical bulwark of American Zionism."[4]

In 1928 the Conservative Rabbinical Assembly, at its annual convention, called for support of colonists in Palestine and aid to the Zionist movement. And in 1978, Rabbi Robert Gordis, a leading Conservative proponent, wrote:[5]

> In particular, no other aspect of Jewish experience is even remotely comparable to the impact of the State of Israel in rekindling the "spark of the Jew" in the hearts of our youth the world over. In a world that has seemed to vow death and destruction for the Jewish People, Israel has given us a new gift of life.

In addition, the affinity to the modern State of Israel should theoretically be more intense among Reform and Conservative adherents than among Orthodox — since Israel's official policy, like their own, is not significantly bound by Oral Torah (Orthodox) tradition.

In the study, the criteria for measuring participants' relationship to the Land of Israel was based on attitudes towards the Jewish State, on knowledge of Middle East affairs, and most importantly on two behavioral indices.

The first index was based on the question: *If things in the U.S. remain as they are, do you have any real intention of ever settling in Israel?* Responses were grouped according to synagogue affiliation.

	(N=318) Non-affiliated	(N=79) Reform	(N=113) Conservative	(N=221) Orthodox
Yes	8%	1%	7%	51%
No	92%	99%	93%	49%

According to the above, the percentages of non-affiliated, Reform and Conservative participants who have the intention of *ever settling* in Israel were 8%, 1% and 7% respectively. In contrast, the percentage of Orthodox Jews who intend to someday settle in Israel was 51 percent.

The second index was based on the question: *How many times have you visited Israel?* Results, according to six individual comparisons, were that the Orthodox group has visited Israel significantly more than the other three groups. In addition, there were no statistically significant differences among the other groups when compared with each other.

The *Israel Attitude* and *Middle East Knowledge* scales (questionnaires) and their results were deemed secondary in importance when evaluating the relationship between American Jews and the Land of Israel, in light of their non-obligatory nature — non-obligatory in that only attitudes and knowledge were required. Nonetheless, Orthodox adherents had significantly more positive attitudes towards Israel than did the other three groups. In addition, the Orthodox group had significantly greater knowledge of Middle East affairs.

Based on the above results, some questions that need to be addressed are: Why is there such a discrepancy between Orthodox adherents and the adherents of Reform and Conservative Judaism? Why have Reform and Conservative leaders failed to stir up their constituencies in relation to the Jewish homeland? Are Orthodox leaders such powerful and charismatic personalities vis-à-vis their Reform and Conservative counterparts? Are Orthodox Jews so inherently different from Reform and Conservative? Moreover, how is it possible that little to no differences were recorded among the Reform, Conservative and non-affiliated? Why do Reform and Conservative constituencies seemingly ignore their leaders' direction regarding their ancestral homeland?!

Jewish Education   JEWISH EDUCATION IS another area in which the policy of all three groups ostensibly converge.

Officially, all deem Jewish education a highly important and integral aspect of Judaism. For example, Rabbi David Einhorn (1809–1879), who made his Reform imprint both in Germany (Birkenfeld) and later in America (Baltimore), stated the following: [6]

> The religious training of our children should be thoroughly Jewish and instructed with the spirit of the Sinaitic teaching. This is a task of supreme importance, a task to which we should bend every effort. Here no obstacle should block our path…. We will point out to our children the world redeeming power, the ever-widening significance of the Sinaitic teaching which is ever enduring; the changeable character of its outward forms, the glorious triumphs it has achieved…. When synagogue, school, home and our life in general are imbued with such a spirit, we can rest assured that we shall have given our heritage an abiding place in the hearts of our offspring.

Accordingly, in the *Guiding Principles of Reform Judaism*, the emphasis on Jewish education was expressed thusly: "The perpetuation of Judaism as a living force depends upon religious knowledge and upon the education of each new generation in our rich cultural and spiritual heritage."[7]

The Conservative approach to Jewish education is seemingly as positive as that of the Reform. For example, a staunch proponent of Conservative Judaism, Rabbi Dr. Israel J. Kazis, declared: [8]

> We must strive to produce, as did our ancestors, dedicated custodians of our heritage who will with equal conviction and devotion cherish it, enhance it and transmit it with love and loyalty to their children and children's children. The development of such devoted Jews requires above all an intensive pursuit of Jewish learning for only in the rich soil of knowledge can the seeds of appreciation and love of our heritage flourish.
>
> The dictum *"Talmud Torah k'neged kulam,"* the study of Torah takes precedence over all other precepts, must guide and inform the philosophy and policy of Jewish community life in America.
>
> Only knowledgeable Jews are in a position to develop the intellectual appreciations and spiritual affinities which are prerequisites for the cultivation of an authentic and meaningful Judaism.

The emphasis on Jewish education was further expressed by Rabbi Robert Gordis (1978) in Principle 4 of his *Seven Principles of Conservative Judaism.* He writes: [9]

> Jewish knowledge is the privilege and duty of every Jew, not merely of the rabbi and the scholar. A Hebrewless Judaism that has surrendered to ignorance and has ceased to create new cultural and spiritual values is a contradiction in terms, and must perish of spiritual anemia. The regular study of Torah on whatever level is incumbent on every Jew, a supreme commandment second to none.

In the study, the index for measuring participants' level of fundamental and elementary Jewish knowledge was a set of ten questions on Jewish history, Jewish holidays, the Bible, the Talmud, the Prophets, prayer and the Hebrew language. The following data represent the complete *Religious Knowledge Scale,* according to synagogue affiliation.

JEWISH RELIGIOUS KNOWLEDGE

	(N=323) Non-affiliated	(N=80) Reform	(N=112) Conservative	(N=231) Orthodox

1. Could you tell me the name of the Jewish New Year?

Correct	76%	80%	80%	96%
Incorrect	24%	20%	20%	4%

2. On what date was the First and Second Temple in Jerusalem destroyed?

Correct	10%	16%	21%	78%
Incorrect	90%	84%	79%	22%

3. On which Jewish holiday do some Jews wave around a palm branch (a *lulav*)?

Correct	36%	55%	61%	95%
Incorrect	64%	45%	39%	5%

4. What were the names of the three Jewish Patriarchs?

Correct	33%	47%	45%	89%
Incorrect	67%	53%	55%	11%

5. Could you give an example of what is meant in the Bible by "an eye for an eye"?

Correct	7%	3%	8%	59%
Incorrect	93%	97%	92%	41%

	(N=323) Non-affiliated	(N=80) Reform	(N=112) Conservative	(N=231) Orthodox

6. Who brought the Jewish People into the land of Canaan after they had left Egypt?

	Non-affiliated	Reform	Conservative	Orthodox
Correct	13%	14%	17%	66%
Incorrect	87%	86%	83%	34%

7. What is the Oral Law?

Correct	14%	17%	20%	69%
Incorrect	86%	83%	80%	31%

8. What is the name of the morning prayer-service?

Correct	10%	11%	28%	88%
Incorrect	90%	89%	72%	12%

9. What is the name of the chief commentator of the Talmud whose commentary is found on the same page as the Talmud itself?

Correct	12%	11%	26%	74%
Incorrect	88%	89%	74%	26%

10. Please spell the word "Shabbat" in Hebrew.

Correct	19%	21%	29%	83%
Incorrect	81%	79%	71%	17%

SUMMARY OF RESULTS

	(N=323) Non-affiliated	(N=80) Reform	(N=112) Conservative	(N=231) Orthodox
0–2 Correct	72%	58%	48%	7%
3–5 Correct	16%	30%	31%	10%
6–8 Correct	7%	11%	16%	25%
9–10 Correct	5%	1%	5%	58%

In summary, the percentage of non-affiliated, Reform, and Conservative participants who obtained scores of 25% correct or lower were 72%, 58% and 48% respectively. In contrast, only 7% of Orthodox participants scored 25% or less.

Similarly, the percentages of non-affiliated, Reform and Conservative participants who obtained scores of 90% correct or higher were 5%, 1% and 5%, respectively. In contrast, the majority of the Orthodox participants (58%) scored 90% or higher.

(Despite the vast difference in Jewish knowledge between the Orthodox group and the others, no significant difference was registered when participants' secular educational level was compared. The average education of all four groups was slightly above the B.A. level.)

Significance of the Findings

WITHOUT EXAGGERATION, THE above results reflect not only a lack of knowledge among Reform, Conservative and the non-affiliated, but rather an abysmal ignorance, most probably unparalleled in Jewish history.

Is it conceivable that 70–80% of the American adult population would be unable to spell the word *"cat"*? And yet, the self-declared backbone of American Judaism (i.e., Reform and Conservative) is unable to spell its Hebrew equivalent.

How are we to understand their leaders' elevated rhetoric concerning Jewish education, assimilation and the importance of the Land of Israel?

How is it possible that the intelligent baby boomers who grew up as Reform and Conservative Jews know little to nothing of Judaism? And how is it that the prior generation, as well, is pitifully lacking in Jewish knowledge?

Does it truly matter that Reform and Conservative leaders have failed to educate their constituents on matters of Judaism? Is it our obligation to worry that a preponderance of their adherents neglect the observance of some of the most explicit and basic commandments of the Torah (e.g., Shabbat, dietary laws, *tefillin*)? Is it our business that their followers have little to no knowledge or appreciation of the Oral Law or of the Jewish concept of the World to Come? And are we our brothers' keepers to bemoan and criticize Reform and Conservative Judaism for fostering the inexorable assimilation process? This author believes that the answer to these questions is an emphatic yes, and some of the reasons, stated briefly, are:

(1) DISILLUSIONED JEWISH YOUTH

A large number of American Jewish youth (i.e., many times their proportion in the general American population) have been recruited, over the past forty years, into religious cults of all types in their search for spirituality. These young people are not products of Orthodoxy but, primarily, from families originally affiliated with Reform or Conservative Judaism.[10]

As long as the Reform and Conservative movements are portrayed as legitimate forms of Judaism these young people will probably never return. Their sincere response is: "We know all about Judaism (that is, Reform and Conservative) and found it devoid of spirituality and meaning, and therefore are looking elsewhere."

If Reform and Conservative Judaism are not publicly decried, these young Jews will probably never return, and others will inevitably follow their lead.

(2) ABANDONMENT OF JEWISH TRADITION

For more than three thousand years, millions of Jews have been pillaged, exiled, tortured and slaughtered because they would not renounce their Jewish nationalism (i.e., relationship to the Land of Israel), Torah study and observance of Torah Law. Yet according to the present findings, and extrapolating therefrom, literally millions of Jews have significantly relinquished these same Jewish treasures in the name of Judaism itself.

The analyses discussed, in this and the previous chapter, indicate that American Jews were led into abandoning their rich cultural and spiritual heritage without truly understanding what they were, in fact, forsaking. In other words, by remaining ignorant of Judaism and continuing to believe in the legitimacy of Reform and Conservative Judaism, the Jewish masses were, perforce, prevented from making intelligent decisions regarding the over three-millennia tradition of their forefathers.

(3) CATALYST OF JEWISH SUFFERING

When the Jewish People act in accordance with their historical traditions they are blessed. Reform and Conservative constituents do little of what is required according to Torah Law and are, therefore, the agents of their own suffering.

If the Torah is indeed true, they are sowing the seeds of affliction by their non-observance — not only for themselves and their descendents, but for the entire Jewish People.

The ruination that Reform and Conservative leaders have inflicted on the Jewish soul and spirit, both individually and collectively, is no less than catastrophic. This one-hundred-year American deception needs to be exposed for what it is. Because these movements have been granted legitimacy, American Jewry has been denied the opportunity of experiencing Torah-true Judaism — for only through the study and observance of our 3,200-year-old tradition can true unity, peace and security be achieved.

NOTES TO CHAPTER 16

1. Rosenthal, G.S., *The Many Faces of Judaism* (New York: Behrman House, 1978), pp. 69–70.

2. Raphael, M.L., *Profiles in American Judaism* (San Francisco: Harper & Row, 1984).

3. Ibid.

4. Ibid.

5. Gordis, R., *Understanding Conservative Judaism* (New York: Rabbinical Assembly, 1978), p. 100.

6. Plaut, W.G., *The Rise of Reform Judaism* (New York: World Union for Progressive Judaism, 1963).

7. Plaut, W.G., *The Growth of Reform Judaism* (New York: World Union for Progressive Judaism, 1965).

8. Kazis, I.J., "Meeting the Challenge to Jewish Survival," in *Roads to Jewish Survival*, M. Berger, J.A. Geffen, M.D. Hoffman (eds.) (New York: Bloch, 1967), p. 167.

9. Gordis, p. 217.

10. Fisch, D.A., *Jews for Nothing* (New York: Feldheim, 1984).

17 | A Look into the Pre-Messianic Era

Rabbi Elazar was asked by his students: "What can a person do to be spared the travail of the birthpangs of the Messiah?" He answered: "One should occupy himself in the study of Torah and in acts of kindness."

(Talmud, Tractate Sanhedrin 98b)

THE TALMUD RELATES THE FOLLOWING INCIDENT:[1]

When they [Rabbi Gamaliel, Rabbi Elazar ben Azariah, Rabbi Joshua, and Rabbi Akiba] were going up to Jerusalem, and reached Mount Scopus they rent their clothing [as mourners witnessing the destroyed Temple]. When they reached the Temple Mount they saw a fox coming out of the area where the Holy of Holies once stood. They began to weep and Rabbi Akiba laughed!

"Why are you laughing?" they asked him.

"Why are you weeping?" he responded.

"A place of which it is written 'an alien who comes near shall die' and now foxes therein reside, and we should not cry?" they replied.

279

> [Rabbi Akiba explained:] "Just because of that, I laugh...
> for if the prophecy of Uriah [who described the Temple's
> destruction] had not materialized then I may fear that
> Zachariah's prophecy (who spoke of the Final Redemption)
> would also not transpire. Now that Uriah's prophecy has
> transpired, we may be assured that the prophecy of Zacha-
> riah will also come about."
>
> "Akiba, you have consoled us," they said. "Akiba, you have
> consoled us!"

Not all Jewish prophecies have been fulfilled. The last
and most important prophecy — for both Jew and non-Jew
alike — concerning the "End of Days" has yet to be realized:
"And it shall come to pass in the last days, that the mountain
of the Lord's House shall be established on the top of the
mountains, and shall be exalted above the hills; and all nations shall flow unto it" (Isaiah 2:2). According to traditional
Jewish literature the Final Redemption (for all humanity) is
assured, but the process of getting there — either through
worldwide destruction or supernal benevolence — is dependent on the Jewish People collectively. For example, the
Talmud states:[2]

> The son of Levi cites a contradiction: In the prophet Isaiah it
> is written "in its time" [i.e., the Final Redemption will come
> in its prescribed time], but it is also written "I will hurry
> it up" [i.e., God will bring the Final Redemption before its
> prescribed time]!
>
> [The Talmud explains:] If they [the Jews] merit, I [God]
> will hurry it up, if they do not merit, it will come in its
> prescribed time.

The Maharsha, Rabbi Samuel Eliezer (seventeenth century), explains: "If the Jews merit [the Redemption] by

repentance and Torah observance, God will have compassion on them [and indirectly on the entire world], but if they do not return to Torah observance, God will delay the Redemption until its 'prescribed time,' and only then will He redeem them [amidst destruction and suffering]."

In the Zohar (the primary source of Jewish mysticism, redacted second century C.E.) it is likewise written:[3]

> We learn that all the time the people of Israel are in exile, if they merit, God will have compassion and take them out of exile; and if they do not, God will delay them until the prescribed time. If the time comes and they are not fit to be redeemed, then God, in the honor of His Own Name, will not forget them completely.

Talmudic and other traditional Jewish literature depict signs of what life may be like preceding the Messianic era. From several places in Talmudic and Midrashic literature it becomes clear that if the Redemption comes in its "prescribed time" it will come gradually, in a seemingly natural manner.[4] For example, the Talmud states:

◆ There is no surer sign for the imminent coming of the Messiah than when the Land of Israel becomes fertile again for the Jewish People.[5]

◆ If you see a period of time where constant and frightful sorrow confronts the Jewish People, anticipate the arrival of the descendant of King David [who according to tradition will be the Messiah].[6]

The Talmud[7] also enumerates various scenarios that may occur shortly before the Messianic era. They are:

◆ The Jewish government will be run by non-observant Jews.

- The wisdom of the Rabbis will be scorned.

- Pious Jews will be ridiculed.

- There will be great inflation.

- This inflation will not be attributed to lack of supply.

- Truth will be lacking. (The Talmud means that the Jews will split up into several groups, each laying claim to the truth and making it difficult to discern true Judaism from the false.)[8]

- Neither parents nor the aged will be held in respect. The aged will be humiliated by the young and a man's household will be his enemies. Arrogance will greatly increase and rebuke will be silenced. Religious students and studies will be held in disdain.[9]

- The generation before the coming of the Messiah will be a lustful one without shame.[10]

- Before the Messiah comes, most people will have given up hope or trust in a supernatural redemption.[11]

- If the Jewish People desire to behave like other nations, the Redemption will come, but with great anger.[12]

In the Midrash we find the following predictions:

- Rabbi Elazar taught that the pre-Messianic Era will usher in a generation with the power to consume itself.[13]

- Shortly before the coming of the Messiah all mankind will be frightened and dismayed by an excess of ongoing wars and tension between nations.[14]

- In the future, God will pay heed to the people of Israel's sorrow, that will be caused by the sons of Ishmael (the Arabs).[15]

◆ Immediately preceding the Messiah, the Ishmael (Arab) kingdom will ally itself with the "Roman" nation.[16]

◆ This last nation from "Rome" will call all peoples of the world to be one people and to speak one language. It will also decree that anyone who says that the Jewish God is God will be executed.[17]

The Zohar[18] states: "In the future the 'sons of Ishmael' (the Arabs) will rule in the Holy Land while it is a wasteland for a prolonged period of time, and will hinder Israel from returning."

The Zohar further relates that prior to the Messiah, the Jewish People will establish for themselves a government in Jerusalem and that the sons of Ishmael, together with other nations, will attack the Jewish state. The Jewish People, it says, will suffer greatly, but will prevail.[19]

The eighteenth-century commentary *Metzudat David* notes that the Jewish People will immigrate to the Land of Israel more out of non-Jewish hatred than of their own volition.[20] The Talmud relates that the pre-Messianic Era will begin with a measure of political independence for the Jewish People in their own land.[21] (This political independence will come with the permission of other nations.[22])

Preceding the Redemption, the Jews, then called Israel, will deny God's help, and will claim that their success is dependent on their own efforts.[23]

Maimonides wrote the following, concerning the awaited-for Messiah:

> If there comes a ruler from the House of David, who is immersed in the study of Torah like David his ancestor, following both the Written and Oral Torah, who brings masses of Jews back to the ways of the Torah, strengthening

the Laws and fighting battles for the sake of Heaven, then it may be assumed that he is the Messiah. If he is further successful in rebuilding the Temple on its prior site and in bringing the dispersed Jews back to their Land, then his identity as the Messiah is a certainty.[24]

Nachmanides (thirteenth century) wrote that during the period from the beginning of the pre-Messianic era to its finale, there will be great fighting and tumult in the world.[25]

Wars predicted to occur immediately before the Messianic era (if the redemption comes in its prescribed time) are discussed in the Talmud. In Tractate *Yoma* it states: "The descendant of [King] David [the Messiah] will not appear until the 'Roman' nation spreads out over the entire world."[26] The Talmud[27] relates that the conquering empire ("Rome") will rule over the Jews nine months before the Messiah comes.

According to the Biblical book of Daniel, ten kingdoms will spring forth from the fourth conquering empire (which according to the Midrash is Rome).[28] Thereafter another and final kingdom will arise from Rome but will be different from the others.[29] It is this last kingdom from Rome who will spread out and attempt to conquer the entire world.[30]

Correspondingly, according to the prophet Ezekiel the final superpower to war with Israel (before the Messianic era) will come from the land of Magog.[31] Josephus, who lived during the first century C.E., wrote that the land of Magog is Scythia.[32] "According to the ancient Greeks, Scythia was a vast, undefined region lying north of the Black and Caspian Seas" (present-day Russia).[33] "Throughout classical literature Scythia meant all regions to the north and northeast of the Black Sea, and a Scythian was any barbarian coming from those parts."[34]

However, the Jerusalem Talmud[35] (fourth century C.E.) notes that the land of Magog is Gothia (Goth), and according to the *Encyclopaedia Brittanica,* the Goths (first century C.E.) inhabited the middle part of the basin of the Vistula River (central to eastern Poland) but migrated into Scythia (again, present-day Russia) under their sixth king (who was more contemporary in time with the Jerusalem Talmud).

In the book *Yov'lot,* which is a history of the periods covered in the Books of Genesis and Exodus, written in approximately 110 B.C.E., the land of Magog is likewise identified as being to the north of the Black Sea. [The book *Yov'lot* is

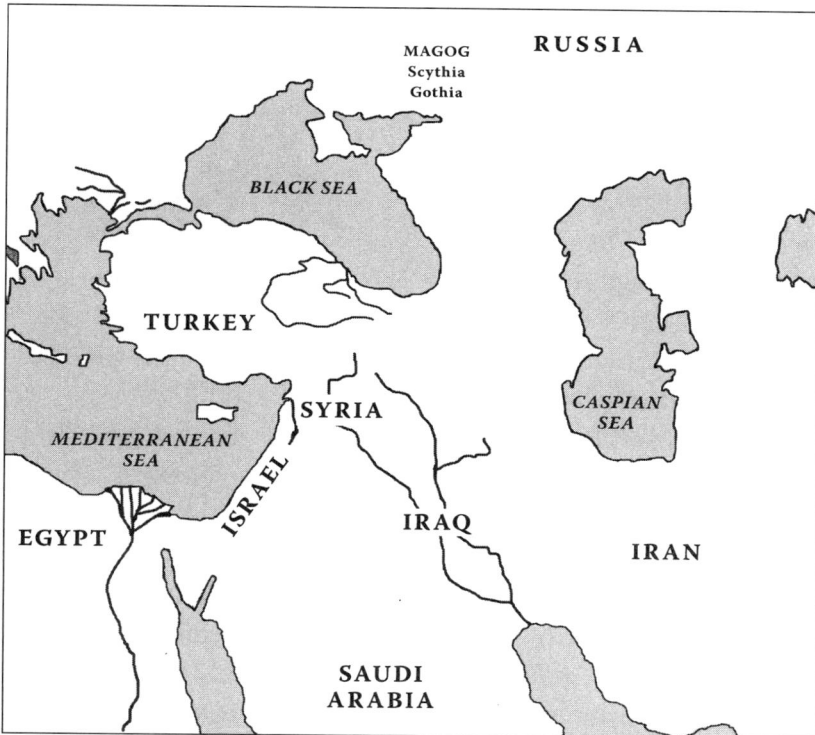

Location of Magog according to above-mentioned sources

the earliest source for much of the material found in the Midrashic works of *Pirkei d'Rabbi Eliezer, Bereshit Rabati, and Midrash Tadshe*.][36]

According to the *Encyclopaedia Brittanica*, after the destruction of the Western Roman empire by the Teutons, only Constantinople remained as the capital of the (Eastern) Roman Empire (i.e., the Byzantine empire). And from the day the Russian king (Ivan III) betrothed the only niece (Sophia) of the last Byzantine Roman emperor (Constantine Palaeologus), Russian autocrats considered themselves the new emperors of the Roman empire. Russian aristocracy claimed that since the Greeks had been punished for their apostasy, their succession had to pass to the third Rome (Constantinople being the second) which was Moscow.[37] In addition, before the Russian Revolution in 1917, the Imperial Standard of the Russian Czar was a double-headed eagle, black on a yellow field, an insignia adopted from the Byzantine Roman Empire of the fifteenth century.[38]

Imperial Standard of the
Russian Czar

Rabbi Saadia Gaon (882–942 C.E.) received the tradition that the final two kings to sprout from the "Roman" empire before the coming of the Messiah, will be the King of Russia (he explicitly mentioned the name Russia) together with the King of Ishmael.[39]

According to the Jewish proselyte and scholar Onkelos (circa 90 C.E.) and Jonathan ben Uzziel (circa 10 C.E.) the cryptic verse in Numbers 24:24 means that immediately preceding the Messiah, the "Roman" nation will send fleets of warships against various nations in the Middle East, and will wreak havoc.[40]

The great Jewish scholar of the eighteenth century, the Vilna Gaon, told his students that when they see the warships of Russia pass through the Bosporus straits they should put on their Sabbath clothes (i.e., their nicest clothing) for the Messiah is close at hand.[41]

Based on Biblical verses in *Daniel* (2:40–42 and 12:1), various medieval Jewish commentators (e.g., Rashi, Ibn Ezra) explain that when "Rome" begins to conquer the Middle East, the peoples of the world will suffer as never before.[42]

Once "Rome" conquers Egypt, it will hear rumors that armies from the East and the North are coming against it. Rome will then go on the offensive and attack them.[43]

The Midrash states that once "Rome" begins to subjugate the Middle East, the sons of Ishmael (the Arabs) will seek help from "Western Rome."[44]

According to the Zohar, the mechanics of the final war (if the Redemption comes in its prescribed time) will proceed in the following manner:[45]

(1) The sons of Ishmael (the Arabs) will attempt to keep Israel from returning to its homeland.

(2) The sons of Ishmael will effect fierce wars, and "Rome" will eventually wage war against them in order to take over their land and the Land of Israel.

(3) "Rome" will succeed in taking over Arab land but the Land of Israel will not be conquered.

(4) *"One nation at the end of the world,"* together with other nations, will then challenge "Rome," but after a period of three months, these nations will be consumed.

(5) After vanquishing all opponents, "Rome" will attempt

an all out attack against the Land of Israel. At that time, God will defend Israel, and "Rome" together with her allies will perish.

The pre-Messianic scenarios discussed in this chapter should not be viewed as scare tactics, but may serve, hopefully, as a wake-up call to both Jew and non-Jew alike. After all is said and done, it is best to always focus on the positive — that is, when the Jewish People return to authentic Judaism, which is indeed happening, the Messianic era will surely be ushered in amidst security, prosperity and unprecedented blessings.

NOTES TO CHAPTER 17

1. Talmud *Makkot* 24b (Jerusalem: Ortsel, 1960).
2. Talmud *Sanhedrin* 98a (Jerusalem: Ortsel, 1960); Zohar (*Parshat Acharei Mot*, 66).
3. Zohar (*Parshat Acharei Mot*).
4. E.g.: Jerusalem Talmud, *Yoma* 3:2; *Midrash Tehillim* (18), in *Midrash Shochar Tov al Tehillim* (Jerusalem: Midrash, 1968); Zohar, in A. Kaplan, *The Real Messiah?* (New York: NCSY, 1985).
5. Talmud *Sanhedrin* 98a.
6. Ibid.
7. Talmud *Sotah* 49b (Jerusalem: Ortsel, 1960).
8. Talmud *Sanhedrin* 97a.
9. Ibid.
10. Ibid.; see Rashi.
11. Talmud *Sanhedrin* 97.
12. Ibid. 105a; see Rashi.
13. *Pesikta Rabati* (end of no. 1), (Vilna: 1880).
14. E.g., *Bereshit Rabbah* 42, in *Midrash Rabbah*; *Yalkut Shimoni* (on Isaiah 60).
15. *Pirkei d'Rabbi Eliezer* 32 (Jerusalem: M. Kilman, 1969).

16. *Midrash Daniel*, cited in Isenberg, R., *Chevlei Mashiach Bizmaneinu* (Tel Aviv: Chidekel, 1970).
17. *Midrash, Pesikta Zutrata*, cited in Isenberg.
18. Zohar (*Parshat Va'era*).
19. Zohar (*Parshat Bereshit*), cited in Isenberg.
20. See *Metzudat David* on Ezekiel 20:33–34, cited in *Mikraot Gedolot* (New York: Friedman, 1971).
21. Talmud *Sanhedrin* 98, cited in Kaplan, p. 90.
22. Nachmanides, cited in Kaplan, p. 90.
23. See Rabbi Joseph Karo (late eleventh century–early twelfth century) on Isaiah 48:1–5.
24. Maimonides, M., *Mishneh Torah, Melachim* 11:4.
25. Nachmanides, *Kitvei Ramban* (516) (Jerusalem: Mossad HaRav Kook, 1964), vol. 2.
26. Talmud *Yoma* 10a.
27. Talmud *Sanhedrin* 98b; see Rashi.
28. *Midrash Daniel*.
29. Daniel 7:23–24.
30. Isenberg, R.
31. Ezekiel, ch. 38.
32. Josephus, *Antiquities.*
33. *Brittanica World Language* (London: Encyclopaedia Brittanica, 1954).
34. *Encyclopaedia Brittanica* (London: 1954).
35. Jerusalem Talmud, *Megillah* 1:19 (Jerusalem: Torah Mitzion, 1985).
36. Kaplan, A., *The Living Torah* (New York: Moznaim, 1985).
37. *Encyclopaedia Brittanica.*
38. Campbell, G. & Evans, I.O., *The Book of Flags* (London: Oxford University Press, 1969).
39. Isenberg.
40. In *Mikraot Gedolot*, Numbers (New York: Friedman, 1971).
41. Isenberg.
42. In *Mikraot Gedolot*, Daniel (New York: Friedman, 1971).
43. See Isenberg; based on Daniel 11:43–44.
44. *Midrash Pesikta Rabati* 37:2; see Isenberg.
45. Zohar (*Parshat Va'era*) (Jerusalem: Mossad HaRav Kook, 1964).

Bibliography

Aban, Ezra. In *Mikraot Gedolot; Daniel.* New York: Friedman, 1971, Abelson, C.M. "Bias and the Bible." In A. Carmell & C. Domb (Eds.). *Challenge: Torah Views on Science and Its Problems.* Jeruslem: Feldheim Publishers, 1978.

Abu-Lughod, LA. (Ed.). *The Transformation of Palestine: Essays on the Origin and Development of the Arab-Israeli Conflict.* Evanston, IL: Northwestern University Press, 1971.

Adorno, T.W. "Types and Syndromes." In T.W. Adorno, E. Frenkel-Brunswik, D.J. Levinson, and R.N. Sanford (Eds.). *Authoritarian Personality.* New York: Harper & Row, 1950.

Adorno, T.W., Frenkel-Brunswik, E., Levinson, and Sanford, R.N. *The Authoritarian Personality.* New York: Harper & Row. 1950.

Aharoni, Y. "Canaanite Israel During the Period of Israeli Occupation" in A. Sutton & Arachim Staff (Eds.), *Pathways to the Torah.* Jerusalem: Arachim, 1985.

Albright, W.F. *The Biblical Period.* New York: Harper & Row.

Albright, W.F. *Archaeology and the Religion of Israel.* New York: Anchor Books, 1969.

Allport, G. *The Nature of Prejudice.* New York: Addison-Wesley, 1954.

Allswang, B. *Anti-Judaism, Anti-Semitism, Anti-Zionism: An Empirical Analysis of the Anti-Jewish Phenomenon throughout history to the Present.* Doctoral dissertation submitted to the Social-Psychology Department of Loyola University at Chicago, 1985.

Allswang, B. *The Final Resolution: Combating Anti-Jewish Hostility*. Jerusalem/NY:Feldheim Publishers, 1989.

Am Segulah. Jerusalem: Dvar Yerushalayim, 1981.

Anti-Defamation League of B'nai B'rith. *Hate Groups in America: A Record of Bigotry and Violence*. New York: Anti-Defamation League of B'nai B'rith, 1982.

Baidawi. Cited in A. Katch, *Judaism and the Koran*. New York: Perpetua, 1962.

Baird, Mitchell G. *Myth and Facts, A Guide to the Arab-Israeli Conflict*. Chevy Chase, MD: AICE, 2001.

Berdkilaev, N. *The Meaning of History*. Cleveland: Meridian Books, 1962.

Bergman, S.H. "Can Transgression Have an Agent? On the Moral Judical Problem of the Eichmann Trial." *Yad Vashem Studies*, 5, 1963, 7–15.

Berkowitz, L. "Whatever Happened to the Frustration-Aggression Hypothesis?" *American Behavioral Scientist*, 1978, *21*, 691–708.

Berkowitz, L., Cochran, S.T., and Embree, M.C. "Physical Pain and the Goal of Aversively Stimulated Aggression." *Journal of Personality and Social Psychology*, 1981, *40*, 687–700.

Bettelheim, B., and Janowitz, M. *Social Change and Prejudice: Dynamics of Prejudice*. New York: Free Press of Glencoe, 1964.

Biberfeld, P. *Universal Jewish History*, Vol. I. New York: Feldheim, 1962.

Bottomore, T.B. *Kark Marx: Early Writings*. New York: McGraw Hill, 1964.

Britain Israel Public Affairs Committee. *The PLO Exposed*. London: Britain Israel Public Affairs Committee, 1982.

Britannica World Language. Edition of Funk and Wagnell's New

Practical Standard Dictionary. London: Encyclopaedia Britannica, 1954.

Bruer, I. *Moriah.* Jerusalem: Mossad HaRav Kook, 1982.

Campbell, A. & Evans, I.O. *The Book of Flags.* London: Oxford University Press, 1969.

Cawley, J. "Canada Accuses German of Writing off Holocaust." *Chicago Tribune,* February 3, 1985, p. 5.

Chafetz, Z. *Double Vision: How the Press Distorts America's View of the Middle East.* New York: William Morrow & Co., 1985.

Charniovsky, A. *Between Science and Religion.* Tel Aviv: Joshua Chachik Publishing, 1965.

Chavel, C.B. *The Law of the Eternal Is Perfect.* New York: Shilo, 1983. *Chicago Tribune.* "Percy Held Talks with Palestinians." December 31, 1981.

Cirino, R. *Power to Persuade.* New York: Bantam Books, 1974. Cohen, I. "Myths and Facts on the Middle East Mishegoss." *Jewish Chicago.* New Year, 1984, pp. 18–22.

Cohen, S. "Divine Origin of the Torah." In D. Kiel (Ed.). *Return to the Source.* New York: Feldheim Publishers, 1984.

Cohen, S.M. *Attitudes of American Jews Towards Israel and Israelis: The 1983 National Survey of American Jews and Jewish Communal Leaders.* New York: American Jewish Committee, 1983.

C.O.M.A *Media Onslaught on Israel.* Santa Monica, Calif.: Committee on Media Accountability, 1983.

Davidowicz, L.S. *The War Against the Jews,* 1933–1945. New York: Bantam Books, 1975.

Davis, L.J. *Myths and Facts* 1985: *A Concise Record of the Arab-Israeli Conflict.* Washington, D.C.: Near East Research, Inc., 1984.

Davis, L.J. & Decter, M. *Myths and Facts* 1982: *A Concise Record of the Arab-Israeli Conflict.* Washington, D.C.: Near East Research, Inc. 1982.

DeBileda, J. In *Am Segulah.* Jerusalem: Dvar Yerushalayim, 1981.

Drayer, M. & Kanner, M. "Fighting Anti-Israel Propaganda." *Near East Report,* 1983, 27, 130.

Dunham, D.C. *Kremlin Target: U.S.A.; Conquest by Propaganda.* New York: I. Washburn, 1961.

Einstein, A. *Comment je Voi le Monde.* New York: Philosophical Library, 1949.

Eliezer, S. *Maharsha: Talmud Tractate Baba Kama.* Vilna edition. Jerusalem: Ortsel, 1960.

Eliezer, S. *Maharsha: Talmud Tractate Sukkah.* Vilna edition. Jerusalem: Ortsel, 1960.

Emden, J. *Sulam Beit Al.* In *Sidut Beit Yaacob.* New York: Mefitzay Torah, 1950.

Encyclopaedia Britannica. London, 1954. *Encyclopaedia Judaica.* Jerusalem: Keter Publishing House, 1973.

Encyclopaedia Judaica: 1973–82 Decennial Book. Jerusalem: Keter, 1982.

Etkin, W. "The Religious Meaning of Contemporary Science." In A. Carmell and C. Domb (Eds.). *Challenge: Torah Views on Science and Its Problems.* Jerusalem: Feldheim Publishers, 1978.

Ettinger, S. "The Origins of Modern Anti-Semitism." *Dispersion and Unity,* 1969, 9, 17–37.

Eybeschutz, J. In *Am Segulah.* Jerusalem: Dvar Yerushalayim, 1981.

Fendel, Zechariah. Legacy of Sinai New York: Hashkafah Publications, 1992.

Fisch, D.A. *Jews for Nothing: On Cults, Intermarriage, and Assimilation.* New York: Feldheim Publishers, 1984.

Flannery, E.H. *The Anguish of the Jews.* New York: Macmillan Co., 1965.

Forster, A., and Epstein, B.R. *The New Anti-Semitism.* New York: McGraw-Hill, 1974.

Fromm, E. *Escape from Freedom.* New York: Farrar & Rinehart, 1941.

Gager, J.G. *The Origins of Anti-Semitism: Attitudes towards Judaism in Pagan and Christian Antiquity.* New York: Oxford University Press, 1983.

Gartner, L.P. "Immigration and the Formation of American Jewry, 1840–1925." In M. Sklare (Ed.), *American Jews: A Reader.* New York: Behrman House, 1983.

Geen, R.G. "Effects of Frustration, Attack, and Prior Training in Aggressiveness upon Aggressive Behavior." *Journal of Personality and Social Psychology,* 1968, 9, 316–21.

Gerol, Ilya. "TV Exaggerates Lebanese Damage." Ottowa, Canada: *The Citizen,* October 30, 1982.

Gevirtz, E. *L'havin U L'Haskil: A Guide to Torah Hashkafah, Questions and Answers on Judaism.* New York: Feldheim Publishers, 1980.

Gilbert, M. *Atlas of Jewish History.* New York: Dorset Press, 1985. Gilbert, M. *Auschwitz and the Allies.* New York: Holt, Rinehart & Winston, 1981.

Ginzberg, L. *The Legends of the Jews.* Philadelphia: The Jewish Publication Society, 1968.

Givet, J. *The Anti-Zionist Complex.* Englewood, N.J.: SBS Publishing, 1982.

Glover, T.R. *The Ancient World: A Beginning.* Westport, Conn.: Greenwood Press, 1979.

Goldberg, M.H. *Just Because They're Jewish.* New York: Scarborough House, 1981.

Goot, A.K., and Rosen, S.J. *The Campaign to Discredit Israel.* Washington, D.C.: American Israel Public Affairs Committee, 1983.

Gordis, R. *Understanding Conservative Judaism.* New York: Rabbinical Assembly, 1978.

Grayzel, S. *A History of the Jews.* Philadelphia: Jewish Publication Society of America, 1968.

Great Soviet Encyclopaedia (1952). Cited in D. Prager and J. Telushkin. *Why the Jews? The Reason for Anti-Semitism.* New York: Simon & Schuster, 1983.

Grosser, P.E. & Halperin, E.G. *The Causes and Effects of Anti-Semitism.* New York: Philosophical Library, 1978.

HaLevy, J. *The Kuzari.* New York: Schocken Books, 1964.

Harris, L., and Associates. Cited in H.E. Quinley and C.Y. Glock, *Anti-Semitism in America.* New Brunswick, N.J.: Transaction Inc., 1983.

Hirsch, S.M. "How Does Our Time Relate to Truth and Peace?" in *Collected Writings of Rabbi Samson Raphael Hirsch.* New York: Feldheim Publishers, 1984.

Hoge, D.R. & Carroll, J.W. "Christian Beliefs, Non-Religious Factors, and Anti-Semitism." *Social Forces,* 1975, 4, 581–9

Hussein. "Interview with King Hussein." *Time,* July 26, 1982, p. 23.

International Center for the Study of Antisemitism. *ANTI-SEMITISM.* Jerusalem: Hebrew University.

Isaacs, J. *Our People: History of the Jews.* New York: Shulsinger Bros., 1975.

Isenberg, R. *Chavlai Meshiach Bizmanainu.* Tel-Aviv: Chidekel, 1970.

Jaakobi, S. "Land of Israel." In D. Kiel (Ed.), *Return to the Source.* New York: Feldheim Publishers, 1984.

Jakobovits, I. Foreword. In H.C. Schimmel, *The Oral Law: A Study of the Rabbinic Contribution to Torah SheBe'Al Peh.* Jerusalem: Feldheim Publishers, 1971.

Johnson, M. *Time Magazine,* August 9, 1982, p. 24.

Josephus. *Against Apion. The Life and Works of Josephus.* Philadelphia: John C. Winston Co., 1936.

Josephus. *Antiquities. The Life and Works of Josephus.* Philadelphia: John C. Winston Co., 1936.

Josephus, F. *Complete Works of Flavius Josephus.* Grand Rapids, Mich.: Kregel, 1970.

Josephus. *The Jewish Wars. The Life and Works of Josephus.* Philadelphia: John C. Winston Co., 1936.

Kaganoff, B.C. *A Dictionary of Jewish Names and Their History.* New York: Schocken Books, 1977.

Kaplan, A. *Handbook of Jewish Thought.* New York: Moznaim, 1979.

Kaplan, A. *The Living Torah.* New York: Moznaim, 1985.

Kapustin, M. "Biblical Criticism: A Traditionalist View." In A. Carmell and C. Domb (Eds.), *Challenge: Torah Views on Science and Its Problems.* Jerusalem: Feldheim Publishers, 1978.

Katsh, A.I. *Judaism and the Koran.* New York: Perpetua, 1962.

Katzir, A. "In the Midst of the Scientific Revolution." In A. Sutton & Arachim Staff (Eds.), *Pathways to the Torah.* Jerusalem: Arachim, 1985.

Kaufman, Y. *The Religion of Israel: From Its Beginnings to the Babylonian Exile.* Chicago: University of Chicago Press, 1960.

Kazis, I.J. "Meeting the Challenge to Jewish Survival." In M. Berger, J.S. Geffen, M.D. Hoffman (Eds.), *Roads to Jewish Survival.* New York: Bloch, 1967.

Keniston, K. *Youth and Dissent: The Rise of a New Opposition.* New York: Harcourt Brace Jovanovich, 1971.

Keller, W. *The Bible as History: A Confirmation of the Book of Books.* New York: Wm. Morrow, 1956.

Kessler, J.S., and Schwaber, J. *The AIPAC College Guide: Exposing the Anti-Israel Campaign on Campus.* Washington, D.C.: American Israel Public Affairs Committee, 1984.

Kondracke, M. *Chicago Sun-Times.* January 25, 1985.

Krsoney & Schmueloff. *The National Jewish Ledger.* April, 1986.

Lamprecht, S.P. *Our Philosophical Traditions: A Brief History of Philosophy in Western Civilization.* New York: Appleton-Century Crofts, 1955.

Levi, L. *Torah and Science: Their Interplay in the World Scheme.* Jerusalem: Feldheim Publishers, 1983.

Liebman, C.S. "The Religion of American Jews." In M. Sklare (Ed.), *American Jews: A Reader.* New York: Behrman House, 1983.

Lindsey, H. *The Late Great Planet Earth.* Grand Rapids, Mich.: Zondervan, 1977.

Lindsey, H. *The 1980's: Countdown to Armageddon.* New York: Bantam Books, 1981.

Lipset, S.M. & Ladd, E.C. "Jewish Academics in the United States: Their Achievements, Culture and Politics." In M. Fine and M. Himmelfarb (Eds.), *American Jewish Yearbook 1971.* Philadelphia: Jewish Publication Society of America, 1971.

Ma'ariv Newspaper. April 17, 1983.

McKay, J.P., Hill, B.D. & Buckler, J. *A History of World Societies.* Boston: Houghton Mifflin, 1984.

Machshavot I.B.M. "Sociobiology-Nature Within Man." In A. Sutton & Arachim Staff (Eds.), *Pathways to the Torah.* Jerusalem: Arachim, 1985.

McLellan, D. *Karl Marx: His Life and Thought.* New York: Harper & Row, 1973.

Maharal. *Netzach Yisrael.* Warsaw: Freedberg, 1886.

Maimonides, M. *Mishnah Torah: Hilchot Melachim.* Jerusalem: Mossad HaRav Kook, 1972.

Maimonides, M. *Mishnah Torah, Hilchot Teshuvah.* Jerusalem: Mossad HaRav Kook, 1972.

Maimonides, M. *Mishnah Torah, Introduction.* Jerusalem: Mossad HaRav Kook, 1972.

Maimonides, M. *Mishnah Torah: Sefer Mada.* Jerusalem: Mossad HaRav Kook, 1972.

Maimonides, M. *Shemoneh Perakim.* In Talmud *Tractate Avodah Zarah.* Vilna edition. Jerusalem: Ortsel, 1960.

Malamot, A. *A History of the Jewish People.* Cambridge, Mass.: Harvard University Press, 1976.

Mandel, R. "Israel in 1982: The War in Lebanon." In M. Himmelfarb and D. Singer (Eds.), *American Jewish Yearbook*, 1984. New York: American Jewish Committee, 1983.

Maslow, A.H. "The Authoritarian Character Structure." *The Journal of Social Psychology*, 1943, *18*, 401–411.

Mason, S.F. *A History of the Sciences.* New York: Collier Books, 1968.

Meiri, S. "Burden of Proof." In D. Kiel (Ed.), *Return to the Source.* New York: Feldheim Publishers, 1984.

Merari, A. *PLO: Core of World Terror.* Jerusalem: Carta, 1983.

Meyers, D.A. *Social Psychology.* New York: McGraw-Hill, 1983.

Midrash Aggadat Esther. Israel: 1964.

Midrash Abba Gurion. In A. Jellinek (Ed.), *Beit HaMidrash.* Jerusalem: Wahrmann-Books, 1967.

Midrash Bamidbar Rabbah. In *Midrash Rabbah.* Jerusalem: Levin Epstein, 1965.

Midrash Beit HaMidrash. Jerusalem: Wahrman-Books, 1967.

Midrash Bereshit Rabbah. Jerusalem: Vaharmon, 1965.

Midrash Daniel. Jerusalem: Mekitzei Nerdemim, 1968.

Midrash Eichah Rabbah. In *Midrash Rabbah.* Bnai Brak: Tiferet Zion, 1963.

Midrash Esther. In L. Ginzberg (Ed.), *The Legends of the Jews.* Philadelphia: Jewish Publication Society of America, 1968.

Midrash Esther Rabbah. In *Midrash Rabbah.* Bnai Brak: Tiferet Zion, 1963.

Midrash HaGadol (Shemot). Jerusalem: Mossad HaRav Kook, 1956.

Midrash Mechilta in *Mechilta d'Rabbi Yishmael.* Philadelphia: Jewish Publication Society of America, 1976.

Midrash Panim Acherim. In L. Ginzberg (Ed.), *The Legends of the Jews.* Philadelphia: Jewish Publication Society of America, 1968.

Midrash Pesikta Rabati. Vilna: n.p., 1880.

Midrash Pesikta Zutrata, Parshat Balak. In A. Kaplan, *The Real Messiah.* New York: National Conference of Synagogue Youth, 1985.

Midrash Pirke d'Rabbi Eliezer. Jerusalem: M. Kliman, 1969.

Midrash Tehillim. In *Midrash Shochar Tov al Tehillim.* Jerusalem: Midrash, 1968.

Midrash Rabbah. Jerusalem: Levin-Epstein, 1965.

Midrash Seder Eliyahu Rabbah. Jerusalem: Vaharmon, 1960.

Midrash Shemot Rabbah. In *Midrash Rabbah.* Jerusalem: Levin Epstein, 1965.

Midrash Shir HaShirim. Jerusalem: *Ktav Yad VaSefer,* 1971.

Midrash Tanchuma. Warsaw: Y.G. Monk, 1879.

Midrash Tanchuma HaKadum V'HaYashan. In *Midrash Tanchuma.* New York: Sefer, 1946.

Midrash Vayikra Rabbah. In *Midrash Rabbah.* Bnai Brak: Tiferet
Zion, 1963.

Midrash Yalkut Shemoni. Jerusalem.

Midrash Yashar Noah. In *Sefer HaYashar HaShalem.* Jerusalem: Etz Chaim, 1968.

Midrash Yashar Shemot. Sefer HaYashar HaShalem. Jerusalem: Etz Chaim, 1968.

Miller, A. *Behold a People.* New York: Balshon, 1968.

Miller, A. *Rejoice O Youth.* New York: Balshon.

Miller, A. *Torah Nation.* New York: Balshon, 1971.

Morse, A.D. *While Six Million Died: A Chronicle of American Apathy.*
New York: Random House, 1968. Muller, H. *Time Magazine.* October 18, 1982, p. 34.

Muravchik, J. *Misreporting Lebanon.* Washington, D.C.: Heritage Foundation, 1983.

Nachmanides, M. Commentary on Leviticus. In *Mikraot Gedolot Vayikra.* New York: Pardes, 1951.

Nachmanides, M. *Igeret* to His Son Nachman. In *Kitvei Ramban,* Vol. I. Jerusalem: Mossad HaRav Kook, 1964.

Nachmanides, M. *Kitvei Ramban,* Vol. II. Jerusalem: Mossad HaRav Kook, 1964.

Nachmanides, M. "Prayer at the Ruins of Jerusalem." In C.B. Chavel (Ed.), *Ramban: Writings and Discourses,* Vol. II. New York: Shilo, 1978.

Negev, A. *Archaeological Encyclopedia of the Holy Land.* New York: Putnam, 1972.

Netanyahu, B. "How Central Is the Palestinian Problem?" *The Wall Street Journal,* April 5, 1983.

Newfield, J. *The Village Voice.* New York, 1981.

New Testament, Matthew. Self-pronouncing edition. Cleveland, Ohio: World Publishing Co., 1941.

New Testament. Hebrews. Self-pronouncing edition. Cleveland, Ohio: World Publishing Co., 1941.

Newton, I. *Opticks.* New York: Dover, 1952.

Nimrod, D. *Peace Now: Blueprint for National Suicide.* Quebec: Dawn, 1984.

Onkelos. In *Mikraot Gedolot: Numbers.* New York: Friedman, 1971.

Or L'Amim. Jerusalem: Dvar Yerushalayim; 1983.

Palestinian National Covenant (1968). In L. Davis, *Myths and Facts 1985: A Concise Record of the Arab-Israeli Conflict.* Washington, D.C.: Near East Report, 1984.

Parsons, T. "Postscript to the Sociology of Modern Anti-Semitism." *Contemporary Jewry,* 1980, *1,* 31–38.

Perlmutter, N. & Perlmutter, R.A. *The Real Anti-Semitism in America.* New York: Arbor House, 1982.

Peters, J. *From Time Immemorial: The Origins of the Arab-Jewish Conflict over Palestine.* New York: Harper & Row, 1984.

Pfeiffer, C.F. (Ed.) Wycliffe Dictionary of Biblical Archaeology. Peabody, Mass. Hendrickson Publishers, Inc., 2000.

Pilzer, J. *Anti-Semitism and Jewish Nationalism.* Virginia Beach, VA: Donning Co., 1981.

Planck, M. *Where Is Science Going?* Woodbridge, CT: Ox Bow Press, 1981.

Plaut, W.G. *The Rise of Reform Judaism.* New York: World Union for Progressive Judaism, 1963.

Plaut, W.G. *The Growth of Reform Judaism.* New York: World Union for Progressive Judaism, 1965.

Poincarbe, H. *The Foundations of Science.* Washington, D.C.: University Press of America, 1982.

Prager, D. & Telushkin, J. *Why the Jews? The Reason for Anti Semitism.* New York: Simon & Schuster, 1983.

Quinley, H.E., and Glock, C.Y. *Anti-Semitism in America.* New Brunswick: Transaction Inc., 1983.

Quran. In *The Koran Interpreted.* New York: Macmillan Co., 1970.

Radday, Y.T., Shore, H., Pollatschek, M.A. & Wickman, D. "Genesis, Wellhausen and the Computer." In A. Sutton (Ed.), *Pathways to the Torah.* Jerusalem: Arachim, 1985.

Raphael, M.L. *Profiles in American Judaism.* San Francisco: Harper & Row, 1984.

Rifkin, J. *Algeny.* New York: Viking Press, 1983.

Rosenman, S. "Psychoanalytic Reflections on Anti-Semitism." *Journal of Psychology and Judaism,* 1977, 2, 3–23.

Rosenthal, G.S. *The Many Faces of Judaism: Orthodox, Conservative, Reconstructionist, and Reform.* New York: Behrman House, 1978.

Ruether, R.R. *Faith and Fratricide: The Theological Roots of Anti-Semitism.* New York: Seabury Press, 1979.

Ryan, W., Pitman, W. *Noah's Flood: The New Scientific Discoveries about the Event That Changed the World.* New York: Simon and Schuster, 1999.

Sachar, H.M. *A History of Israel: From the Rise of Zionism to Our Time.* New York: Alfred A. Knopf, 1981.

Saenger, G. *The Social Psychology of Prejudice.* New York: Harper & Row, 1969.

Said, E.W. *The Question of Palestine.* New York: Times Books, 1979.

Sancton, T.A. *Time Magazine.* June 28, 1982, p. 17.

Sanford, R.N., Adorno, T.W., Frenkel-Brunswik, E., and Levinson, D.J. "The Measurement of Implicit Anti-Democratic Trends." In T.W. Adorno, E. Frenkel-Brunswik, D.J. Levinson, and R.N. Sanford (Eds.), *The Authoritarian Personality.* New York: Harper & Row, 1950.

Sartre, J.P. *Anti-Semite and Jew.* New York: Schocken Books, 1976. Scherman, N. Foreword. In M. Prager, *Sparks of Glory.* New York: Mesorah Publications, 1985.

Scherman, N., and Zlotowitz, M. *History of the Jewish People: The Second Temple Era.* New York: Mesorah Publications, 1982.

Schimmel, H.C. *The Oral Law: A Study of the Rabbinic Contribution to Torah SheBe'Al Peh.* Jerusalem: Feldheim Publishers, 1971.

Schurer, E. *The History of the Jewish People in the Age of Jesus Christ.* Edinburgh: T & T Clark Ltd., 1973.

Schwartzman, S.D. *Reform Judaism Then and Now.* New York: Union of American Hebrew Congregations, 1971.

Sefer HaIkarim. Jerusalem, 1960. Seidman, H. *United Nations: Perfidy and Perversion.* New York: M. P. Press, 1982.

Selznick, G.J. & Steinberg, S. *The Tenacity of Prejudice: Anti-Semitism in Contemporary America.* New York: Harper & Row, 1969.

Sherif, M. *In Common Predicament.* Boston: Houghton Mifflin Co., 1966.

Shultz, R.H. & Godson, R. *Dezinformatsia: Active Measures in Soviet Strategy.* Washington, D.C.: Pergamon-Brassey, 1984.

Sierksma, K.L. *Flags of the World 1669–1670.* Holland: S. Emmering, 1966.

Simon, E.H. "On Gene Creation." In A. Carmel and C. Domb (Eds.), *Challenge: Torah Views on Science and Its Problems.* Jerusalem: Feldheim Publishers, 1978.

Sklare, M. *The Conservative Movement/Achievements and Problems.* In M. Sklare (Ed.), *American Jews/A Reader.* New York: Behrman House, 1983.

Smith, W.E. *Time Magazine.* July 26, 1982, p. 25.

Sutton, A., & Arachim Staff. *Pathways to the Torah.* Jerusalem: Arachim, 1985.

Tal, E. *Now the Story Can Be Told.* Tel-Aviv: Achduth Press, 1982.

Talmud. Tractates *Avodah Zarah, Avot, Baba Batra, Berachot, Chullin, Gittin, Chagigah, Ketubot, Megilah, Nedarim, Pesachim, Sanhedrin, Shabbat, Sotah, Sukkah, Ta'anit, Yoma.* Vilna edition. Jerusalem: Ortsel, 1960.

Talmud. Tractate *Uktzin.* Jerusalem: Hotzaot HaTalmud.

Talmud, Jerusalem. Tractates *Megillah, Yevamot, Yoma.* Jerusalem: Torah Mitzion, 1968.

Talmud, Jerusalem. Tractate *Ta'anit.* New York: M.P. Press, 1976.

Tapsell, R.F. *Monarchs, Rulers, Dynasties, and Kingdoms of the World.* New York: Facts on File Inc., 1983.

Targum Yerushalmi.

Time Magazine, February 5, 1979, p. 51.

Trachtenberg, J. *The Devil and the Jew: The Medieval Conception of the Jew and Its Relation to Modern Anti-Semitism.* Philadelphia: Jewish Publication Society of America, 1983.

Tumin, M. "Anti-Semitism and Status Anxiety: A Hypothesis." *Jewish Social Studies,* 1971, 4, 307–16.

Twain, M. "Concerning the Jews." *Harpers Magazine,* September, 1899.

Twain, M. *The Innocents Abroad; or the New Pilgrims Progress.* New York: Harper & Row, 1911.

Uzziel, J.B. In *Mikraot Gedolot,* Numbers. New York: Friedman, 1971.

Van Loon, H.W. *The Story of Mankind.* New York: Liveright, 1984.

Velikovsky, I. *Ages in Chaos.* New York: Doubleday, 1952.

Wald, G. "The Origin of Life." *Scientific American, 191*(2), 1954, 45–53.

Wasserman, E.B. *Kovatz Ma'amarim.* Jerusalem: Gitler & Associates, 1963.

Wyman, D.S. *The Abandonment of the Jews.* New York: Pantheon Books, 1984.

Yaneev, S. *Remez BePardes and Sofot Nestarot BaTorah.* Gush Dan: Machon Meir, 1985.

Zohar. Jerusalem: Mossad HaRav Kook, 1964.